Also By Chris Stroffolino

AnTi-GeNtRiFiCaTiOn WaR dRuM rAdIo (Boog City, 2016)
Life In A Tin-Can (e-book, 2015)
Single-Sided Doubles CD/LP (Pop Snob, 2010)
Speculative Primitive (Tougher Disguises, 2005)
Scratch Vocals (Potato Clock (2003)
Spin Cycle (Spuyten Duyvil 2001)
Shakespeare's *12the Night,* with David Rosenthal (IDG Books, 2000)
Stealer's Wheel (Hard Press, 1999)
Light As A Fetter (Situations, 1997)
Cusps (Aerial/Edge, 1995)
Oops (Pavement Saw, 1994; backyard press, 1991)
Accident (at the corner of happiness and health) (Iniquity Press, 1991)

Notes Toward An M(F)A In Non-Poetry

(& Other Essays on Poetry, Academia & Culture)

Chris Stroffolino

SPUYTEN DUYVIL
New York City

Earlier versions of these essays have appeared in: Konch, Jacket, The Rumpus, The Bigtakeover, The Newark Review, Imaginary Syllabi (Palm Press), Journal of Poetics Research, Poets & Writers, and The Laney Tower.

©2017 Chris Stroffolino
ISBN 978-1-944682-31-6
Cover art: Nelson Enrique, *The Path Of Understanding*
(Constellation Cassiopeia)

Library of Congress Cataloging-in-Publication data applied for.

Contents

Preface (File Under Cultural Criticism)   vii

Introduction
Culture Crash:
The Killing Of The Creative Class, Scott Timberg   2

Section I

How Post-Structuralism Was Used To Marginalize Black Studies   20
Crisis? What Crisis?   26
Teaching The Conflicts & Learning To Curse   37
Beyond Preparing Students For Beowulf   5
Creative Writing Is Critical Thinking   52
Ye Shall Know Us By Our Taboos!
Thomas Sayers Ellis's "The Judges Of Craft"   57
Literary Activism At Its Best: Craig Santos Perez's Anti-Racist MFA   67
Notes to an M(F)A in Non-Poetry   75
A Yearly Anthology Or Two   89
Ebonics and College Radio   95
The Interdisciplinary Music Class   102
Community Outreach For Creative Writers   111

Section II

A Poem With Histories: Dudley Randall's "Booker T. And W.E.B."   122
The BreakBeat Poets   131
uPhakamile uMaDhlamini   179
The Two Underdogs: Sly Stone & The Great Fillmore Whitewash   183
"Rich:" Beme The Rapper In Oakland (2010)   223

Section III

If Facebook Won't Listen, Will City Hall?   243
The New 7th St.   258
Appeal To Musicians   264
Inside Oakland's Art (& Housing) Crisis: A Dialogue   269
Bridges To Be   277

Preface:
File Under Cultural Criticism?

This book was inspired by my students, especially the ones who fall through the cracks. Every issue addressed in it is based on classroom discussions about contemporary social issues or questions students have asked me in individual meetings, questions that have caught me off-guard, questions that have no easy answers and that remind me that writing is a necessary part of teaching. These questions may be better understood as challenges, and sometimes my students have made blatant challenges: *if you're going to force us to write a sonnet for next week, you better write one for* **us** *to critique too!* (which made me realize that I had never written a sonnet, at least one I was even semi-proud of).

And, just as I wouldn't have started writing poetry again (insofar as a sonnet, *sui generis*, is a poem) had it not been for the honor and privilege of teaching a creative writing class, so I never would have started writing cultural criticism again were I not teaching freshman composition. Reading student papers on the childhood obesity epidemic, racial bias in the corporate mass media (specifically TV), or on possible anti-displacement strategies that could solve Oakland's housing crisis challenges me to get my own thoughts in order more than I have to in class conversations.[1] Even if I don't always show these essays to my

---

[1] When I discovered that my literary and academic training hadn't prepared me for this, I flung myself into writing journalistic puff pieces for an Oakland monthly (*The Oakbook,* circa 2008—2010)— to hone some of these skills that could ground my writing, though I don't include any of these pieces here—as well as to rock criticism, especially for *The Bigtakeover* (and these essays on music, especially after the illegal corporate buyout of a local college station, inevitably became more general cultural criticism; you can say, a love of music, more than anything, drove my civic conscience).

students, they serve as useful reminders when I'm preparing lesson plans, and refining my syllabi for the next semester. It also challenges me to be an ambassador for my students' concerns, which often are not addressed by those who determine the civic (and cultural) policies in our country.

So, despite the book's title, many of these essays attempt to appeal to a more general reader/listener who cares neither about poetry nor academia. But what is a general reader if not my students? Does this "average reasoning man or woman" even exist (anymore)? Did it ever? Can we write to one specific general audience without running the risk of appealing to the lowest common denominator (which is not the same as "common sense"), or must we appeal to several specificities and run the risk of creating a stylistically and/or thematically inconsistent book?

In my experiences, I've found most publishers (and record labels) prefer a book (or album) that's more stylistically and/or thematically consistent, by which they often mean appealing to one particular main audience, or niche (or as some put it "tribe"). But if one's primary social life is made up of people from many—and potentially all—walks of life,[2] who are rarely writers or even professional readers, one may soon discover that one must let their various vocabularies set the terms, and speak in different languages or codes (what one person refers to as God as Jesus another may refer to as "the wisdom of the body" for instance)—even if you're monolingual as I, and many Americans, alas, are. The limits of such professional niche, or specialized tribe, kind of thinking become all too apparent.

You may find yourself arguing with those who published your celebrated niche writing ("excellent scribbling in a period style"), trying to explain the fiscal logic in the equation: "I'd rather that 100 people each intimately engage one or two chapters (or songs) each than 10 people intimately engage with the entire book (or album)." In order for this to make sense, one may have to appeal to another equation: "You may learn more about someone else's writing, as well as the art of writing in general, by closely reading 10 pages than less closely reading 100

---

2   And, if I must specify further, I'll say mainly non-white, both poor and what's left of the middle class....

pages: re-reading matters, less can be more."[3]

Once you understand and accept that such an alternative to what Roland Barthes—in his intro to S/Z—calls "the ideological and commercial habits of our society" that value acquisitiveness and quantity over quality is possible, you won't necessarily feel *ripped off* if a teacher assigns you one 333 page book for the semester, but only discusses at most 1/10th of the book in class. Nor will you necessarily feel ripped off if you buy a book and only *like* 26 pages—for those 26 pages, *really speak to you,* and inspired you to write your own book or even—*hint hint*—fund a series of yearly anthologies,[4] or a series of 45RPM chapbooks to complement the 33 1/3 series.

In the conflict between these two world-views, I believe this latter more flexible attitude is more conducive to conversation and collaboration and especially needed in a time of cultural crisis, and a *perma-temp* economy when eclecticism becomes a survival skill. When confronting the failed promises of stability-through-specialization and the failed strategies of "putting all your eggs in one basket" still institutionally encouraged-if not entirely mandated—by academia, no wonder so many feel a need to cast a wider net (if not necessarily go so far as to use "the kitchen sink strategy") even if it takes us out of our so-called "comfort zone."

One of the reasons I begin this book with a review/essay of a recent book of general culture criticism (*Culture Crash*) is because it appeals to a generalist even in a world in which the broad-based middle class has turned into a mere niche. By including individual chapters on various specialized fields, it manages to cast a wider net that can navigate the middle ground between appealing to the specialist and the "general reader." On the one hand, it runs the risk of alienating or boring many readers in today's specialized society (picture two musicians thumbing through it at a bookstore: "Cool, there's a chapter on music," "Yeah, but I don't want to read that chapter on journalism or architecture.") Yet, *Culture Crash* understands that showing these analogies between/across these segregated decimated disciplines is a

---

[3] See Chapters 4, 5,6.

[4] See Chapter 10.

necessary precondition to any coalition building so necessary in the absence of any assumed (ready-made) "general reader," whose loss that book clearly laments.

I don't entirely share that lament for the loss of a general reader, but I do agree with much of its diagnosis of the crisis. So, while *Notes To An M(F)A In Non-Poetry* doesn't explore as many professions as *Culture Crash* does, it does get deeper into a lesser number of professions, and hopefully the relative depth here can complement that book's broader approach to further the necessary coalition building.

2. Gathering Places (or must we destroy to create)

At the core of every essay in this book[5] is a burning general question: How can we, in a corporate dominated culture characterized by the over-specialization of professional fields, niche marketing, gentrification (urban removal), "every man for himself" individualism, institutional racism, the dominance of Big Food and Big Pharma, privatization and the loss of public spaces, make room for a more truly democratic, vital and empowering culture?

In every culture industry I work in (writer, teacher, musician), I am confronted with complaints about today's culture. Often these justified complaints—or you could call them, "the cries of the colonized"—are accompanied by a despair or resignation that we can't do anything about them on a structural level. Too often, people don't even realize that many others have the exact same complaints, or analogous complaints in their particular specialized field of activity.

It's difficult, in this fragmented society, to find safe places to actually meet and share our complaints and try to propose realistic solutions, or even the "unrealistic" ones that are often a necessary precondition to finding realistic ones. While I am not a "community organizer" or "activist" as those terms are often understood, my research and work in the culture industry as writer, musician and teacher have shown that the most successful coalitions and alliances have occurred when artists and activists, thinkers and doers, introverts and extroverts, edu-

---

5   with the possible exception of the review/essays of poems and songs in Section II

cators and entertainers, experts and populists, academics and non-academic public intellectuals, etc. can put aside their differences and work together across disciplines for a greater common cause. Bridges must be built between genres and the social scenes they imply, whether we call it "an interdisciplinary approach" as academics do, or "unity in diversity" as the Philly punk/hip hop scene did.

Indeed, as my experience in the Philly underground music scene showed me, dances can be one of those safe spaces where such gatherings can take place, and this is not only true in America. In Guinea-Bissau under Portuguese rule, political meetings were forbidden, but organizers could meet at dances.[6] And, in America, even after many neighborhood clubs shut down in the 70s, placing cardboard on your block and blocking it off to traffic could create those spaces for gathering and organizing (even though, under the watchful eye of the police, these spaces were not as safe as dance clubs could be).[7]

Yet college classrooms can also facilitate such gatherings, even in an era that is trending, alas, to the MOOC model of Phoenix University and the (re-)banning of ethnic studies. In the (non-online) classroom, I've found that conversation, and the writing that is part of it, can create safe spaces. Many of the Black Panthers, it must be remembered, met each other at Merritt College (and, later, Laney, SF State et al).

Furthermore, college may also facilitate safe spaces *for dancing* in the increasing absence of other safe, affordable, under-aged venues and community centers. My first moshpit experience (which lead me to be on the editorial board of a local underground newspaper) happened through the auspices of Temple University's student union. I heard about this event through Drexel University's community run WKDU radio station. And, back in my day, college radio meant *dance-radio* and local radio, and I firmly believe that political rallies and teach-ins would draw more people deeply in if they included dancing just as I

---

[6] See, "Thinking With Our Own Heads and Walking With Our Own Feet, Augudta Henriques and Miquel Barros of *Tiniquena*, Guinea-Bissau in conversation with Molly Kane," *No Easy Victories* (302-217, especially 209).

[7] See Kevin Powell, "Kool Herc." http://www.vibe.com/2011/02/activist-kevin-powell-talks-kool-herc-hip-hop-and-healthcare/

believe that music scenes would be less transient if their live performances also included organizational discussion.

3. Why Academia?

I've worked in academia for 30 years, and hope to continue to work there until the day I die (though it would be nice to have summer's off), and most of these essays in Section I take stock of the state of that profession today. Many are love letters to those who work in that field, whether in MFA programs or community colleges, especially those of us for whom our intellectual relationships with our students become our most important social life, who may sit at dinner with our significant others unable to stop thinking (or some might say worrying) about our students, who try to gracefully bear the burden of being the unacknowledged public intellectuals of our time, knowing that we could serve our students better if the institutions in which we work would be open to structural change, beyond the salient need for "more funding."[8]

Having taught every level of College English (from foundational courses to graduate seminars), I've become aware that my ideal job would synthesize the work I do at a community college with the work I do at an MFA Program: The MFA program obviously had advantages: better pay, students who don't feel forced to be there, smaller class sizes, and not having to grade on the quality of the work. Yet even though teaching required composition classes in an overcrowded, underfunded, environment has obvious disadvantages, it also has the advantage of more diversity, and can even be said to exist on the front lines of today's culture clashes (as every semester we collectively work to come

---

8 When teaching at a school more often in a budget crisis than not, it's easy to become more curious about alternative models of fiscal management without sacrificing the *human* dimensions. This is not necessarily an anti-bureaucratic argument. Though I have taught free-lance non-accredited creative writing classes (and one on one writing and piano tutoring), one advantage of academia's middlemen is that the teacher doesn't have to hustle to get students, and thus can devote more time and energy to one's work in the classroom and the curriculum committee.

up with a new common language).[9]

As a community college teacher, I'm strongly encouraged and certainly permitted to "teach the conflicts"—and not merely the aesthetic/ethical conflicts between say imagism and symbolism, or mainstream and avant-garde, or prose and poetry, but the less specialized socio-political conflicts which often undergird these. Creating a comfortable space for airing out these conflicts becomes the first task, and, when it works, the class conversations can further a culturally syncretic vision that could transcend the culture wars with as much equanimity as, say, **Patrick Rosal's** essay of poetics ("The Art Of The Mistake: Some Notes On Breaking As Making") does.[10] I welcome this challenge.

In a pre-transfer level composition class, I'm reading a student paper which compares the Black Panthers' demand for reparations with their demand for full employment and concludes that the demand for full-employment is more realistic in part because it can be easier to convince and persuade the skeptic than the demand for reparations would. This brilliant thesis (that he came up with on his own) basically argues that the two demands are just two different ways of saying the same thing—since the reparations would be used to create the full employment, and that full employment is in fact at the essential heart of the promise for reparations as it was first made at the end of the Civil War, a promise that was never delivered and thus the African-American was never truly freed. "Necessitous men are not free men," and, lacking that payment of start-up capital promised at the end of the Civil War, the overwhelming majority of African-Americans were not able to compete on equal footing with the whites.

As I sit here, grading and commenting on his paper, thinking about the stakes of what he's writing about and his need to *persuade the skeptic*, I realize that this kind of argumentative thinking (the bread and butter of composition classes) is generally not encouraged in the more "advanced" literature and creative writing classes that I, in many

---

9   If I can't synthesize these two radically different roles institutionally, can at least do it conceptually, to "decolonize my mind" as it were, to enhance students' learning experiences?

10   For a more detailed discussion of this essay, see BreakBeat Poets, Chapter 15

ways, prefer to teach. Poet Bernadette Mayer used to teach a creative writing workshop where she'd ask her students to *create a utopia*, but, as the specialized genres, disciplines and professions are currently structured, this utopian striving is actually much more permitted in freshman composition classes than in more "advanced" and "elective" classes.

What if MFA Creative Writing programs made more room for these kind of students, or assignments, and what if we took the best that graduate creative writing programs allowed, and applied it to community college, and vice versa? I believe that room should be made for this kind of thinking in these "advanced" courses (call me a traditionalist who believes that an artist who paints abstractions has more cred if she can also paint figures), and that there's a way to do that without watering down "high literature" to some bourgeois notion of "self-expression" held as standard. Yet, we need to rethink this hierarchical relationship.[11]

4. What does this have to do with Poetry? (part one)

Though it's been over a decade since I published a book of poetry, I still love teaching it in literature and creative writing courses, as the review-essays in Section 2 (on Dudley Randall, Thomas Sayers Ellis, jessica Care moore, John Murillo, Krista Franklin, and others in the *BreakBeat Poets* anthology) attest. Readers who enjoyed—even if only to disagree—with the review/essays that made up the bulk of my earlier collection, *Spin Cycle* (2001), who would otherwise ask, "what does this have to do with poetry," may find in these essays a useful entry point into the cultural discussion. Yet the category of "Non-Poetry" this book proposes is a (semi-playful?) response to the repeated realization that the social institution of poetry too often acts like a jealous god that excludes the very things it could benefit from.

When I taught in an M(F)A program, the one black student in my class began her presentation on Baraka by talking about 1) how her

---

11   It must be said, on the other hand, that poetry should be allowed a little more currency in the "remedial" and "basic skills" classes as well as I argue in Chapter 6, "Creative Writing Is Critical Thinking."

dad taught her that separation of church and state didn't exist in the black community the way it does for most whites, and 2) that, in many ways, things are worse in today's ostensibly "desegregated" era than they were in the days of blatant segregation. Before we got a chance to discuss this, however, another (white male) student rudely interrupted her and asked (but it was really a statement), *what does this have to do with poetry?*

I knew it had everything to do with poetry, but it was too late—the damage had been done.

In other contexts as well, I've heard people who like to speak for poetry smugly ask this question (after all, the "poem that stands on its own two legs" is a staple of New Criticism as much as many contemporary theories of poetry and poetics), but this experience made me see, on the front-lines, as it were, the human toll such attitudes have, and wondering about my complicity in it challenged my aesthetic habits which were encouraged—if not (exactly) mandated—by the institution in which I worked.

Indeed, when I was a "young and upcoming poet," there was a strong taboo against exhibiting any public intellectual ambitions (parallel to the taboo against telling and end-stopped 'sing songy' rhymes). Yet, being a teacher, even a student-centered teacher, tends to demand this role. When I'm teaching a composition class, in which I'm trying to get students to write critical argumentative essays more than poetry, of course it makes me want—even need to—write essays of cultural criticism myself (to not be a hypocrite). Although I was known primarily as a "poet" by trade, it becomes an imperative to not let the narrow demands of poetry get in the way of my intellectual commitment to my students.

Regardless of my lack of cultural clout as a "public intellectual" writer in the mass cultural sense of the word, I know that part of being a college teacher, especially in composition classes, is playing the role of the public intellectual much more than in my public artistic endeavours as musician and poet. And, as a teacher of composition classes at a community college, you may even reach more people than lecture circuit/radio show heroes like Richard Wolf, Chris Hedges, or Ta Nehisi Coates (100 students a semester adds up).

Notes Toward An M(F)A In Non-Poetry

And it occurred to me that since so many poets and published writers do make their living as teachers, the literary presses would do well to make room for the diverse kinds of writing assignments the writers' job requires. The failure to do this often leads to an internal split in many teacher/writers, in which teachers devalue their students' work for their *art*. It may help explain why it's a common complaint that "the best writers are often the worst teachers."[12]

By contrast, I find that my basic writing students have not only been my toughest "audience," but have also provided tremendous help in grounding me, and slowing down the kind of leaps that can be an "occupational hazard" of the overqualified demands of the literati. And I ask the poets: you don't have to be what I'm calling a public intellectual to write poetry, but could you at least acknowledge that they could ultimately enliven contexts for your own poetry, and increase the potential audience pool—if that is a concern for you or your publishers?

Even though my students are not the primary audience for most of the pieces in this book, I try to translate some of the life I find in our classroom discussions into these essays (the best essays, like the best poems, often come alive most between their lines). I still have a long way to go, but in the meantime I can devote more time to reading each of their papers more slowly, even if it robs from the time a "good citizen" of the poetry world is supposed to be devoting to new works of poetry.

A review of my last collection of prose essays wrote, "Stroffolino holds out an olive branch between warring literary factions, but sometimes that branch seems to be on fire."[13] Or, as the old song puts it,

---

[12] It also explains why many colleges' claims to serve the community, and instill civic pride (often in Latin, as in the University of San Francisco's *"Pro Urbe et Universitate"—for the City and University—*), in practice are usually empty words. http://bigtakeover.com/essays/open-letter-to-president-privett-on-the-sale-of-kusf-by-the-university-of-san-francisco. For the beginning of a corrective to these, see Chapter 13 "Community Engagement For Creative Writers."

[13] "The branch is on fire" is Steve Tomasula's poetic way of saying, the book is too poetic for the olive-branch prose crowd. http://ameri-

"you wanna be a bridge/ but you're falling through the cracks." And I believe this can be said for this current collection; though its concerns are less specifically literally and more broadly cultural, I cannot simply write to one general audience, but rather several specialties, just as I must in a diverse classroom.

5. The Ghost Of Martin Luther King (*there's a spectre haunting…. Oakland*)

"I am sure that none of you would want to rest content with the superficial kind of social analysis that deals merely with effects and does not grapple with underlying causes."

Letter From Birmingham Jail

If any white friends from back east would visit me in Oakland, one of the first things I'd like to do is take them for a walk up or down Martin Luther King. I want to show them Marcus Books, an amazing black owned bookstore. I also need to show them the scene of a crime.

For those for who can't picture this street, I refer you to Chris Rock's joke in which he asks why the most crime-ridden street in many towns he's been to is called Martin Luther King. *Triste Triste Triste.* Isn't it ironic?[14] Perhaps, but it's also systemic. And even my little superficial tour could show you why. We could start right at the 880 underpass at 23rd Street where the homeless are setting up tents again, after being cleared out by cops the night before, and walk 5 blocks. It won't take long. See the grassy hill at the end of the cul de sac. It used to be houses torn down to make way for the interstate (and Bart).

Dig that building with its beautiful "Welcome To Oakland" graffiti on it. You can tell it was a hamburger joint or Soul Food restaurant with picnic tables and maybe even a jukebox. There used to be 3 or 4 beauty salons, even a blues club with dancing. The building I lived in for years was featured in the Sun Ra *Space Is The* Place movie. And on West there's the church where the Black Panthers started their free

---

canbookreview.org/issueContent.asp?id=32

14   https://www.youtube.com/watch?v=7hJxWr1TKK8

breakfast programs that put the feds to shame. A few abandoned black owned garages, and a burnt out church. On the corner of MacArthur you can still see, beneath an RCA logo with Nipper the Dog, an electric sign for Terry's TV.

For decades now, many of these buildings have remained empty. I'm told this neighborhood is called "Ghost Town" (though not, of course, by developers, who probably now call it East KONO or something). Many of the younger people have told me that this is because of the high murder rate, but the older folks have told me that it was called "Ghost Town" *before* the murder rates rent up because the businesses were disappearing, and these buildings stand as gaping wounds, as a sea of corpses, casting a shadow on what used to be called the ghetto, and reminding us of *a crime that was committed in white people's names*, and that has analogies with parallel historical developments in every area of our culture—as seen from the history of jobs, housing and police brutality to the histories of music and academia.

Our education system rarely speaks of this crime, nor do the official histories we're taught by mass-cultural mediums like movies, TV, or the baby-boomer rock critic establishment passing the torch to the 33 1/3 Books generation. Neither do they provide us with the facts and the conceptual apparatus to make connections between these specialized arenas of culture, or between the past and the present. If anything, these ideological organs of our culture worked to actively undermine attempts to expose these connections.

In this light, the mere name of the street (Martin Luther King) is part of a cover-up that compounded the crime. For, in cities across America, the name MLK was given to a street that had been one of the main corridors for black owned businesses, and it's not an accident that most of these streets are in close proximity to interstates (in Oakland, it's even *beneath* the interstate). The urban planners found these streets to have the most "expendable" real estate on which to build (In West Oakland, we also see "limited access" (placeless) highways casting similar shadows on 7th Street, and MacArthur Blvd, which had also been thriving business/cultural thoroughfares). Thus, the destruction of these businesses was no mere "unfortunate, if unintentional side-effect" of the construction of highways, but clearly part of a plan to "devise a system that recognizes that....the whole problem is really the blacks....without seeming to," as Nixon was caught putting it,[15] as well as make people more dependent on cars

As these "urban renewal" (more accurately called "urban removal") projects were underway,[16] renaming Grove Street for Martin Luther King added insult to injury, placing a band-aid of unconvincing appeasement over a wound that only makes it worse. The name "Martin Luther King" can also allow some whites an easy way to account for the discrepancy between the "promotion" the street name signifies, and the demotion of quality of life to be found on this street ("See, they got less obstacles now than they did before, so it must be *their* fault their blocks are so run down. I *told* you they're inferior.")

Historically, such a decimation of these business districts and communities was a necessary precondition for the subsequent wars on the black community in the 80s. Do you really think the Crack the CIA brought in to black communities would have served as a pretext for The War On Drugs[17] had Urban Planners not destroyed these non-revolutionary Black Capitalist businesses around the same time the police and FBI were burning Black Panther offices a decade earlier?

Once one knows enough of the facts, it's hard not to imagine the murder suspect saying these exact words: "*So you demand self-determination!!* Well, we'll show you; we'll take away what slivers of self-determination you've already got. You uppity folks." And call it progress at that, just as surely McDonalds is progress over Art's Crab Shack and Target and The Apple Store infinitely better than Terry's TV.

I've lived in this "Ghost Town" neighborhood since the year Katrina, and its aftermath, hit New Orleans (2005) and, in the decade I've lived here, these ruins have remained to tell their story to anybody

---

15   http://www.washingtonpost.com/wp-srv/style/longterm/books/chap1/smoke.htm

16   The 1960s version of what today we'd call gentrification., see also Chapter 17 for how this occurred in San Francisco as well.

17   Even though, as Michelle Alexander points out, the War On Drugs was begun *before* the crack epidemic had begun, and the percentage of whites and blacks who use crack cocaine has been roughly the same (*The New Jim Crow*, especially 98-125).

who will see through the cover-up clouds and listen. This is not to say there isn't a vibrant culture amid these ruins, but I can certainly understand why some rappers have made a connection between growing up in a Palestine bombed by Israelis, or an Iraq bombed by the US.

As gentrification sweeps over Oakland, coming at this neighborhood from the north, south, and even west, the days are clearly numbered for even the *signs* of these ruins like Terry's TV. So, increasingly, if you tell visitors, *"this was once a thriving black neighborhood!"* they won't even be able to see the ruins that testify to that. Meanwhile, the generation of the wise elders who have seen, and lived through the "before" and "after" picture, is dying. I fear this history lesson will get lost, and feel more urgently than ever that it needs to be taught, to passed on to my students (if they don't already know), and even to 6 year olds who are being taught about Washington crossing the Delaware, etc.

These crimes were certainly not the founding murders, nor are they the last, but they could be the subject of a great Hollywood blockbuster (after all, it would be about block busting) that could be an important antidote to the "happy ending" of *Selma*, for instance. This is not just black history, but American history, and knowing it can help make more sense of our present cultural crisis.

6: Troubling Frames and Planting Seeds: Book Outline [18]

Calling mostly non-white neighborhoods like "Ghost Town," home—on and off (but mostly on) since I moved to North Philly 30 years ago informs the world view of this book at least as much as looking out from the so-called ivory tower does. Besides, by some definitions, where I've taught for the last decade is hardly an ivory tower, but a campus of short squat brick buildings (with a theatre, pool, and community garden, mind you), and the people I work with (I won't say teach here) live in similar—and sometimes the same—neighborhoods. They've often taught me as much about these neighborhoods as the wise elders at the YMCA do.

---

18   I like the sound of that, but from a certain perspective I'm sure it sounds too male

In this world, the (mostly white) literary cliques in which my works used to circulate seem far away, alien, even. So, yes, I do fear a tone of contempt towards "my white supremacist training" may be seen in some of these essays, but I do try to argue in more race-neutral terms in others, and that's another reason I start the book (proper) with a book review/essay on *Culture Crash*. The diagnosis of today's cultural crisis in Timberg's book is presented in race-neutral terms more likely to appeal to the white mainstream public intellectual audience (Yale, KPFA), and I deeply admire—and even envy—his ambassadorial ability to speak in a tone more likely to be called rational discourse than my book will likely be.

With a clear sense of "the big picture," *Culture Crash* sets a standard for civic discourse that can serve as a kind of short-hand "launching pad" for the diverse ruminations in this book, even as I strain uncomfortably to fit within the rhetorical parameters it sets, and I include this essay first in part to *dramatize the straining*. Ultimately, it would be unfair to say that my essay/review accurately represents either *Timberg's* position or *my* position, but I hope to dramatize a dialogue at least as much as to elaborate my own position in a monologic way.

You could say *Notes To An M(F)A In Non-Poetry* starts where *Culture Crash* ends.[19] Taking some statistics from Timberg's book to flesh out his account of how this contemporary cultural crisis exists in academia, Chapter 2 ("**How The Rise Of Post-Structuralism was used to Marginalize Ethnic Studies**") moves beyond Timberg's parameters to offer its own (alternative) explanation for what caused this crisis. This more intimate and immanent account of how academia may be guilty of self-inflicted wounds attempts to complement *Culture Crash's* by making a case for why Black Studies Matters that could appeal not just to Timberg's more general (white) reader, but to fellow educators and even fiscally conservative college administrators.

While the fight for Black Studies was waged primarily on the undergraduate (and K-12) level, it has historic parallels with the demands for more Graduate Creative Writing programs to challenge, or

---

19 Some readers (who have no interest to the academic and literary-world basis of Sections 1 and 2) will want to go directly from this chapter to the Section 3

supplement, traditional English degrees. Chapter 3 ("**Crisis? What Crisis?**") again shifts its appeal to more race-neutral terms to show how Creative Writing programs have come to co-exist (somewhat uneasily) with traditional English Departments. It also introduces how the struggles for a more equitable and financially solvent model for Creative Writing programs are waged on both a pedagogical/aesthetic level as well as an institutional level. The crisis can be, and perhaps must be, approached from many different angles.

On the other hand, "**Preparing Students For Beowulf**" speaks from the perspective of a community college teacher attempting to appeal on behalf of his students to college administrators and educators to address the disconnect between more diverse community colleges and the more inflexible monoculture-dominated curriculum demands of universities, while also offering a defense of poetry and close reading (which, pedagogically, are almost synonymous terms for me) and a more diverse curriculum. "**Learning To Curse (with apologies to Stephen Greenblatt)**" speaks more directly to students by invoking a "post-colonial" reading of Shakespeare's Caliban to champion diversity more than the Euro-American common core curriculum allows. This appeal to students as well as fellow professors aspires to the syncretic vision and pragmatic spirit I find so admirable in the **Patrick Rosal** essay discussed later in this book,[20] and which I try to apply to general civic issues in Section 3.

In these two essays, I try to restrict my comments to what we can do in the classroom in good times as well as bad ("I'm not suggesting any radical changes to our transfer-level curriculum,") but I do begin to suggest such changes in the next essay, "**Creative Writing Is Critical Thinking**," This essay extends the defense of poetry—in more race neutral terms by arguing for why creative writing courses should be required, or at the very least permitted to fill one of the basic writing requirements should students so choose.

The chapter on **Thomas Sayer's Ellis "The Judges Of Craft**," reminds us, however, that even championing creative writing in composition classes can only go so far to address the crisis, when even

---

20 See chapter 15 for a lengthier discussion of Rosal's essay.

the institution of poetry, insofar as it is separate—with some autonomy—from academia, is based on racist assumptions. The publishing world—especially small, independent presses—may not seem to be as much of an *institution* as academia, but TSE's "Judges Of Craft" shows how it is.

Here, I borrow from some of strategies of academic close reading to appeal to poetry editors, critics and scholars (often poets themselves) more than to teachers and administrators. Ellis' poem/essay uses "close reading" of a non-literary text to create Civic Poetry of the highest order (he also uses the *They Say, I Say* template so beloved of freshmen composition teachers). It serves as an example of the kind of aesthetic/pedagogical challenges needed to liberate the institution of poetry, and I find it instructive to note the way the critical establishment reacted to it.[21] By dramatizing the conflict, TSE leaves the reader with the facts needed to make an informed choice when asking, "are the poetry police really working *for you?*" His struggles in the publishing division of the cultural superstructure complement the work Craig Santos Perez is doing on the level of the academic institution, which is the subject of **"Literary Activism At Its Finest: Craig Santos Perez's Anti-Racist MFA"**

Non-Academic (or Academic) Public Intellectuals may write brilliant books that show a clear grasp of the cultural crisis, but are often unwilling (or discouraged by publishers) to risk absurdity in proposing solutions.[22] Luckily, I find some solutions to aspects of the problems specifically in MFA programs in **"Dr. Craig's 11 Step Program For Curing 'Mainly White MFA' Sickness."**

Perez has graciously given me permission to republish his piece in full, and in many ways it is the centerpiece of the book. With flair,

---

21 As we shall see in the title essay (Chapter 9), letting students in creative writing classes know about these struggles they're likely to encounter (if they haven't already) is, in my opinion, one of the most important tasks of an honest creative writing teacher (and, no, we don't have to waste a lot of time on it, and let it get in the way of doing *their* work!)

22 Timberg, for instance writes that "conditions are changing so rapidly" that specific solutions would "be pointless."

sharp humor, and absolute sincerity, Perez has certainly mastered the form of the pithy bullet point, the manifesto-like sound bite, more than I have. Perez is one of the best poets writing today, and "Dr Craig's 11-Step Program to Curing 'Mainly White MFA' Sickness" is perhaps my favorite poem by him, even if he doesn't refer to this piece as a poem.[23] I'm tempted to because I believe the form of proactive solutions should be allowed into the realm of 'poetry' as much as any "I do this, I do that" list poem or lover's complaint.

Perez's appeal to college administrators and fellow educators, on behalf of underserved students, may have a more "radical" tone compared to my **"Notes to an M(F)A On Non-Poetry,"** but both essays suggests how making structural changes to encourage more diversity can actually benefit an M(F)A program economically, create more job possibilities for *all* students, and provide more contexts for creative writing. Neither of these essays are content to resign themselves to accept that the hunger for pro-active solutions to today's cultural crisis is simply non-poetic.

Though the term "Non-Poetry" may seem somewhat tongue-in-cheek, the term was born in great pain. The essay was originally written a response to an essay written by Dale Smith in 2005, in which he argued that poets should consider writing for a non-poet at least as much for other poets, and as I questioned the way the term "poet" has come to circulate as a quasi-ontological category for quite a few, I came to the realization that the only way (for the poet) to reach the non-poet was to write "non-poetry." This essay, however, is only concerned with the aesthetic insofar as it is already social, and spends more time arguing for the advantages of a multi-genre creative writing workshop than either a single-genre workshop, or even the standard ideas of "poetry readings" as a gathering place for the social-exchanges "in the name of poetry" to take place.[24]

---

23 Perhaps Thomas Sayers Ellis would refer to Perez's piece as a "perform-a-form" (See chapter 7).

24 My proposal for an MFA in Non-Poetry is no mere attempt to "justify integration under the umbrella of the capitalist centre," (Cabral 162). If it seems that way, please let me know so I can make the necessary corrections.

The essay on a proposed yearly **Anthology (or Two)** continues to investigate possible structural changes, and attempts to show one way in which the MFA Creative Writing Programs, community colleges, and civic leaders can work together to achieve some of Craig Santos Perez's vision to the mutual benefit of each. "**Ebonics and College Radio**," shows one small intervention I'm making with my ex-student Chris Brown on the community college level while "**The Interdisciplinary Music Class**" speaks from the perspective of the community college English teacher again, but this time more interested in bridging a gap with the music department to serve the currently unmet student needs.

It's an appeal on behalf of students who fall through the cracks between the music and English Department (there's more of them that you might think). Its somewhat superficial account of the history of college music department curriculum (if compared to my earlier accounts of the institutional history of College English in the last 50 years) is an attempt to start a discussion across these departments. And what I say about this hybrid course could be applied to other interdisciplinary ideas (for instance, the playwrights in my creative classes would welcome a team taught class with the theatre department faculty).

Many of these threads come together in the chapter "**Community Outreach For Creative Writers.**" Informed by the spirit I see in Craig Santos Perez's essay and what a loved about college radio at its best, this ambitious essay comes closest to "imagining a utopia" by investigating the possibilities suggested by a brief course description in an existing M(F)A program in the Detroit area. Imagining a college course that can transcend the "town/gown" distinction (even if I have to invoke Motown and the WPA to do it) could suggest other ways we can more truly educate, empower, and employ students (as well as non-academic citizens in the community). These issues dovetail well with the civic proposals and anti-displacement strategies discussed in Section 3.

Close Reading Civic Poetry (With Apologies To Alissa Quart)

The essays, hybrid texts, and dialogue pieces in section 3 shift the emphasis away from academia to circle back[25] to the more general cultural concerns introduced in chapter one, but with an emphasis on a shared local commonwealth. With a hope that these essays are relatable[26] to the non-academic or "non-artistic" activists on the front line of the anti-gentrification struggle, for instance, this humble audition for activism strives to act less as a specialized professional and more of a **concerned citizen**.[27]

I begin with some attempts to flesh out a utopian vision that could foster a sense of civic pride and unity (in diversity) and a vibrant local culture that could transcend the class division and help liberate us from Hollywood's colonization, while also creating more jobs and more wealth. Taking as a backdrop a city in the midst of a post-Panther (cold) civil war that has been getting hotter in recent years, I attempt to apply my academic rhetorical skills to the front-lines of these civic conflicts in what, I hope, are patient and reasonable terms that may be of use to (general) readers even if they don't live in the same city.[28]

Despite the authoritarian tone that's an occupational hazard of mo-

---

25 Hopefully it's more of a spiral rather than a mere Spin Cycle, leaving gaps and plenty of room for discussion...

26 yes, I'm using that word "relatable."

27 *and I try not to worry about the poets as poets* (There's got to be some other way in between standing with thousands blocking off a highway after the latest police shooting (police are the shock troops of gentrification) or getting to speak for 2 minutes at a City Council meeting on one hand, and devoting a few years to writing a well-organized mindblowing novel that will be pubished 4 years from now and later be deemed "so 2016."

28 if they can forgive my local and topical emphasis. I know when I read a detailed essay about an analogous battle happening in another city (Flint, New Orleans, Newark, Ferguson, Jackson, Ms.), I learn much that could be applied to Oakland, and the "merely topical" reveals the structural conflict.

nologic prose essays, it' probably best to think of each essay as a question, or a series of questions. For instance, what does it mean to act locally, especially if writing, talking, listening (and music) is your mode of action? Can we use our writing skills to effect civic and governmental policy? And, if so, how? I confess to not knowing the answers to these questions. Obviously, some do, or seem to. Would Donald Trump have been possible without 3 decades of Rush Limbaugh? And would Rush Limbaugh had been possible without the deregulation of radio which allowed monopoly control of radio airwaves? And could the Big Food/Factory Farming industry have been able to gradually introduce more unhealthy foods into the standard American diet without the help of wordsmiths like Richard Berman, of the Center For Consumer Freedom?[29]

On the other hand, there are many muckraking journalists and culture critics or silver tongued populist preachers who have successfully used words to change minds and empower people against the corporate/government propaganda machine, but often the policy changes they suggest fall on deaf ears or get proposed in name only (like "elevating" Grove St. to Martin Luther King, or a recent declaration of a Black Arts Movement and Business District in my town). Their speeches become aestheticized, which is fine if they did not also become depoliticized.

Yet I sincerely and humbly ask any activist reader who is genuinely trying to solve my city's real estate crisis, "can analyzing the double-speak of the property owners and the city officials who cover for them be of any use for your cause? Can close reading be activism? Can showing how a specific proposal by the Creative Development Partners is civic poetry of the highest order convince the poets that they have something to gain by joining the fight to save an auditorium?[30]

---

29 For a more detailed account of Richard Berman, the father of ex-Silver Jew frontman David Berman, see Chapter 18

30 It may be "old news" now, but it is also news that stay news, as this struggle is played over and over again (and I'm sure your city has something like *the mayor's toothless "made in Oakland" campaign*). In addition to its aesthetic beauty, it also could also help address the academic crisis, and would have certainly brought us closer to fulfill-

Do we need to convince white folks that a self-governing Black Arts and Business District would benefit them too?

Or I ask the venture capitalist, "can you see how these ideas could be fiscally solvent?" Over and over again, I ask, is there a way to appeal to the shared common self-interest of many who might otherwise stand on opposite sides of this civil war? And is a live/work community performance center/art studio that is also a community owned radio station really such an absurd and unrealistic idea?

As these essays speak to several audiences from different angles in hopes we can achieve "strength in numbers," and "power-to-the-people," they're ultimately a thinker's appeal to the doer, whether activist, bureaucrat, or even enlightened venture capitalist who understands the importance of "mom & pop shops" in the struggle against the soul-crushing monopolies and duopolies that dominant a culture. They may fail by the standards of the high-art of *agit-prop,* but I'd rather try and fail by those standards than once again succeed by standards that taboo the attempt.[31]

So, ultimately, the book may seem to contradict itself, trying to argue against specialization in essays that probably only have a niche appeal (I can see the reviews now. "Stupid, or too ingenious for its own good." Shop talk suited for a niche so small, even Stroffolino himself can't fit in it!")...but that may be necessary if we live in a society in which the middle, the commons, is largely gone. Maybe someday I can do something more truly populist, though I don't think I can do it on my own (and that's part of the point)....

But it's rather more like a conversation that anyone can enter and disagreements are more than welcome. Although this book may appear, as a product, to be a collection of monologic essays, I see it ul-

---

ing Santos Perez's vision, and create better contexts for community engagement for creative writers (so a little old English Department doesn't have the full burden of having to reinvent the wheel).

31 (and forgive my omission of my essays on visual artists like Bettina Hubby, for instance, or my close reading of PJ Harvey and The Silver Jews; I devote much more space to David Berman's father here, but if we don't reunite, I'd still be glad to write a 33 1/3 book about that album).

timately as part of larger process, a dialogue—whether through panel discussions (with dancing) or a discussion board that can develop plans for collective action, or at least a *revised edition*, which will be better and more collaboratively written. I will maintain an active discussion board for one year after publication of this book....and if anybody wants to talk about any of these issues on *The Chris & Chris Show*,[32] even if they haven't read the whole book, there's an open invitation.

So now that I've written an introduction to this book which may not really be clear, or make sense, of the book unless you read the book, or at least some of it first, I could end by just saying this book needs no introduction....and if the poets won't call it poetry, or even Civic Poetry (though there's no logical reason why they wouldn't, after all Ashbery's prose *Three Poems* was called poetry, and Kenny Goldsmith is called poetry), rest assured, dear students, they'll always be concerned citizens, or teachers, like me will honor it as Non-Poetry.... and, yes, dear student, if you devote enough of your life work to it, and re willing to risk trial and error in public, your funeral could turn into a rally that hopes get your son elected mayor of a major U.S. city.....

---

32 See Chapter 11

Notes Toward An M(F)A In Non-Poetry

1. Book Review: *Culture Crash: The Killing Of The Creative Class,* Scott Timberg (Yale University Press, 2015)

"Kodak—a company that once employed 144,000 people and supported an entire region of upstate New York—has been sold to Instagram, an online photo sharing service with thirteen employees. What happened to all those middle-class jobs, all of that wealth?"
—Jason Lanier (77)

"Every single person I've ever talked to has said that doing Kickstarter is the hardest thing they've ever done. You have to live it everyday—you're not a songwriter anymore, you're planning, you're making promises, you're going to people's houses…It becomes an all-consuming thing to get that money. *It's like the grind of going on tour, without the joy of performing.*"
—Stew, The Negro Problem (84)

"But I won't be homeless; I can teach. I'm really concerned about a generation who won't get a chance…But as an educator, I feel like an ayatollah sending kids running into the minefield"
—Oliver Toraine (132)[33]

These quotes, and many more like them, are a few of the fragments Scott Timberg's *Culture Crash* gathers together from hundreds of interviews/case studies done with culture workers across the disciplines since the great Crash of 2008. He takes pains to remind us that he is a journalist first and foremost to connect the dots between today's cultural, economic, and political crises, which the mainstream media encourages us to keep separated. While Timberg's book is not as deeply theoretical as some books of culture criticism (for instance, he doesn't get into a detailed nuts and bolts economic analysis in an attempt to answer Jason Lanier's question about "what happened to all that wealth"), his applied theory nevertheless synthesizes many

---

33   Of course, teaching is no guarantee of not being homeless, as the increased number of homeless teachers attest

strands to show the human toll of what Thomas Frank calls *The Wrecking Crew's* diligent dismantling of America's Middle Working Class Culture. Like Frank, Timberg offers a well-researched diagnosis of today's cultural crisis.

By devoting chapters to how the cultural crisis affects a wide array of specialized professions/vocations/culture industries (from visual art, including graphic design, to music, journalism, academia and even architecture), Timberg shows the common roots between them, and hints at possible coalitions that need to be formed in order to address them.

Yet, in contrast to Frank, Timberg does not focus on the agents who've caused this dismantling (It's not called, The Culture Crashers, The *Killers* Of The Creative Class). Thus, while Frank shows how the destruction of America's economic infrastructure was a policy designed by the ruling elite, Timberg tries to spread the blame around, including targeting the self-inflicted wounds that made many culture workers forget that culture is a negotiation, struggle or war (and, as a result of this forgetfulness or hubris, the 1% is winning, while the rest of us are losing).

In discussing the Wrecking Crew, or the 1% who hires them, Timberg characteristically uses the passive voice, as seen, for instance, in this sentence: "*Citizen's United*, the 2010 Supreme court decision that dropped limits on political spending by corporations, means that plutocratic influence on U.S. politics will only increase." (221). This could be translated as: The Plutocrats and Corporations have been successful in gaining control of US Politics, and its culture. Therefore, we must stand up for our rights against its tyranny!" Pick your tone—both, I believe, are needed.

Culture Crash tends to emphasize the language of negotiation over that of war, clearly preferring a capacious inclusive bipartisan American culture, which he passionately terms the "middlebrow consensus." Yet, despite his rhetorical use of the passive voice, which has earned praise by M.G. Lord for its "coolness and equanimity," Timberg does show how it's not an accident that the corporations have been able to take over the politics, economy, and culture of this country, but the result of policy. This book still manages to trouble the frame even as it shies away from revolutionary rhetoric to appeal to the Yale/NPR crowd.

At the core of this book's class analysis of how this culture crash occurred is Timberg's insight:

When the affluent class shifted from owning land to owning part of a business, the wealthy "proprietor" began to dislocate himself from a town or community. Multinational corporations took this a step beyond. When the world economy went global in the 1990s, and digital technology pushed it even further along,....the changing culture at the top...lead to an abandonment of public spaces as well as the notion of shared culture." (232)[34]

Timberg is careful to concede that today's billionaires may be "intelligent and decent," but adds: "Plutocrats of the 21st century have no real hometown or home team of any kind. Their dedication is entirely to capital and to its frictionless international exchange." (233) The result is a world in which local prestige, and local culture, no longer matter. No wonder that this class consolidates its power with the rise of the placeless, globalized, internet, rising rent (and, before that, the growth of toxic individualism in the post "me decade" era). Cultural institutions like book, record, video stores, art centers and locally owned newspapers and radio stations clearly provide too much human "friction" for these capital loving plutocrats.

But why did local prestige, or even national culture, *ever*

---

34   This doesn't mean that they no longer own the land, only that the landowners often don't live in the town where they own land....

matter to the super rich? Part of the reason for this is that corporations had been regulated by a government which, to some extent, looked out for the interests of the working class. This occurred most profoundly in mid-20th century America. In "the '40s, '50s, '60s and most of the '70s—the United States did not have a winner-take-all society. It had instead what economists call the Great Compression, a structure of wages, government investment, and progressive taxation that led to a large and solid middle class, as well as steady economic growth"(230).

It's not a coincidence that America's culture, and its creative class, grew and thrived during this time, for "culture, as we understand the term, tends to originate in the middle class" and "depends on a middle class audience for its dissemination and vitality" (8).[35] Yet the relationship between culture and the economy is symbiotic; such a culture also *creates* and propagates this middle class: "A broad-based class making its living in culture ensures a better society."(14). The fate of the middle class and the creative class are linked; they rise and fall together.

Given this somewhat Reichian historical economic/cultural analysis, it's surprising to hear Timberg argue, "I'm not advocating for a new WPA" (265), a staple of the New Deal policies that not only "kept writers, photographers, theater actors, and others alive during a difficult time" (234), but also laid the groundwork for this Great Compression that characterized America's mid century cultural flourish.[36] Neither does he advocate for

---

35 Note that it is primarily the *consumption* of the culture that defines origins for Timberg. Producers may come from the lower-classes, but the *middle class* audience is what makes them. While I agree with Timberg that such culture does not generally originate from the upper class, must we assume that it originates from the "middle" as opposed to the poorer classes? For instance, if I were to argue that culture originates from the poor (as say jazz is rooted in the blues, and hip hop was founded in one of the poorest neighborhoods in the USA), would Timberg's argument fall apart?

36 For those who would still entertain the possibility that something

bolder Socialist policies to place checks on the post-Reagan winner-take-all Monopoly Capitalist economy, in which the rich get richer, the poor get poorer "and the middle withers."

Timberg, instead, seeks to rationally persuade the wealthy global elites that they, too, may benefit from the better society. He invokes the largely lost, but once "widespread idea of loss leaders or *noblesse oblige*—a sense that some culture mattered for reasons outside its exchange values." (230). Timberg suggests that if we can bring *noblesse oblige* back (with no ideological strings attached—in contrast to the Koch Brother's buy outs of esteemed cultural institutions), perhaps we don't need a new WPA, much less socialism. We may, however, need the sense of nationalistic cultural pride that characterized the Cold War era when the U.S. Government underwrote culture—admittedly for dubious reasons (for instance, jazz artists were sent overseas to "paper over racial tensions," domestically [234])—but nonetheless with tangible consequences that benefited American society as a whole certainly more than the current state of affairs does.[37]

Such appeals to the wealthy, however, may continue to fall on deaf ears as long as Poptimists, Individualists, Technological Utopians and proponents of "free" culture dominate today's cultural discussion. In fact, it is this class of faux-populist (151) culture workers that Timberg has the harshest words for, as they serve, whether intentionally or not, as the plutocrats' propaganda arm. In a letter to the editor I wrote in 1995,[38] I made a similar argument against the tech utopians. Tech Utopianism was very fashionable circa 94-96 among many I knew (at U-Penn,

---

like a WPA could help ameliorate today's crisis, and in the long-term be more 'fiscally solvent,' see my Chapter, "Community Outreach For Creative Writers" (Chapter 13) for a smaller-scale intervention.

37   For A Similar Argument about how the breakup of the USSR caused American culture to atrophy, see Ian Svenonius' mordantly brilliant *The Psychic Soviet* (2006)

38   see *Spin Cycle*

the Kelly's Writer's House argued how it would make use of this cutting-edge technology to help de-specialize and de-hierarchize literature and similar arguments were made in the Ph.D program I was enrolled in at Suny-Abany by Chris Funkhouser, Don Byrd, even Robert Creeley).

I was skeptical then, or even fearful ("tech will do more harm than good. It's still not too late to stop tech from taking over, but we gotta act soon!") and, in retrospect, I could say prophetic. For indeed this technology has been used to separate people from each other even more today than in the 90s, as *Culture Crash* amply shows.[39] Though some of his criticisms of these folks seems based more on Timberg's own aesthetic standards, which he takes as self-evident, one doesn't have to agree with his taste in music, literature and art to see the soundness of his broader diagnosis of how this ideological work has helped cause the culture crash from above.

On The Cultural Value of Cheap Rent

Timberg begins his analysis from the ground up, from the "street level," (15) the everyday world that the vast majority of us can relate to, even if we don't care about "culture" or "art." Consider skyrocketing property values, "The boom-bust-flip phenomenon," in which the housing market has been turned into a Casino, that "benefits the upper class while brutalizing the middle class"(223)...to say nothing of the poorer classes.

The unregulated real-estate market, or what Allen Sanford calls "government sanctioned racketeering"[40] allows developers, for instance, more incentives to raise rent and drive small

---

39   I discuss these issues further in the section "Techquity & The Erasure of the Local"

40   https://www.facebook.com/RealEstateFraudOrGovernment-SanctionedRacketeering/?pnref=lhc

businesses out, because they can make more money leaving the buildings vacant (sometimes for more than 20 years) before they find an outfit who can pay their inflated rent. And, in the first decade of the 21st century, Timberg writes, "next to disruptive technology, it's skyrocketing rents that are pushing culture merchants out." (64) This "doesn't just cut into the number of people who can make a living from working in culture. Every time a shop selling books or records, or renting movies, closes, we lose the kind of gathering places that allow people oriented to culture to meet and connect; we lose our context, and the urban fabric frays."(64)

This thus has ethical implications, as the novelist Pico Iyer says, an independent bookstore with its human touch and element of surprise "frees me from my habits as a website seldom does." (68) As Jonathan Lethem adds, "With bookstores, you go in and you find things you weren't looking for...you develop a loathing for the false canon—the two books each year that everybody is supposed to read."(56). Such small retail outlets help create a grassroots counter-balance to the trickle down culture the oligarchs prefer; store clerks may teach people more about culture than the corporate media and schools combined, and their absence leads a void that an internet algorithm can never fill.[41]

The rising real estate prices have not only affected these gathering places. According to Chris Ketchum, a freelance writer who is struggling to stay in Brooklyn during the onslaught of gentrification. "Rent is the basis of everything. For any artist or creator who wants to live with that dynamism of dense urban spaces, he can be saddled with rents so high that they take up 50% or more of his income. It's impossible to do things outside the marketplace because you're constantly working to pay rent"

---

41 Is it the burden of teachers to take up this slack, and inhabit the void left by the bookstores? Note to publishers, if you really want to sell more—and better—books, support local bookstores!

(80).[42]

It wasn't always this way, at least for some. According to legendary art-funk-rocker David Byrne, "Cheap rent allows artists, musicians and writers to live without much income during their formative years. It gives them time to develop...and it gives the creative communities that nurture and support them time to form." (26).[43] This was certainly true of David Byrne during the 1970s (along with a little money from mom and dad as his song "Pull Me Up" reminds us), but it's even more true for people not as lucky as Byrne to become rich off their art, and who thus need cheap rent beyond their formative years, as a sustainable middle class life-style.

Consider New Orleans. As late as 2004, this storied city was known as one of the poorest cities in America, but the flipside of that was that it was also cheaper, and thus less difficult for local celebrity street musicians, young and old, to survive and create a less corporate mediated popular culture. No wonder this city was the birthplace of jazz and, debatably, R&B (and rock and roll). After Katrina, however, it's a different story (especially after BP's war on the "small people").[44]

As Timberg puts it, "real estate prices have begun to wage

---

[42] ""Doing things outside the market place" doesn't just mean working on art, but also activism. In NYC, even in the 90s, many of my artist friends loved to joke, "sorry I couldn't make it to the affordable housing rally. I was too busy working my three jobs to pay rent." Quotes like Ketchum's also provide amble evidence to show that contemporary "economic justice" movements like the $15 dollar national minimum wage or the more ambitious "guaranteed basic income" movement) are but band-aids on the wound (that might even make the wound worse if the underlying real estate prices remain unregulated and unaddressed).

[43] Of course, Byrne himself lost touch with the local communities that nourished him once he became a "star."

[44] *https://www.youtube.com/watch?v=th3LtLx0IEM*

the economic equivalent of ethnic cleansing on the middle class."(65). Indeed, ethnic cleansing, and urban removal, has been an economic policy the Black Creative Class is all too familiar with. It just took a few decades to trickle up from the African-American creative class to the middle class; as a black friend put it, "we're the canary in the coalmine." The same process that has made San Francisco rents skyrocket 30% between 2011 and 2013 began many years earlier, as the black population decreased from over 20% in 1970 to less than 4% by 2010, and neighboring Oakland is following suit.

Timberg does not go so far as Ian Svenonius' *"The Seinfeld Syndrome"* –let alone Ta Nehisi Coates' "The Case For Reparations,"[45] in arguing that this process is part of a systematic long-term plan that began with the corporate engineered "white flight" during the 1940s, but his analysis of the street level economic consequences gives ample evidence for the necessity of developing strategies to reverse this process.

Culture Crash suggests that if we value culture, we must advocate for stringent rent control, truly affordable housing, and other anti-gentrification strategies…or a recalibration of earnings. Artists and the creative class must make it clear that we align ourselves with the inner-city poor who have been systematically driven out by "urban renewal." The developers and gentrifiers have too often used the creative class to help make the city more "livable" for the elite class who have been pouring in from the suburbs, and then price them out.

Even culture workers in the creative class who just want to, need to, continue to make their art or entertainment, who don't have a political bone in their body, inevitably became politicized—if only we had time and places to meet and organize (which is exceedingly different in this "permatemp" economy

---

45 http://www.theatlantic.com/magazine/archive/2014/06/the-case-for-reparations/361631

of content serfs), and were not increasingly separated from each other due to the dismantling of the public sphere, the war against the compact, affordable waking city, the growth of the placeless, privatized, Web, insecure jobs, longer commutes and work hours.

Culture Crash does go beyond complaints and making excuses to challenge the way the middle class has internalized the ideology of individualism that benefits the wealthy at our own expense; how we let our enemies create our spokesmen, and Timberg, at times, adopts the zealous voice of the recently converted evangelist in challenging the myths of his upbringing. You could say he "got religion" when the Crash of 2008 cost him his job and home, and made him question everything he believed was his birthright, as he watched the "middlebrow consensus" his parents could take for granted "fade away like a pale ghost" (225) during the last few decades of the 20th century, as the broad middle class turned into a mere niche (221). [46]

No wonder he tries to warn others of making the same mistakes he did. And no wonder he sometimes assumes his audience is more likely to think the way he did before the crash, and may need to be "reprogrammed," when he preaches that the only way to save culture, so that it is "not made up exclusively of feudal lords and struggling content serfs," is by *"fighting against the assumptions we inherited"* (252—emphasis added).

The Necessity of Challenging *Free Lance Nation* to bring back The Middle Class

In fighting these inherited assumptions, Timberg looks beyond the official histories of heroic geniuses, the corporate propaganda machine that characterizes what Adam Curtis calls *The*

---

[46] I can identify with Timberg here, as a white so-called "generation Xer" who achieved success in the culture industry only to see it come crashing down in the 21st century

Century Of The Self; indeed, he is at his evangelical best, when he takes on the individualistic "winner-take-all" ethos, which is such a deeply rooted, insidious presence in today's culture, to remind us, as the Gang of Four would sing, that history is "not made by great men." In order to "create a world that is not predatory" (252), we have to fight against this official reality that, at the very least, doesn't mind if we forget (or never knew) that "artists did much of their best work laboring together, in cities and the subcultures they made possible."(24)

Understanding art as, at its essence, collective in its creation may require a different sense of ontology than the false, or destructive, conscience of the every-man-for-himself, winner-take-all rugged individualism pushed by the Elite through their cultural outlets, whether in the "fine arts" or in mass-culture.[47] Timberg sees this old-fashioned "all American" ideology of rugged individualism revised and updated for the 21st Century Tech Economy in influential books such as *Me, Inc.* by business guru Tom Peters ("Where we are all CEO of our company" [74]). Such slogans underpin the vast majority of TV advertising and are virtually omnipresent in the alleged democratic culture of social media. Yet, Timberg shows how these ideological winds of "Freelance Nation" reveal a profound misunderstanding, or intentional obfuscation, of the words "democracy" and "freedom."

In the first place, such freedom, isn't really free, just as "free" downloading is not really free when you need to have a $1,000 laptop, a $500 iPHone, or a $400 Samsung Tablet" as David Lowery points out, [104]. Furthermore, although the near-universal commodification of "self" is sold as democratic, and even a possible cure, to the loss of physical gathering places the real

---

[47] Timberg certainly believes that the American Dream was to be middle class (as if that's an honest buck) rather than "he who dies with the most toys wins."

estate market caused (with tax dollar assistance),[48] there was never a vote on whether we should have an internet instead of bookstores, etc (and it's possible that if there were, most voters would have rejected it, just like Nafta). Surely, there are advantages to the virtual communities of a facebook newsfeed that enables a rapid exchange of opinions, and maybe even creates a kind of "safe space" for difficult discussions on race which wouldn't happen otherwise (the verdict is not yet in on whether #BlackLifeMatters has been able to effect positive lasting change through this medium).

Even acknowledging these possible benefits, social media also tends to appeal to the lowest common denominator of reactive/reactionary thinking, and I know, from repeated experiences, that some of the most hotly contested cultural and ideological clashes on my newsfeed could have a better chance of finding common ground if people felt the vibrations of each other's voices (or were out dancing).

We may all be CEOS of our own company (even if it's just a "trying to get laid" company), but as "free agents," these atomized, uncoordinated array of individual content providers (so-called self-reliant individuals) are simply no match for the coordinated efforts of the large corporations.[49] It can't provide the necessary push-back, or resistance, that a local collective effort could to help create more truly two-way forms of communication on an institutional level. The fact that mass-culture's propaganda mechanisms have done a great job of convincing many white-collar workers, including those celebrated in the creative class, including the literary arts—that they're not workers, with any sense of collective identity, certainly doesn't help fight the

---

48 "Who needs a physical gathering place, when we got an on-line church, where, by comparison, even talking heads seem embodied enough to speak in tongues."

49 Only corporations, not mere companies, get to be called "persons".

downsizing, outsourcing and robotizing of the work force.

As long as culture workers (content providers, content serfs) conceive of themselves, and act primarily, as isolated individual commodities, they will be cut off from the social creative source, from the clash of cultures, that potentially productive negotiation, the *churn* of culture so needed for a truly democratic society ("if everything is flat and even, the winds don't blow" [50]). A culture *clash,* culture war (even if it's as seemingly benign as the clash between Motown and white album oriented artists in the 60s), is needed in order to avoid a culture *crash!* And today's placeless tech culture tends to sweep that clash beneath the increasingly concrete rug.

From the plutocrats' perspective, the fact that many in the working class have drunk this Kool-Aid of "self" has been a brilliant strategy to divide the enemy, an enemy who may have been blindsided and has forgotten that there's a war. In my life, a common and oft-repeated story in so-called "underground" (i.e. local) music scenes (whether punk, hip-hop, or other forms of dance or art-music) is that a large corporation comes in like a colonizer to cherry pick 2 or 3 artists, thus helping to fragment the scene and eliminate the threat to its monopoly. Timberg certainly doesn't mean to cast any aspersion to artists who let the corporations play them that way (David Lowery, for instance, is one of the books heroes), but his argument does challenge the media-pushed myth that this way is better ("These artists were pursuing their own unique vision! Community was holding them back!" "The corporations gave them freedom," etc)—even if this ideology has produced some great art.

Yet this anti-collectivist ideology is especially insidious when we find it manifest in the lyrics of some of our favorite songs, songs we were raised on, and may still cherish. For instance, Timberg is clearly a fan of music and art that has much more of an individualist than collectivist ideology: larger than life figures like Dylan, Davids Byrne and Bowie, or Waylon, Willie, and Townes Van Zandt.[50] Since many of these pop song sentiments, past and present, are many people's first poetry, they may have the subliminal power (as if the sounds were the sugar to coat the bitter pill of the words), to contribute, along with the schools and the infotainment biz, to the anti-collectivist ideology Timberg is struggling (with himself, even) to weed out, and be free of.

And of course, one doesn't have to entirely reject the anti-collectivist sentiments of these lyrics (especially if they got a good groove), if one understands the behind the scenes collectivism *Culture Crash* foregrounds, and in this sense the book points in the direction of a great "behind the music sociopic"[51] that could complement the similar scope of earlier book-length classic analyses of cultural decay like Nelson George's *The Death Of Rhythm & Blues*.

Culture Crash, by drawing on a few representative examples from different arenas of how culture worked well in the past, points to possible ways of reversing this trend. All of Timberg's positive examples that could help reverse these trends occur during that era of The Great Compression, when the cultural means of production were more "mom and pop" operations owned by more folks in the middle class who had no "winner-take-all" ambitions and were content to work "successfully in a single city"(229). For instance, Motown in its early days approached this, and studying such models deeper may allow us to come up with new ways to learn from their successes, and

---

50 So called "classic rock" is littered with such outdated—or never really applicable—sentiments as (to name but one of a million examples) "get a second hand guitar/ chances are you'll go far/ if you get in with the right bunch of fellows"—a big *if* of course

51 A sociopic—in contrast to the "great man" and/or "debunking *biopic* genre beloved of Hollywood: http://chrisstroffolino.blogspot.com/2014/09/get-on-up-and-limits-of-bioptic-or.html

avoid their failures.[52]

In the meantime, *Culture Crash* attests to the increasing number of people colonized, whether they like it or not, by the ideology of "free lance-nation," who, since the crash of 2008, have increasingly made the connection between the Kool-Aid and the fact that we must "fight to keep a home (or even a flat), a livelihood, or medical coverage" to say nothing of a community or family. The killing of the creative class may very well be an "unintended consequence" of Big Tech and the corporate control of the means of production, as Timberg argues throughout—but it may very well have been intended. Either way, we must struggle to take it back.

Yet, just because one understands this selling, this branding, and this ideological indoctrination as a disenfranchising lie doesn't mean it's going to be easy to know how to reverse it. The question remains: How can we restore, reinforce, or replenish what Thom Hartmann likes to call "the commons" or the "radical middle" or what Michael Moore calls a "we society"? Can we put down our egos or our aesthetic differences and allegiances, our hopeless resignation, to make common cause to reground culture in the *vox populi*, even if the elites deign not to be part of it, find unprofitable and, for some reason, feel threatened by?

What Is To be Done? (Anti-specialization strategies)

Ultimately, *Culture Crash* is either a call for artists and culture workers to become activists, or at the very least a call for artists and activists to join forces.[53] Timberg closes his book by

---

52 See Chapter 13 on "Community Outreach For Creative Writers" for a more extensive account of how Motown achieved this, and Chapter 17 "The Great Fillmore Whitewash" for an analogous example from the San Francisco Bay Area

53 "Artists, cultural icons, can highlight, reflect, and support a movement, but those of us with real organizing skills, and consis-

stating that even though "technological and economic trends work against the creative class" and the culture he values, and even if we are helpless to fight Big Real Estate or Big Tech, he argues "some things are within our control." (267) He claims "it's pointless to offer specific solutions" because "conditions are changing so fast," but he does offer a vision for what he'd like to see happen. Though his list doesn't read like a manifesto of demands, I believe that taking this list as a starting point, we could start a *Culture Crash* discussion group or think tank devoted to considering ways to get from where we're at now to this envisioned world.

To put it another way, *Culture Crash*, like any good book, needs a sequel—ideally a collaboratively written sequel, perhaps to be published on Timberg's website in a discussion board format, along with videos of Q&A sessions that occur during his book release parties.[54] This considering of "ways and means" to go along with unmet hopes and deferred dreams will require the collective communal effort, and would be open to anybody with a stake in culture, *and feel free to risk specific solutions even though they may be outdated later.* So-called "hair-brained" ideas are welcome. In fact, I'll offer up a few to put on trial:

One of the things Timberg would like to see is:

A world in which people who aren't poets read poetry and draw sustenance and wisdom from it. In which non-dancers attend dance concerts, and folks who are neither professional musicians nor foreign businessmen go to jazz shows.

This, of course, is easier said than done. In thinking about

---

tent activist mindsets must be the ones to make movements happen," Kevin Powell, *Kool Herc*, 37.

54   I'd love to be on a panel discussion with him, especially if I could bring my musician friends

how we could achieve this less specialized, fragmented world, I feel we have to start with the young just as the corporations and the culture crashers do—for children don't think in specialized terms as much as adults and may have a lot to teach us older folks and our "inherited assumptions." We may not have access to the mass media that can reach kids in their preschool years, but we still do have access to the schools, and I don't want to feel like that ayatollah sending kids running into the minefield that teaching the creative arts (including critical thinking) have become these days.

I am reminded of an ex-student of mine who wrote a brilliant, beautiful paper titled, "Life Is Dance." She hopes to be able to work as a dancer, dance teacher and writer, but she is forced into choosing a specialized field to work in. She chooses dance, and her passion for writing atrophies, just as another student chooses writing and loses his balance as his passion for dancing atrophies. Over and over, I see this consequence of the specialized education system. People don't complain about it too loudly because that's just the way things are, yet many people struggle with the necessity to overspecialize in our society, and this is one of the main causes for why dancers and poets don't patronize each other's art as much as Timberg would like.

I want to tell my student, "Look, there are older people, with some cultural clout, like Scott Timberg, who want to help create a culture in which you'd thrive, who are willing to fight for your need to bring these scenes together. You're onto something that could help save our culture from such isolated specialization and help make people more productive and happy." Of course, it will be a fight, and would take at least a generation to achieve. In the meantime, I personally have been frustrated by how poets (and to a lesser extent musicians) seem to be content to huddle in the corners to which they've been assigned—but I know many struggle with these institutionally opposed limits.

This is one reason why team-taught interdisciplinary classes that emphasize what the arts have in common is so crucial for creating the better society Timberg envisions. School, like church, can offer temporary shelter from the relentless push of market values, and provide that gathering place that has not yet been replaced by MOOCs or on-line churches. Teachers have the power to require their students to attend dance and poetry events, and the duty to make it engaging for their students, especially given the failure of standard individualized, specialized American education to meet the needs of students. We should make use of these institutions before they, too, get defunded as education is privatized.

Starting from a students' passion, and building on that, teaching them about the existing structures and rules the better to change them from within, could also increase—rather than decrease—students' employability—all the more so if we include a service component, an internship/practicum in which local culture would be emphasized over what Timberg calls the all-or nothing blockbuster culture. Of course, in order for this to happen, we need to emphasize the racism in the culture industries (from Hollywood to academia) more than Timberg's argument does. In fact, it's a strong possibility that white institutional racism towards blacks, and other POC, has had a lot to do with causing the crisis that more whites now feel acutely in the 21st century.

2. How Post-Structuralism Was Used To Marginalize Black Studies (& How This Contributes To Today's Cultural Crisis)

In looking for the roots to today's cultural crisis, Timberg believes some of the fault lies with academic Humanities Programs and English Departments. In his book *Culture Crash* (2015), Timberg recognizes a disturbing trend. "In the 1970s, the percentage of students studying English and the Humanities, which had been rising for two decades, plummeted. Humanities majors went from 30 percent in the 1970–71 academic year to 16 percent by 2003–04" (193) and "the Yale English Department graduating majors dropped 60% from 1983 to 2013" (187).

Timberg claims that this statistical decline is not primarily due to economic factors (i.e. of course Business and Marketing become more attractive majors than English or other Liberal Arts in the post-Reagan economy), but rather because English and Humanities departments had lost their connection to a common language, and were essentially "speaking in tongues" due to the dominance of post-structural discourse in these fields. Timberg believes that had not post-structuralist theories and lexicons been imported from Europe (especially France) in the last three decades of the 20th century, more people would still want to be English majors. Before this, Timberg believes, academia did speak in a more common language—but what does he mean by a common language? Did academia ever have that? Can we achieve it (or restore it) today? Certainly this requires closer scrutiny than his 8 page historical summary provides.

While I find aspects of Timberg's argument attractive (especially as one who, as a grad student in the 90s, struggled with the faux-leftist regime of Post-Structuralist theory and jargon, and tried to find a way to subvert its hegemony from within), I must question some of his assumptions. First, just because the percentages have dropped, the absolute number of English majors is still larger than it was in the 1950s as college attendance, in general, increased during this time.

Most significantly, I believe that Timberg ignores some important socio-cultural factors within academia, and bases his theory on a reductive binary that opposes the post-1970s post-structuralists with the pre-1960s academics like the Joyce scholar who laments the loss of the culture in which teachers would "Champion with passion the books they teach and make a strong case to undergraduates that the knowledge in these books, and the tradition in which they exist, is a human good in and of itself." Sure, if new academic books with Shakespeare in the title are more likely to be about the kind of underwear Elizabethans wore, no wonder there's less passion for books. Yet, these need not be the only two options. In fact, if we look at the history more closely, we find other—and somewhat erased—factors within academia during the turbulent 1960s that intervened in between the reign of these two eras that came closer to proposing a more common language than either the Joycean or the post-structuralist. We must, at the very least, envision a triangle

While Timberg mentions that "the failure of the student/worker rebellions of 1968 Paris" lead to the rise of post-structuralism, he entirely ignores the student/worker rebellions occurring during the same time in America, as the growth of cheap, and in some cases free, publicly funded colleges and universities increased both the numbers as well as the diversity (in terms of race, gender and class) of first generation college students during the '60s, on a broader scale than the post WW2 GI Bill. It must be remembered that before 1960, the vast majority of college students in America were primarily white, male and upper (or at least upper-middle) class, and the "tradition" had been perpetuated to benefit *those* people.

Yet in the '60s, academia stood at a historical crossroads as many of these new students saw how the traditional "great books" curriculum and/or established ways of reading and discussing them reflected an anti-populist, elitist and Euro-centric agenda devised to justify and perpetuate the elite's hold on the culture industry—hardly a common language. One of the most pronounced—but often erased— American student protests and/or rebellions during this time occurred when a coalition lead by the Black Student Union managed to shut down San Francisco State. They wanted a *humanities* that gave a true knowledge of self that acknowledged the decadent nature of this society, as the Black panther Ten Point Platform put it.

These students demanded structural changes to the institution—-a more inclusive curriculum, and the development of a Black Studies Program. They didn't demand doing away with "white" or "European" studies (for those who have a stake in it), but were interested in supplementing it to make the humanities more relevant to the communities they were a part of, stressing practicums and internships and providing a new paradigm that contrasts with, and challenges, the dominance of the traditional "ivory tower." As a result of their struggles, Black Studies (and, more broadly, ethnic studies) departments were instituted around the country. Yet many of their demands went unmet. For instance, they didn't manage to create a university curriculum in which a course on the Black Arts Movement would be required alongside of Shakespeare. Though the structural demands went largely unheeded, "identity politics" grew. Lip service was paid: Tokenism and admission quotas were debated. And it is in *this* context that post-structural ideas began flooding into academia from the top down.

While Timberg makes it seem like those who considered the canon "too white" and "too male" came to academia *after* the post-structural challenge, it's important to note that the challenge Black Studies presented to the traditional academic culture in English and Humanities departments *preceded* the rise of deconstruction. Considering this chronology, it's very plausible that the rise of post-structuralism in American universities was at least as much a *reaction* to these popularizing, democratizing student movements of the 1960s as it was a reaction to the old-school professors. The same academic power structure that resisted the revolutionary challenges the Black Student Union made found post-structuralism much less of a threat to the established ways of doing things.

It's perhaps not a coincidence that just as blacks and women and other previously disenfranchised people were beginning to empower themselves *as subjects* that the fashionable new trend of post-structuralism *did away with the subject*, and rendered it "outré." What happened in the 70s and 80s was the academic equivalent to White Classic Arena Rock (AOR) in mass culture; it presented itself as progressive while serving to reify a new exclusionary, racist and (thoroughly mediocre) anti-neighborhood elitism. Though some proponents of the old academic establishment would later lump all these challenges together, proponents of Black Studies ask what can "The Humanities" mean in a society that treats some as less than human. Their challenge was not merely about "the death of the author," but about trying to make the humanities more human (if that word can have any positive meaning, and not be at the expense of non-human nature).

By contrast to the poststructuralists, proponents of black studies did not "distance themselves from good books." They just rejected the taken-for-granted standards by which certain books (usually by white males) and traditions are judged great, while others are not given an equal hearing. It asked, among other things, why, in America, do we still call it an *English* department? What does it mean to be a "humanist" when the humanities have been used, more often than not, to justify segregation and the belief that white institutions were categorically superior?

Black Studies also challenged (and challenges) the specialization of genres, a model of education that became dominant during the "enlightenment." It didn't need to resort to the overly specialized lexicon and codes of post-structuralist approaches. Black studies understood that one could express the most sophisticated intelligence and imagination in a common language—certainly much more than post-structuralism did, but also much more than the old school professors with their Eurocentric "eternal verities" did.

On the contrary, Black Studies made room for the oral, verbal intelligence that Derrida and his ilk would deride as phallogocrentrism, just as traditional humanists would deride it as "afro-centrism" or "ebonics" as earlier slave-masters considered Africans less "civilized" because they didn't write things down. These aspects of Black Studies could also come to benefit English and Humanities programs in general, and could play a part in truly opening up public discourse to the full spectrum of opinions and perspectives that are still largely unheeded in academic Literature programs. This philosophy also encourages collaboration more than the specialized, individual-centric Euro-American model of education.

In being more inclusive and less specialized, the language of black studies was too clear and too common for those who have a stake in *exclusion*, as do both the new fangled deconstructionists an the old-fashioned New Critics, an outgrowth of white southern "fugitive" aristocrats. Was the new "post-structuralist" way more elitist than the old way? Probably not, but neither was it unequivocally better especially if one is looking for more inclusiveness, and values honesty as Timberg does.

In short, Black Studies, with its more inclusive, functional, approach understood how to create more utility and *a wider demand* for an academic degree in ways that what we now call The Humanities could benefit from. If Academia had chosen to allocate more of its resources to an Afro-centric Black Studies Curriculum, I believe we wouldn't be in the predicament we are today—manifested not merely by a declining number of humanities students, but also by a higher unemployment rate among college and grad-school graduates. In this sense I agree with Timberg that the dominance of post-structuralism has indeed contributed to the crisis both within the academy as well as in American culture as a whole. I just disagree that returning to the pre-1960s notion of "The Humanities" is the best way to address it.

As post-structuralism came to dominate the academy, so did academic inflation (the devaluing of the degree). In the 1970s, you could land a full-time tenure track academic position with only a M.A.; by the 1990s, even a PhD couldn't guarantee that, and not because of a declining percentage of English majors, but rather because there was more of a supply of graduates than there were employment demands.

The exclusionists argue that crisis occurred because standards had been lowered to make room for people who are clearly unqualified (as if the proof of "being unqualified" is found in their inability to get jobs), but it's clear that this new, post-1970s culture, crammed more people into a smaller room when it could have created a larger room, by tearing down some exclusionary walls as black studies programs would have.

Hence, a new labor force of over-educated and overqualified graduates emerged, armed with post-structuralist discourse that promised to give them a competitive edge in an increasingly bureaucratic profession. The proliferation of academic creative writing programs in the last third of the 20th century took up some of the slack, and did some work in creating a larger room by bringing English Departments closer to "the masses" than they would have been without them, before Black Studies and after Post-Structuralism, but, today, as in 1968, we stand at a crossroads, as it's not only the supply of people with PhDs that has increased while the market demand for them has decreased: MFA programs too have come to cram more people in a smaller room when they could've created a larger room....

3. Crisis? What Crisis?
The Rise (and Plateau) of the Academic Creative Writing Program

The growth of post-structuralism during the 70s also parallels the proliferation of M(F)A Creative Writing programs under the broader auspices of the academic English department. In some ways, graduate Creative Writing programs are the opposite of graduate programs in post-structural theory. While the latter may be more elitist, the former may seem more populist, less hierarchical and not as specialized. Yet, the two have some similarities, as both can be seen as reform efforts, or even reactions, in response to the mid century populist upswell and culture clashes of the 50s and 60s.

Coming to poetry in college during the 80s, I inherited the myth that n the 1950s and 60s, the percentage of, as well as absolute number of, people who read poetry and other forms of literature had risen (and not because of Iowa's Writing Workshop). Affordable, quality, mass-marketed paperback books and middlebrow publications encouraged a more literate populace and made literature seem much more inclusive and relevant to the needs and demands of the first generation college students during this time. Ginsberg, Baraka and others could use the mass cultural media, and cheap affordable paperbacks by viable independent publishing houses, as a bargaining chip in negotiations with the more exclusionary academia. Ginsberg, for instance, could become a popularizing poet and public intellectual due to a mass-cultural industry that publicized a censorship trial (and a corporate think-tank that assumed that even "radical" beat poetry and communist folkies like Pete Seeger were less of a threat to the established order than the more dynamic poetry of contemporaries like Chuck Berry), and their popularity trickled up so even less "populist" poets could benefit (Creeley's *For Love* sold over 10,000 copies, which rarely happens today).

Because the culture producers and culture consumers of this time were the last generation who weren't so raised by TV, mass media needed "high literature" to lure people in, and this worked both ways (since mass media created more interest in poetry—and literature in general—than academia did). By 1960, the hegemony of the old elitist guard of academic formalists had been chipped away by the somewhat wide coalition that was collected in Donald Allen's *New American Poetry* anthology. The 1972 *Norton Anthology of Modern Poetry* that was used as a primary text in many colleges through 1987 brought together an even wider array, including many populist public intellectual poets like Ginsberg, Baraka, and Adrienne Rich alongside the more traditional "poet's poet" (say Wallace Stevens, Elizabeth Bishop, John Ashbery or Robert Creeley).

By Timberg's definition, one could see this anthology as emblematic of the Middle-brow consensus at its best: it brought a populist groundswell in closer dialogue with the more traditional "trickle down" canon. Sure, there wasn't an absolute agreement over literary merit, but the debates were exciting and empowering as "high culture" and "counter culture" clashed with each other, and even found common ground against the mediocrity of corporate "mainstream" culture. Finally, literature could be more capacious, and not simply at the mercy of the whims of the aristocratic patrons. Since this new, more eclectic "canon" included more than a few writers from the Black Arts Movement who had a very populist aesthetic, I believed that being a populist poet or public intellectual speaking to a general audience could be a viable option. Working class writers were finding working class readers, both inside and outside of the academy,

By the '70s, Creative Writing Programs seemed to be a way to empower these consumers of culture to become cultural producers, as there was a widespread assumption that literacy would continue to grow (kids thought it was cool to read, and not just because of *Schoolhouse Rock* or *Sesame Street,* etc.). M(F)A Creative Writing programs during the last third of the 20th century were sold as more progressive and inclusive than the standard degree in English, and in some ways they are. For a while, it permitted more aesthetic freedom (without having to be necessarily intimate with the canonical Euro-American tradition many questioned), and a temporary autonomous zone, an island, a green zone of contemplation, somewhat sheltered from market demands—in short, a false economy. These programs even created more jobs for writers in the absence of large scale public funding; theoretically, it could spread the "gospel" of contemporary American literature—especially in a country in which most of us only become aware of poetry and contemporary literature in general by attending college. I certainly have found working within these programs to be very useful in widening the range of legitimate academic options for those who wish to reach a more general audience and speak in a more common language than specialized post-structuralist discourse and conventional English Literature degrees allow.

But, even as Creative Writings were expanding and thriving during the 80s, it became clear when the second edition of the *Norton Modern Poetry* anthology came out, that trends were turning the other way, that populism was less and less a value in the academy, and poetic fashions were imitating Reagan's trickle down economics. Meanwhile during the 80s, Hollywood and TV gained in influence over American culture and realized they really didn't need poetry anymore as paperbacks and college tuitions rose in price, while schools became increasingly underfunded. Proposition 13, for instance, took funding away from K-12 programs, so increasingly there became less demand (if not need) for literature at the same time the supply of potential producers increased.

So even if some of the work that emerged from Creative Writing programs over the last 40 years has been able to seduce and challenge readers and listeners and yet be accessible, and that accessibility didn't water, dumb, or tame it down to the lowest common denominator for those raised (razed) on violent sit-com propaganda, such work increasingly would not find its readers or audiences because of external and internal structural obstacles that were becoming rigid, insular, and reified. The institutional structure and culture of M(F)A programs eventually fell prey to the law of diminishing returns for potential students (consumers).[55]

55 Things To Do When Your MFA Students Ask For Advice

When I taught in an MFA program, my students often asked me for advice on whether they should consider enrolling in a Ph.D. program. Of course, I can't make the decision for them, and I tried to be as neutral as possible in considering their needs and abilities, and today's economic/cultural landscape (which I don't want to reduce to a "job market"), in weighing the advantages and disadvantages of each. They also wonder why I needed a Ph.D. to get a job in an MFA program, when the other teacher was able to get published and find this job with only an MFA?

I offered a historical interpretation: In the 70s when the other teacher received her degree, it was much more common for professors to get hired with (only) a Master's degree than it was for my generation at the turn of the 21st century. Many of us in the 90s who probably wouldn't have tried to get a Ph.D. if we had been around in the 70s, found ourselves enrolling in Ph.D. programs after getting creative writing degrees because we needed to hedge our bets, or not put all our eggs in one basket in the more competitive market of the 90s.

"And from what I can see, the market is even tighter now (this was the Bush2 years before the Great Crash of 2008). For these reasons, I might be more likely to advise that it would be prudent to work towards a Ph.D, but that degree is also a victim of academic inflation, and offers no guarantees, and even the likelihood of more debt. On the other hand, another advantage of the Ph.D., for me, was that it allowed me to buy time; for while I was working on my Ph.D., I was also publishing my first three books, as well as in many magazines,

Notes Toward An M(F)A In Non-Poetry

I refer to the law of diminishing returns of graduate creative writing programs as a crisis, but some argue that these programs are actually doing what they were set out to do in encouraging an "Amway Pyramid" of elitism and de-valuing populism ("the system isn't broken, it's fixed!").

As studies such as Eric Bennett's recent *Workshops Of Empire* show, the MFA Creative Writing program was initially designed to "discourage the abstract theorizing and systematic social critiques to which the radical literature of the 1930s had been prone, in favor of a focus on the personal, the concrete and the individual. While workshop administrators like Paul Engle and Wallace Stegner wanted to spread American values, they did not want to be caught imposing a particular ideology on their students, for fear of appearing to use the same tactics as the communists. Thus they presented their aesthetic principles

---

so that by the time I received the degree (which itself wouldn't have been enough to get this job), I already had a national poetic reputation which I didn't have when I graduated from the M.A. program. But that, too, may be harder for your generation, especially because I had the advantage of paying for my Masters degree with a TA that allowed me to be a teacher of record, which, alas, this program doesn't allow."

As I witnessed students laboring amidst the increased cost (and devaluation) of the Graduate Degree, I felt a crisis bubbling up beneath the surface. I saw brilliant young writing communities form among Graduate students only to fall apart they second they graduate, once the harsh economic realities of "the real world," compounded by being saddled with debt, hit them with *post-degree hangover*. I questioned how long can this last? I could understand why some thought it was a scam, almost like a soldier coming back from Afghanistan or Iraq who questions his or her youthful idealism. And I wondered if the MFA programs are ultimately a sustainable business model, and if, as teachers, we're powerless to lower the costs, can't we at least create more opportunities to counter academic inflation and the devaluing of the degree?

as a nonpolitical, universally valid means of cultivating writerly craft. The continued status of 'show, don't tell' as a self-evident truth, dutifully dispensed to anyone who ventures into a creative-writing class, is one proof of their success."[56]

In the broader scheme of things, this anti-populism is nothing new. In post-enlightenment European and American culture, poetry had largely been an elite endeavor, not meant for the masses. The literary Modernism that developed in the first half of the 20th century—Pound and Eliot, etc—continued this tradition with its often explicit snobbery (and classism and racism) toward mass people's poetry such as song lyrics, jazz saxophones and collaboration. From this perspective, what was happening in the 1980s was a "return to normalcy" after the challenge of the 60s (except maybe some first generation college students—including previously excluded women and nonwhites—could now be tapped as creators). But, despite this, some of us still hoped that the heroic struggles that allowed the populists to cross over in the previous generation effected some change and was not just a passing fad.

But in the (protracted) meantime, the proliferation of college creative writing programs thus came to create a new consumer, one who would have to *pay to play*, as it were (analogous to what was happening in the music industry at the time). The rise of graduate Creative Writing programs created a climate in which one paid for the privilege of being read by a select few (mentors, gate keepers) who had risen to their position of prominence through the old pre-MFA system in the post WW2 era, or increasingly in the MFA era. And, as Creative Writing Programs proliferated, the disconnection from popular culture widened. I don't primarily blame the MFA Creative Writing programs for creating this debt plantation dynamic. They were institutionally

---

56   http://www.nytimes.com/2015/11/29/books/review/workshops-of-empire-by-eric-bennett.html?_r=0

powerless to fill the void that had been left when mass media began to abandon literature; as a result, literature, like pop-music, had lost whatever grounding it had during the 50s and 60s and even into the 70s.[57]

This increasingly lead some poets and writers to scorn the whole grad school paradigm. But as that recent book, *MFA Vs. NYC* points out, Creative Writing Programs were increasingly becoming the only game in town—at least if you don't consider hip hop or rock music as poetry. Others of us thought we could work within academic structures in hopes of changing them from within, though it became increasingly obvious that academia was becoming as insular as its Riot-Proof Campuses built during the 70s as it was in the early 1950s. And, for the most part, very few people who didn't identify themselves as poets read poetry or attended the forum called the "poetry reading."

Today, the number of unemployed and underemployed graduates of Creative Writing programs is higher than ever, while there's also a crisis in public education on a K-12 level: high-drop out rates, terrible student-teacher ratios, and miseducation (that tells students that Columbus discovered America while relying on a "common core" literary curriculum that reifies the traditional white male standard of excellence, even when it occurs in 'black face,' as if Phillis Wheatley's "Twas Mercy That Brought Me From My Pagan Land" is the founding poem of a Black Art Aesthetic).

While such aesthetic/ideological underpinnings still dominate the landscape of many of today's Creative Writing programs, it's clear—as I discovered as a teacher in an MFA Program—that there's an increasing feeling of discontentment

---

57 The devaluing of the degree, and the academic inflation that occurred as the academic factories churned out more of a supply of potential culture workers resembled an Amway Pyramid, or the bubble economy of the housing market. Eventually it would have to crash.

coming *from within in the academy*—by student/consumers, first and foremost, as well as some of the best and brightest minds who are either turned away or not offered enough incentives to consider a possible career (or vocation) in creative writing.

Interventions such as the annual *Rethinking Its Presence: Racism in MFA Programs* conference at the University of Montana show that many writers and teachers understand that the need to change the academic (as well as the non-academic) cultures in which creative writing circulates, and is "vetted," must be addressed in two distinct, but overlapping fronts: the **aesthetic/pedagogical** as well as the **institutional.**

On an aesthetic/pedagogical level, we need at the very least to expand the repertoire of stylistic strategies, and content, taught and encouraged within Creative Writing programs, but in order to do this I believe we must think and work both *within* and *outside* the academy, and consider the depth of the rift between "academic" and "non-academic" creative writing that still exists today, despite some "crossovers" and what remains of schools like Naropa.

In his manifesto, "*The New Perform-A-Form* [A Page Versus Stage Alliance]," Thomas Sayers Ellis brilliantly diagnoses today's (aesthetic) crisis, and suggests the kind of conceptual re-orientation of consciousness that needs to occur to help address these issues, and make more room for our fellow "straddlers." You could say he creates a new genre, or he just gives a name for practices that have existed but fall through the cracks in the reductive economy of naming. For instance:

> "*A perform-a-form occurs when the idea body and the performance body, frustrated by their own segregated aesthetic boundaries, seek to crossroads with one another. This coupling, though detrimental to aspects of their individual traditions, will repair and continue the living word.*"

"Perform-a-forms do not lie (on the page or on the stage), frozen in little boxes or voices, unable to interact with the reader or listener, as if on a table in a morgue."

"Perform-a-formists seek a path around both Academic and Slam Poetry, to eliminate the misconceptions between them, and to balance the professional opportunities (in publishing and employment) opened to each. "

"You can't workshop a perform-a-form but you can participate in its creation and correction." (Ellis, 2009, 71-73).

TSE acknowledges that such a move could be "detrimental to their individual traditions," but it is his belief that the advantages would far outweigh the disadvantages, especially if they can "balance the professional opportunities opened to each." I wholeheartedly agree, and hold these truths more self-evident than the wisdom of "show, don't tell." Ellis, I believe, gives eloquent voice to the frustrations of many I've encountered both inside and outside academia, who often get turned off to "poetry" by teachers and their force-fed Frost, and their "segregated aesthetic boundaries." That Ellis uses the word "segregated" instead of "specialized" is also highly significant, because in the official reality the distinction between "academic" (page) or "slam" (stage) is still highly racialized: "And while it is rare to attend a poetry festival or a conference and see poets (established and emerging, white and black, academic and non-academic) being treated as equals, consequently it is even rarer to discover literary editors and publishers open to "all" levels of class intelligence. The first task of activism of any perform-a-formist is the removal of all one-dimensional judges of craft."

As a teacher of creative writing at a community college with a very diverse (and mostly non-white) population who has seen my students (young and old) not being treated as equals to the writers at the (mostly white) schools I've taught at, this issue is something I try to address in the classroom. But there's only so much one can do in a classroom, and in the confines of an English department (whose segregated aesthetic boundaries still don't make enough room for the kind of poetry that's called Hip Hop, for instance). We need to consider institutional change; in fact, that could be a great collaborative assignment in a creative writing workshop....in which we could each participate in the creation (and correction) of our works in progress.

On an institutional level, if MFA Creative Writing programs could mandate practicums in which grad students would be sent into elementary schools as, say, Kenneth Koch did, it could 1) widen the audience for literature, 2) provide a community service for underfunded K12 schools and 3) create job possibilities for grad students. Since there are many unmet needs in K12 schools, and many unemployed workers in MFA programs taking out debilitating loans for a very expensive "lottery ticket," this can address several crises at once. But MFA programs have, for the most part, gone on pretending there's no crisis. And, for some, I'm sure there isn't.

In conclusion, the rise of the MFA programs, like the rise of post structuralism, in academia was a reformist movement. Both were a reaction to the challenges raised by students, and others, during the 1960s.[58] Whether or not these trends were intentionally devised to crush the potentially revolutionary plans being proposed to make academia a more truly broad based institution at the time, it's clear that many who have tried to work within these structures have come to the conclusion that the

---

58 As well as a reaction to the earlier "forgotten" non-academic public intellectuals of the 30s and 40s who had lost much of the source of their livelihood after the defunding of New Deal writer community service programs, and the era of McCarthyism).

ideological underpinnings need to be rethought to liberate literature from its hierarchies, and make the degree more valuable.

Addressing the structural racism in both Literature and Creative Writing programs, and considering other practical solutions (whether seen as pragmatic or revolutionary) could benefit the profession, and, more broadly, American culture as a whole. If it is simply not possible within the confines of academia, or in the mass media marketplace, we should at least consider the need for a new community-run model of education, or grass roots cultural institutions that can educate, entertain and employ us.

4. Teaching The Conflicts & Learning To Curse:

a. Teaching The Conflicts

As English Departments notoriously lag behind the perpetual flux of an American language and culture in transition, the dated designation of "English" department may take some time to change on an official level. In the meantime, we will be a country divided, between so-called "high" English and "low" American. To be successful in this backdrop, we must become culturally amphibious, ambidextrous; we must know how to code-switch, to translate between specialized vocabularies and the audiences they imply. Double-consciousness can be made a positive if seen as a form of cultural bilinguality that allows you to pass without losing the right to your own identity in the process.

Such thoughts have lead me to teach William Shakespeare alongside of Amiri Baraka in courses that introduce students to the study of literature. It's a way to "teach the conflict" inherent in our language and culture. We could start with Shakespeare for his work remains the best example of the standards of white European-centric literary excellence, and his works have profoundly influenced—for better or worse—contemporary drama, novels, poetry and essays, as well as the more popular—if not necessarily more populist—arts of Hollywood films and pop songs. Even today, Shakespeare is most invoked as common ground among those who can't agree on much else about a shared canon that doesn't reduce itself to the tepid "moderation" of the lowest common denominator. That doesn't mean Shakespeare has to be a sacred cow, especially if you can learn more about your self from watching and reading him than you can from any self-help app. Unfortunately, many teach it as a sacred cow, with little knowledge that by doing that, they lose their effectiveness as teachers.

Like many others, I had "stuffy" teachers in college who turned me off to Shakespeare, as to *Beowulf*, Chaucer, Spenser, Milton, Pope and Pound among other writers I was supposed to read. In the meantime, I found other work, like Amiri Baraka's, that spoke more to me, but these were rarely taught on the fringes of proper academia. I knew this wasn't because of the literary merits of the work, the lack of intelligence, passion, relevance and the virtues of complexity and difficulty, but rather because of politics, habit, or "the tradition" (if anything they might have been excluded precisely *because* of their acute contemporary relevance). [59]

As a result of this, I resisted Shakespeare initially, yet after receiving my M.A. (which I had managed to do without knowing Shakespeare, to the chagrin of some traditionalists), I had become comfortable enough with an alternative tradition that I was able to read and watch Shakespeare in a different light, not as the "stuffy" guy my teachers presented his works as. I'd read it on my own and enjoyed the weird poetry which, to its credit, could be read like a freestylin' Coltrane solo not necessarily tied down to the burden of making sense (meaning). Sure, I didn't know what exactly was being said, and how it contributed to the story I was supposed to care about, but that didn't matter the first time I read these plays because it helped inspire my own writing.

Then, I took another Shakespeare class, and learned what I call the "soap opera side" of Shakespeare, the more popular story side, and I realized how part of the fun, and even the political importance and moral imperative, of reading Shakespeare was getting to engage in the debates over *how to read, interpret and act* him (or it). There were so many interpretations, so many different ways of being acted, so many different critical approaches

---

59 And many things they'd accuse him of as basis for exclusion was found—often in worse forms—in the writers they championed.

that I found many scholars wrote 300 page books on just one play. In reading Shakespeare, I found I could bring the burning ethical, moral, and socio-political issues of our time with me in a way a lot of 20th century canonical writing didn't make room for. I could put my self, and put the soul, into Shakespeare as I could non-verbally do with punk/funk dance music. Not only that, I could be legitimized for it.

I couldn't find a way to make an honest buck as a dancer, but I could get gigs teaching Shakespeare and, through that, other literature. In this sense, Shakespeare is like the New York of the song: "If I can make it there, I'll make it anywhere." Its structures may demand more attention than lyric poetry (more like "livin' for the city" than "workin' for the weekend"), but it offers a pedigree and skills you can take with you to the provinces of your daily struggles. So, I found myself having both intrinsic and extrinsic, both personal and professional, incentives to pursue immersion in Shakespeare while there were no professional incentives to pursue, say, Amiri Baraka.[60] While in the short term, this may be a kind of 'moral sell-out,' in the long term it may be the same kind of compromise that learning how to communicate verbally in English involved as a toddler.[61]

Coming through the back door, as it were, to study Shakespeare this way proved in the long term more *efficient*, a way to artfully dodge much of the dross that too often comes with the study of literature. The labor-saving device it provided is something I wish to pass on to my students. In some ways, learning to "master" Shakespeare enough to publish a book about him was analogous to the art of "passing."

---

60   Unless, of course, I marketed myself primarily as a tech-utopian; I know a few who got over that way, and you can sneak in more diverse content if you got tech skills)

61   SG (the second guesser): does this sound too children's book-like, and even condescending. Or is telling a story sometimes the only way to make a point?

b. "Learning To Curse"
(with apologies to Stephen Greenblatt)

It is for these reasons that some of the Shakespearean lines I find myself most quoting are from a late play, *The Tempest*. This play (not one of my favorite Shakespeare plays, for reasons I won't get into here) can be read as a colonialist fantasy, especially if understood historically as written concurrently with King James I's policy to step up the transatlantic slave trade (which Spain and Portugal were further along with) and become a colonial empire.

The Tempest's most memorable character, Caliban, is a native of this colonized island. From the colonizer's point of view, he is a hostile presence, a threat, a savage—at best a necessary evil whose labor must be "tamed" or harnessed to the rich exiled Duke (Prospero)'s will. Shakespearean traditionalists will tell you that the emotional structure of the play is designed to make both viewer and reader sympathize with the colonizer, and against the colonized.[62] But a play, lacking a reliable, omniscient narrator to tell us what to think, almost demands to be read in more than one way. And many have also interpreted Caliban as the more sympathetic character (ignoring Miranda and the so-called 'love plot' for the time being).

Some critics of the play have even gone so far as to *rewrite* the play—in order to make their argument clearer. For instance, Negritude poet Aime Cesaire's play *A Tempest*, written during the height of the mid-20th century internationalist Black liberation movement, is a great text to consider next to Shakespeare's play if you ever find yourself forced to teach or read *The Tempest*.

One of Caliban's (and I'd add Shakespeare's) most memorable lines occurs when he's responding to the colonizer who

---

[62] "Oh, he's not even a colonizer; he's a conjurer, a magician," they protest.

(in the form of the "good cop" sheep's clothes of his beautiful daughter) brags about his 'kindness' and 'mercy' in 'civilizing' him by teaching him proper English. Caliban replies that the *best* thing this "education" (or indoctrination) has afforded him is the ability to *curse* in the language, to speak the language of the oppressor, to use the master's tools to help destroy the master's house, as Audre Lorde would put it: "You taught me language, and my profit on't/ Is I know how to curse (*Tempest: Act I, Scene ii, 368-69)*.

Caliban, in this play, is not successful in destroying the master's house, and, for centuries, enough people in high places have read his attempt to do so as unjustified, as proof of his savagery, as "Caliban" has become a highly racialized cuss-word lodged deeply—even if unspoken and unacknowledged—in the white supremacist psyche of our culture. Today, it's easy to see how corporate media outlets like MSNBC and CNN are pushing an updated version of the Caliban myth in the stereotype of the too loud, black beast. Yet Caliban's voice speaks, and bleeds, beyond the confines of the play's "dramatic closure" and can be heard, among many other places, in J.Cole's 2014 song, "Be Free" or in recent books by Danez Smith or Ta-Nehisi Coates.

I also hear this voice in the young bright students who would only consider being an English major if there's a chance they might be able to succeed in changing it from within. As a teacher, I simply can not sit idly by and enforce these academic standards without considering that they are in need of reform at the very least. So I welcome, and even demand, your skepticism. The master's tools may not be able to destroy the master's house, but at least you can use these tools to help *reform* it, and reform efforts can be the incubator for revolutionary consciousness and action. Shakespeare reveals some of the tools the master uses, and knowing them may help you understand better exactly what you're up against as a writer, and as a person.

All of this is to say that the debate that occurs in *The Tem-*

pest is still relevant to the most pressing contemporary issue of our day, even if the apologists for Prospero (who they see as a stand-in for Shakespeare himself) are clearly on the wrong side of history. Yet as long as Shakespearean studies stands as a shared point of agreement among the vast majority of Literary-Academic gatekeepers, you will be afforded a greater respect for knowing how to speak this language, even if you're trying to curse 'mo better in it. If you're not free to curse in literature, it is hard to be free to transcend cursing by grounding it more proudly and clearly in a greater love (as Baraka's oeuvre shows). If you're not free to talk back to the voices of officialdom that run this society (Google, Geico, Bank Of America, Kaiser Permanente, Clearchannel, for instance), and be heard and taken seriously, your right to free speech means nothing. This is part of how many learn to censor themselves.

Instead, I strongly encourage you to curse in this course, and I will do my best to provide you some of the master's tools to do it with (some new toys, like perfectly legal deflated footballs, corked bats, or performance enhancing substances).

At the same time, I'd be remiss if I didn't also show you an increasingly legitimate *alternative* to the master's tools, some opposing candidates, a movement or at least the writing of a man who devoted his entire life to learning how to dig himself—and others—out of the trap made by the master's tools that had banned many people's "oom boom ba boom." Amiri Baraka accomplished much in this regard, even if his task inevitably remained unfinished at his death. And, we may learn from his failures and successes without sacrificing any of the literary pleasures that draw folks to Shakespeare. A lengthy essay could be written on the many points of similarity between these two writers, yet it must be stressed that Baraka can't be read merely *aesthetically*; he must be read for his ideas (whereas with Shakespeare, you can never tell if they're his ideas or just his characters').

If one were to say, "Baraka is our Shakespeare," he'd likely be criticized from at least two different fronts (or angles): 1) those who consider that statement a preposterous elevation of Baraka to the level of Shakespeare who is clearly superior: no contest. And 2): Champions of Baraka who feel the comparison *reduces* his achievement by (merely) aestheticizing it; why do we even need to legitimize Amiri Baraka by roping him into the confining standards of an imperialist retro-canon? That is what Baraka and The Black Arts movement were fighting against. Yet, even if Baraka hated the uses to which Shakespeare has been put by today's culture industry, he clearly admired and defended this writing, if understood historically. So, if the snobby Shakespeareans press me, I could back up the "Baraka is our Shakespeare" claim. In the meantime, I will teach the two of them side-by-side, to further your culture bilinguality, as some teach classes that compare the Biblical accounts of creation with the Darwinian more scientific view.

I am not arguing that all legitimate literature can be contained by, or falls between, these two polar opposites. After all, they're both male and we need to hear women's voices and writing just as loudly (including feminist critiques of Shakespeare alongside of Audre Lorde, Gwendolyn Brooks, and jessica Care moore). But devoting more time to these two approaches in an "Introduction to College Writing on Literature" course can help prepare you for the more advanced requirements of a 4 year college's English requirement.

In the spirit of full disclosure, I must let you know that this "learning to curse" approach may seem off the beaten track if you're intending to pursue English as a possible major, but thinking about literature this way—focusing more deeply on less texts and writers—is ultimately more efficient because it emphasizes your confrontation with what kind of work writing about reading can do. It can provide you with an edge in this highly competitive field over those who have a more superficial knowledge of a greater quantity of texts, and it just might allow you to learn how to use the language of the oppressor against him. We shall test—and probably refine—this hypothesis this semester.

5. Beyond Preparing Students For *Beowulf* (for Roger Porter)

At a recent English Department meeting, one of my fellow faculty members offered a personal testimony about his experience as a graduate of this community college who transferred to UC-Berkeley's English Department. While finding himself taking a British Medievalist course, he found a near absolute disconnect (or culture shock) between what is taught at Laney and what is taught at UCB as a typical, representative, 4 year English Department. He felt alienated from those students' snobbery, as they bragged about having been to Canterbury or attending the Globe Theatre, and ill-prepared for the canonical English literature curriculum because we generally teach a more culturally diverse one.[63]

Granted, many of the students who take our English courses have little interest in pursuing a B.A., much less M(F)A, in English, but it's not hard to see why some would argue that we need to align our courses more with what the 4 year colleges do, even if it runs the risk of alienating, or losing, more of our students. Yet the disconnect that Roger spoke of—between what Major Universities require (teaching for the GRES, etc) and what we do at Laney—does not necessarily necessitate that we should begin offering medieval or early modern literature courses (Beowulf, Caedmon's Hymn, The Faerie Queen, Chaucer, for instance).

I am certainly not advocating that, nor do I think he is (though I don't presume to speak for him). One of the reasons we both love teaching at Laney is because we offer a strong alternative to the "limited vision of American missionary education

---

[63] In this connection, one may think of the story of David McKemster and the non-academic public intellectual in Gwendolyn Brooks' *Maud Martha*

that's driving Blacks and Hispanics from the classroom," yet can we offer this alternative in a way that also lets students know what they'll be up against in the more "real" world—for you have to know what you're up against if you have any hope of being able to change it.

At the other extreme from the status quo, we may consider a utopian, if comically "unrealistic" proposal to help put this disconnect—or culture shock—in a broader perspective. In Ishmael Reed's novel, *Japanese By Spring,* a fictional Oakland University is bought by a group of Japanese investors. The new regime believes that "The reason that the Americans are so backward is because of what they call their core curriculum," and undertakes some changes to the curriculum:

"We're going to close down the Department of Humanity and move it into Ethnic Studies. You have African Studies, Chicano Studies, Asian-American Studies, Native-American Studies and African-American Studies. We will have a new department, European Studies, with the same size budget and faculty as the rest. My backers would like to eliminate all of these courses which allow for so much foolishness, but they also want to show to the faculty and students how conciliatory we are. We will allow for these frills. Are they really necessary? All they accomplish for these people is to glorify some mythic past and to promote such dubious claims that Europe is the birthplace of science, religion, technology and philosophy. I've been reading this so-called philosopher, Plato. All about such foolishness as to whether the soul has immortality. What nonsense. Hegel and the rest are full of such nonsense also. The ignorant man maintained that the Chinese had no philosophy. What rubbish. No wonder the Americans can't make a decent automobile. Their intellectuals spend all of their time on these fuzzy and useless Greeks and German idealists. If one were to apply the empirical razor to all of these so-called theories, the entire history of

Western philosophy could be covered in one-week. Also, I am considering dropping the inordinate number of courses devoted to the work of John Milton." (160 Ishmael Reed reader).

Beneath Reed's comic exaggeration, there's a serious point here: Why do we still, in 2015, refer to Literature and Rhetoric departments as *English Departments* rather than American departments? Why is a community college education that may devote far more time and emphasis to fields that are currently consigned to "Ethnic Studies" considered less relevant, practical, and useful than the "Great books" in dead languages that students are still required to read?

Even if we wanted a change like what Reed suggests in the culture of what a B.A. or M.A. in American English currently requires (and many of us don't), I am well aware that we do not yet have the power collectively as an English Department to make any significant overhaul. On a practical level, I know we have to resign ourselves to *serving* the standards of the hierarchical status quo at least as much as we are serving the needs of our students.

Yet, this doesn't stop me from getting hopeful when I hear about a school like UCLA deciding to do away with their Shakespeare requirement. And, I must add, I say this *as a Shakespearean,* as one who would love teaching Shakespeare again. I see no contradiction here. In contrast to the vocal "old school" professors who get up in arms about the dumbing down of America if these trends continue, I'm not worried about a Shakespeare class failing to attract students even if it's *not* required. Since the "Shakespeare industry" or brand is still doing very well in mass pop culture, knowledge of Shakespeare thus becomes practical or desirable for students in a way knowledge of Beowulf does not.[64] This doesn't necessitate any "dumbing down," it just re-

---

64 And, yes, I'm aware that Hollywood deemed *Beowulf* militarized

quires the Spenserians (as well as Poundians) to do a better job of selling their product, and appealing to the skeptical student.

As the English Department at a community college, we can perhaps best prepare students for a B.A. (as well as M.A.) degree that requires texts such as *Beowulf*—without sacrificing a curriculum that is more relevant to them—by "teaching the conflicts." By letting students know that the "common core curriculum" is a highly contentious, and politicized, field (regardless of which side of the debates they're on), we can let students decide for themselves whether canonical texts are better than what's excluded.[65] Students should be encouraged in their skepticism, and we can at least provide them with the tools that acknowledge the classist and racist assumptions of much canonical literature. This can help create an environment in which the degree is pursued with a knowledge of self that can allow the students to negotiate with their teachers from a position of strength that demands respect, especially if we agree with Amilcar Cabral that "identity is an informed choice with which to affirm or negate a given culure."[66]

For instance, if one considers a Kendrick Lamar lyric, or a Tyler Perry movie, as worthy of literary close analysis as another student (who brags about having been to Canterbury or The Globe Theatre) considers Chaucer (or loves to get "lost and found and lost again" in John Ashbery), both can still share a knowledge of the same critical/analytical skills and tools in writing about these diverse texts. This is one way to help lev-

---

enough to be worthy of the blockbuster treatment.

65 Ishmael Reed makes a point that my own experience confirms: "When I began mixing the poetry of the masters with those of students from previous classes in my "verses" course at Berkeley, I received a more enthusiastic response than when I merely covered the classics.... Fifty percent said the student was canonized and about an equal number said the canonized was the student" (Totems, xxviii)

66 *No Easy Victories*, 152

el the playing field between "High" and "Low" (or "art" and "entertainment"). By encouraging this, the community college English Major could become more valuable and, in fact, exemplary—even, dare I say it, a model program if we embrace this richness, diversity, vitality...and seriousness....of American culture *en toto* (remembering that, in his day, Shakespeare too was "popular art," performance art—heard and seen more than read).

When I listened to Theatre Department chair Michael Torres wax enthusiastically about how the Theatre Program provides students with "A conservatory education at Community college prices," I asked myself: If this can be achieved in the theatre department, why not something similar in the English department? I believe we should at the very least consider—and debate on—possibilities on a broader structural level....but grounded in some concrete strategies on a micro level, on the practical level of individual courses and syllabi.

On a practical curriculum level, I'm not suggesting any radical changes here to our required transfer level writing courses, or the various currently non-required courses (from Shakespeare to African-American Literature), but I do want to emphasize two strategies that I believe can be very useful for preparing our students (and whet their appetite for) pursuing an English B.A. or grad degree.

1)   Devote more time to close-analytical readings of Op. Ed "think" pieces and literary texts, including "secondary texts"— regardless of whether the "primary text" is "high" like Shakespeare or ""low" or "pop" as in song lyrics. In my experience, it's more effective and efficient if the student has a deeper appreciation of a lesser number of literary texts than the more superficial knowledge that survey courses (with their promise of "coverage") provide.

Over and over again, I see students so saddled by a high quantity of reading, that it doesn't give them enough time to step away from it with the critical detachment that allows them to do more than merely *react* to a text. Instead of saddling them with so many readings, I found myself assigning fewer texts.

For instance, in a semester-length Shakespeare class. I discovered that a student may learn many more long-term useful tools if, rather than trying to cram at least 6 plays into one semester, we only use 2 or 3 plays (as well as a few sonnets) as primary texts. (and if for some reason, students need to go faster, I can easily adjust on the spur of the moment: *syllabus subject to change* is perhaps the most important line on the syllabus). This is especially true if more time is devoted to some of the critical arguments that a particular play, or even scene, has engendered. For instance, Is *The Merchant of Venice* a comedy or a tragedy? Is it Anti-Semitic, or simply a play *about* anti-semitism in Renaissance Venice, and England? Both views are plausible, legitimate and many books and articles have been written from almost every perspective imaginable.[67]

Or, in a pre-transfer level basic writing course, students may learn more when they analyze closely page-length poems, ten-point platforms, comic monologues or dialogues, and political sermons. Even juxtaposing a quote from a bumper sticker with an advertising slogan can engender a lively class discussion, and a 3-5 page essay. We don't need to emphasize *quantity* of texts to teach higher quality writing and thinking; less is more (much to the textbook companies' chagrin), and depth does have some advantages over breadth.

By emphasizing *ways of reading* as much as the particular text, students can become more aware that literature is a discussion, a debate, and that these different critical approaches—once understood—can be applied to all literature. This can be done without an over-reliance on the specialized high theory that currently dominates graduate departments, and can offer

---

67 Similar questions also arise when considering more recent "controversial"—less canonical—works by Amiri Baraka and others.

students *equipment for living* for looking closely, and skeptically, at non-literary texts like contracts, the news, and advertisements. If they can read Shakespeare closely, they have a chance of understanding what one of my comp students calls the "legal jijutsu" (or Orwellian Doublespeak) of Supreme Court decisions. Even if Laney students never learn *Beowulf*, they can enter a B.A. program with the knowledge of ways people talk and write about such texts, and this can be applied to any canonical, and non-canonical text.

2) Consider the usefulness of poetry—not simply in literature classes, but in critical thinking and basic skills classes, since reading, and writing about, poetry requires "close reading" more than any other form of literature.

The study of a lyric poem that can suggest multiple plausible meanings allows us to see how "less is more"—how focusing on the most micro level of the individual word, line, stanza or paragraph, can empower the student as a meaning-maker rather than a passive recipient. As teachers, we often find ourselves "falling behind" on our ambitious syllabi—not getting to everything we planned, and it's easy to feel like we've failed because of this. However, if we give ourselves permission to spend over 3 hours on a poem (or other text) we had only planned to spend 30 minutes on, especially if the discussion is very interesting, we may find that this yields deeper long term rewards.

The study of poetry, and other short forms of creative writing, then, may be very useful for critical thinking classes—as it brings to the foreground strategies of reading the co-existence of multiple, contradictory interpretations. Even the *Beowulf* teachers they will inevitably confront in most English departments will be impressed (especially when these students who brag about having been to Canterbury are found to be lacking in critical skills, and thinking for themselves).

6. Creative Writing Is Critical Thinking

When I first started teaching basic writing at Laney Community College in 2008, I had a student who could be called "shy" insofar as he kept to himself, and never participated in class discussions nor even the many side-conversations that some students seem to prefer and some teachers are known for trying to rope in, if not shut down. When it came time to turn in writing assignments, I managed to get him to speak enough to tell me, "I don't write," without any sense of defiance, but matter-of-factly: "I can't write." I fumbled for some well-worn strategies to help him overcome his resistance to writing, but, clearly, he was blocked….or so I thought.

One day, during class break (it's a 3 hour class), I saw him sitting on the cement slabs that pass for benches at my school, with his head down, staring intently at an 8X11 inch artist's sketch notebook on which there were pages and pages of lyrics to raps (alongside ideas for graffiti) written in magic marker. I asked him if he had written them, and he said "yes," with no visible sense of pride, but not really shame either. He was hard to read. "I thought you said you don't write," I replied; "that's writing." "I'm just messin' around." "Not really…," I countered. I had found an opening. "Do you write them down first, or memorize them and then write them down?" He told me he mostly memorized them first, and then wrote them down, but sometimes he'd change it up when writing it down! "You're definitely a writer," I said. "But I don't know grammar and all that stuff you talk about." "Yeah, but you got ideas, you got something to say, and shapes for it. A lot of people who got better grammar in this class don't have that." After that, he paid more attention in class, and began to turn in more assignments. He's still got a way to go, but don't we all?

I bring up this anecdote to show the wide chasm in our society, acutely felt by many of our students, between what we call "creative writing" and what we call "critical thinking." This student clearly would have done better in a creative writing course than in this mandatory comp. class, and he'd thrive more in the composition class to the extent that it made more room for the standards of creative writing. His story shows just one of the ways encouraging creative writing (even if they still think poetry is nothing more than 'self-expression') can foster the critical thinking skills needed for collegiate writing in the 'liberal arts,' and is thus an especially useful tool given the crisis of our low student success (graduation) rate.[68] This lead me to ask, and to investigate: What are the benefits if, as a school, we'd offer institutional incentives for taking a creative writing class so it would help fulfill requirements of our writing sequence?

A Defense of expanding the Creative Writing Offerings in Laney's English Department to help foster better student success in meeting the school's Critical Thinking ILO…

This year, our department is asked to submit findings about how we meet the district's "Critical Thinking" ILO, and proposals on how we could better meet it to serve students' needs. As part of this, I believe that expanding creative writing courses, albeit currently consigned to the "ghetto" of elective, rather than required, courses, can help us achieve the goal of aiding students' critical thinking and communication skills in ways that could enhance student success, lower attrition rates, aid accel-

---

[68] This is also why, I've tried to make it a practice to invite local non-academic (independent) public intellectuals into the classroom, such as BEME, Khafre Jay, D. Scot Miller, Oba T'Shaka or Davey D. There's no ONE SIZE FITS ALL method.

eration, and help make Laney an exemplary model school.[69]

Some fear that we wouldn't be able to fill these elective classes, and that they shouldn't be a priority when recruiting. Given the recent statewide push for "acceleration" of our pre-transfer level writing sequence, which has lead BCC to streamline its 4 semester pre-transfer sequence into a 2 semester sequence—to use one example of the new trend—, I expect there to be skepticism toward *adding* another required course to this sequence, much less a creative writing one. It could be perceived as adding yet another hoop in the way of our students' achieving equity with those at 4 year schools.

Yet there are ways that requiring a multi-genre creative writing course could actually assist the goal of acceleration, especially if we are mindful that these pre-transfer level courses are designed not only to "remediate" the basic writing skills that the public school's K-12 system rendered them deficient in, but also to serve as "an introduction to collegiate studies"—not just introducing them to the academic study of English, but to collegiate studies, including the other liberal arts, in general, and understanding what a learning community is and can be.

Creative writing courses may serve this second function by dramatizing sharply some ways in which the college learning environment differs (and, I'd argue, is superior to) the standard K-12 environment they are used to. Since understanding the heightened freedoms and responsibilities of the collegiate learning experience is, categorically, something that takes immersion (and there can be no short-cuts in immersion; immersion takes

---

69 There's clearly a need—among students and the community—for an expanded offering of courses. For instance, when my students tell me that fellow Peralta school, BCC, offers two popular creative writing courses we don't offer (Playwriting and Screenwriting, and Autobiographical Writing), they wonder why Laney doesn't offer these classes. After all, our school has a far bigger English Department than theirs.

time, especially if you must commute to campus), a required creative writing workshop can help foster that immersion because it's even more democratic than most college classes are, and because it does not overemphasize grammatical correctness over critical thinking (even if calls its critical thinking "creative writing"), and because students aren't graded on the quality of their work.

Emphasizing the practical value of creative writing, even in its most rarefied and aestheticized forms, can be a secret weapon in the arsenal of critical thinking without taking anything away from creative writing as it's usually taught, with a degree of autonomy from the demands of the public voice of the standard transfer level English requirements, a kind of temporary safe haven for those who feel their true voice can't be heard, or even expressed, in required writing classes.

As long as there is a specialized distinction between these two kinds of courses, I believe there must be a symbiotic, mutually beneficial, exchange allowed to occur between them, a more conscious trafficking between the two major subgenres of College English to help build a bridge, a foundation, to give our students an edge in this highly competitive market.

Although there's a wide institutional chasm between "critical thinking" and "creative writing" on the collegiate level, at their most basic they have much more in common with each other. Critical Thinking, Literature and Multi-genre creative writing courses all require students' written mastery of the rhetorical mode of comparing and contrasting abstract concepts, and explore a variety of strategies to persuade and convince readers.

Clearly, we need to rethink this hierarchical relationship. After all, despite the hierarchical relationship between these genres, for many celebrated poets, the "basic" demands of persuasive argumentative prose are actually *more* difficult to write than the mandates of poetry (or what passes as poetry) are (just as some great abstract painters just can't do figures)—yet, until we make room for a creative writing option that fulfills this requirement, we may be institutionally forced to fail a student who would be one of the better students in a creative writing class.

7. *Ye Shall Know Us By Our Taboos*! Revisiting Thomas Sayers Ellis's "The Judges Of Craft" In Light Of Current Poetry Wars

If you're happy with the status quo in the literary world, you probably don't want to read this: it could make your angry, defensive and/or smug.

I asked a professional poet I admire who has published and been celebrated for her work which, in quite a few cases, sticks its neck out on important social and political issues: Do you still struggle with publishers who will publish your work only on the condition it's not too (blatantly) political? She wrote back that she was lucky that her book publisher never objected to her "overtly political stuff, " and adds: "I made sure it was my best work at the time." On one level, this is very refreshing to hear; it offers hope that a possible ideal conjunction of ethical and aesthetic standards can be achieved in writing published by what is referred to as the "mainstream" or "establishment" press (in relatively small poetry circles at least).

Her statement makes clear: if any more radically political work is rejected, it's because of aesthetic grounds rather than content. While this may be true today for her, and for many others, I am also aware of many who have not been so 'lucky,' and who've had a very different experience with editors, one that is much more like the transactions we see in Thomas Sayers Ellis's piece, "The Judges Of Craft" in his book *Skin, Inc. (2010)*. In this piece, TSE takes the "found objects" of three rejection letters of literary publications, almost as if he were a "conceptual writer"—recontextualizing, baring the device, peeping behind—or through—the scars, exposing a seedy underbelly of the status quo's standard *modus operandi*. Yet, TSE makes use of these "dry texts" that do not stop at the mere (though fashionable) "massaging" characteristic of "uncreative writing," but rather take that gesture as its epigrammatic starting point (and dialogic foil) for a "hybrid text.[70]" Here's the first example:

Thanks for your note. We're actually very interested in poems that address issues of race and racism and wish we could run more of them. Most of what we get in that regard is mere subject matter; that is, there's not enough craft to carry the content (though this is certainly not the case with "Spike Lee at Harvard," which I am sure you'll place somewhere very good).

This is not just any rejection letter, but one with "race and racism" as its subject matter. The editors (speaking as a "royal we") claim to be rejecting TSE's work because they prefer "craft" to "mere subject matter" as the main criteria for acceptance, while duplicitously adding that the poem TSE submitted does have "enough craft to carry the content," so logically, one would think, the editor would be in favor of publishing....unless of course.....what? It's hard not to at least consider the possibility that race has a lot to do with it. So what does this publishing venue (and many others like it) mean when it uses the word "Craft?"

Ellis takes the occasion first to tell you what *he* thinks about "craft" in his own ABC of Writing:

ABC
The art of breathing is the first craft,
the carrier from which
all content pours.

While the rejection letter occasioned this, the poem also has

---

70 The terms I use here from Kenneth Goldsmith, a pre-eminent "conceptual" writer. See Ken Chen's essay in footnote #72 for a good breakdown of the controversy his writing has caused.

power as a statement of poetics in its own right, if one considers the liberating implications of this definition of craft. *Breath is community....Often craft carries you, off the page, away from control.* The ABC of TSE's poetics is easy as 123:

> *A well-made compromise*
> *Allows the shape of exchange into it.*
> *Other currency. Social balance.*
> *The policy of public poetics.*

Ellis' "The Judges Of Craft," itself is a "well-made compromise." TSE could have started it by screaming that the editor is a racist, but instead allows "the shape of exchange" into his poem, by deepening, and lyricizing, the dialogue on "craft." He refreshingly bares the device, by exposing the protocol of "textual exchange" between writer and reader (a reader who becomes a critic, an autocratic judge—as opposed to, say, a jury of one's peers) as he judges the judges in hopes of moving beyond an economy of judgment toward a "social balance."

The second "dry text" Ellis uses doesn't invoke racial content or "weak craft" as the reason for rejecting work, but focuses on another (albeit overlapping) literary taboo:

> **I have disappointing news, but there's a big silver lining. We discussed your poems at length and with admiration and excitement, but in the end we didn't find one in THIS batch that we felt would be a great début for you in the magazine. It's just that so many of them are about writing, and we try to shy away from poems explicitly addressing the subject of writing—much less the politics of the writing scene. But you are definitely on the screen here, and I'm only (and deeply) sorry I took so long.**

In *shying* away from "poems explicitly addressing...the politics of the writing scene," these editors, here, are, strictly speaking, rejecting the content more than the craft, yet "shy away" is the operative verb here. What exactly are these editors afraid of? Though this letter is all we have to go on to determine the motivations of these particular (anonymous, though probably white) gate-keeper editors, Ellis' "The Judges Of Craft" did itself occasion similar responses from other quarters of the literary establishment after it had been published in *The American Poetry Review* (who, to its credit, was less queasy about this poem than other journals).

In his review of Ellis' book, Gregory Orr criticizes Ellis' gesture of including these rejection letters:

"Imagine a gifted and widely acclaimed operatic tenor pausing mid-song to deliver a rant about how *Opera News* once failed to mention him in an article, and you'll have some idea of the jarring note this performance strikes.... The problem is not that these criticisms are undeserved. Maybe the editors who sent Ellis rejection notes are indeed insensitive... The problem is that these criticisms seem unambitious when compared with the provocations in Ellis's better work.... A writer this good ought not spend his time peeling potatoes this small. That said, the motivation here isn't hard to fathom, or to sympathize with. There's a lingering insecurity behind the swagger in some of these poems, and because Ellis is a tough-minded poet, he's reluctant to admit (much less surrender) to that uncertainty. So he stands his ground; he pushes back. The instinct is entirely to his credit, but when the thing that makes you feel belittled is itself tiny, then the consequences of such a response can be unfortunate. And there is almost nothing tinier than the poetry world, just as there is almost nothing bigger, stranger, and more disturbing than the bloody country that contains it."

While Orr's nuanced critique may not be as "insensitive" as

the anonymous authors of the (potentially fabricated) rejection letters, and he clearly appreciates Ellis' poetic "gifts," he's still rattled enough by TSE's chutzpah in calling attention to the inhumanity of the literary world throughout this book to lash out against him in the tones of a paternalistic psychoanalysis: *"there's a lingering insecurity behind the swagger."* Orr makes the mistake of reading TSE's criticisms of the poetic establishment in terms of TSE's personal psychology, as if TSE is driven by mere 'instincts' rather than a collective struggle. This is precisely what Ellis' work taken as a whole, is attempting to expose, a racism so entrenched in the standard protocols of the "literary scene' that even well-meaning proponents of aspects of Ellis' book succumb to it. Ellis is speaking of injustice in the workplace, and trying to counter it. In this light, Orr's comments feel like a scold: *It's okay to think globally, but don't act locally! Don't trouble the sacred frame!"* In this sense, even his largely positive "well-intentioned" review (that can be mined by publishers for blurbs) mimics the very letters TSE takes to task in "The Judges Of Craft."

The most lengthy review of the book, in *The Nation*, also gets deeper into TSE's "personal psychology," by tracing his "career trajectory" with much more attention than it traces what the poem does: "I'm prepared to say this is the inescapable sophomore jinx, which in music usually takes the form of a track by the new star settling scores with people who rejected him back in the day. And sure enough, 'The Judges of Craft' intersperses rejection letters with off-point remarks on craft and life and line and form."

Both points are debatable to say the least. In the first place, Ellis' remarks on craft, life and form are only "off point" if one fetishizes the 'autonomous' poem, the sublime object, a be-all-and-end-all that is its own reward: and renders that object into an absolute standard for judging poetic integrity. In the second place, Ellis is acutely aware of operating in a literary world in which the "ratio of us to them" is "far worse than/ commas to words," as he puts it in the sequence's final section (before he says his 'anapest goodbye'). The poem is "not about me, it's about us" and he just stands as an example of "one of us." Ellis is not the first, nor is he the last, person to have gone through this trial (even if he doesn't confess that he loves this "cultured hell that tests my youth" as Claude McKay's "America" puts it). This sense of identity, of ontology even, is clearly not understood and/or appreciated by the white critics of *Poetry* and *The Nation*.

These white poetic establishment critics praise TSE's work insofar as it works within certain parameters, but it's more challenging, and enlightening to consider it on its own terms. The poem is not simply about the 'politics of the writing scene,' but about the politics that is part of the poem's—any poem's—*essence* (the politics that defines what is and is not a poem as a *genre*, not simply whether it is a good or bad poem):

"In the classroom   the work
on the table is a corpse
surrounded by   other equally

decomposing economies.....

Another lengthy case,
a crack in the craft
to crawl through, the trial of proving
 you are flat, worth paper...."   (88-90).

(Dig the consonants!) The medium of exchange affects not only the shape of "the work" but also of the writers, in academia and publishing. The writing workshop becomes a grand metaphor for what Orr calls "the bloody country (or, more accurately trans-national NGOs) that contains it." The global is in the local; the world is in the workshop. And so far nothing in these lyric passages is specifically about race or racism...until TSE gets to the penultimate section of this XII part poem:

They allow you among them
without a hood.
a type of vitiligo typeface
taught taste

You make the ghetto Greek
Reference, begging.

The word "hood" for instance could refer to "them" (they took off their Klansman's 'hood') or to 'you' (they'll only let you among them if you don't bring "the hood" with you; especially if you help them destroy—I mean gentrify—it) and *Skin, Inc.* is full of such brilliant, illuminating and mordant double-meanings that go beyond mere 'textual play.'

TSE includes a third, shorter, rejection letter that rejects the poem "The Obama Hour" for being "too strident," but if TSE's work is stridency, I believe we could use a lot more of this in the poetry world today. I'm sure even white people have felt the alienation of the workshop and "submission" process, of the protocols and conventions that "guide" poetry performances, have felt straightjacketed by the narrow definitional norms of "poetry" as well as the marginalization of poetry in this world, and Thomas Sayers Ellis, like the Black Arts Movement at its best, may help provide a corrective for many of these ills that were indeed caused by the way white supremacy has institutionally manifested itself in the poetry world....not that he could effect this corrective alone.

From my perspective these are hardly "small potatoes." He's fighting on one of the many front lines of the institutional biases that are a precondition to "legitimate" discussions about poetic craft. In the process he champions a more inclusive, permissive, eclectic lexicon of poetry as his book itself attests to in its range beyond the opposite "extremes" of the Vendler-Perloff continuum—including concrete poetry and manifesto-as-poem, but also his "perform-a-form, photo-elegy with footnotes for feetwork" (on the "cooked" side) and beyond to his enthralling musical collaborations with James Brandon Lewis and company (on the "raw" side).

TSE's relentless attempts to create alternatives to overly narrow specialists, and tyrants of the post-Poundian lyric (an institutional problem with race and class implications) is a fight hardly finished, and today few dare to fight the real life struggle by ruminating on the power dynamics of the literary world with the brilliance and force with which TSE does, but it is at the heart of what Baraka calls the Black Arts aesthetic, which is still rarely afforded equal status in our academic and quasi-academic institutions of poetry.

2. *Screw The "Ever-Fixed Mark"*

Aesthetically, I crave a poetry that errs on sides, a poetics that errs on sides—the more sides the better. I do sometimes crave poems that appeal to the sophisticate (TSE names Ashbery), but also poems that feel that they must yield before the wisdom of a child (which Kenneth Koch championed).—or at least a brilliant 18 year old community college student writing at a "6th grade level." I crave work that lets different standards talk to each other, revolutionary dialogue poetry that questions, interrogates, the anti-populist structures and institutions, and attempts to provide alternatives, to build and organize decimated communities. One audience's great poem is often another audience's lousy poem, you could either try to write a poem that pleases both and ends up pleasing neither, or write two "opposite" poems that can please each separately, and hope to build a wider coalition: This may take years to do (consider the phases of Philip Guston or The Isley Brothers), but I believe TSE is further along in doing the latter than the vast majority of his contemporaries.

The fact that something as commonsensical as a "perform-a-form" is still considered "too radical" for some should tell you a lot about how far we have to go. As Ellis puts it, "breath is the first craft." This simple statement also challenges more than merely the small potatoes of "official verse culture," but beyond it to the western metaphysical tradition based on Descartes' "Cogito" or the notion of the word as essence that precedes, come before, the flesh. Once one sees this dimension to TSE's critique, it's easy to see how these metaphysics (which even Eliot knew ushered in a "dissociation of sensibility" at the dawn of imperialism) were, and are still, used to justify colonialism and white supremacy (as "mind" is more like an enlightenment writer sipping coffee in the Netherlands while the "body" is the people enslaved and displaced to pick the beans—to name but one ramification).[71] Of course, this doesn't mean we can't compromise, can't wear "kid gloves" and not be too heavy handed (I'm sure TSE's too subtle for some as well)—but sometimes you have to scream—or at least shout—and you could either aspire to do it as artfully as James Brown or John Coltrane or maybe just like those guys who dug up the outdated Allen Ginsberg poem "America" to read at an occupy rally in 2011.

Recently, in his long essay, "Authenticity Obsession, or Conceptualism as Minstrel Show,"[72] (especially in the section titled "Writing While Black"), Ken Chen breaks down how the exclusionary economy of scarcity drives the critical presumptions of Perloff and Vendler (and Logan) across the "wide" spectrum of

---

71 See Fred Moten's work on how "imagination" is racialized in Western metaphysics.

72 http://aaww.org/authenticity-obsession/

today's acceptable poetry. Yet, if we take seriously the appeal to reason and passion that is TSE's perform-a-form manifesto, we may yet be able to save the word—and institution—"poetry" from itself if it's worth saving, if we find we have a stake in it, a stake that is not an oil drill as much as a hoe to help plant enough tomatoes to help feed the 'hood and create better paying jobs than the Jack In The Box our actions could put out of business.

8. Dr. Craig's 11-Step Program to Curing "Mainly White MFA" Sickness[73]

Does your MFA program suffer from "Mainly White MFA" sickness (symptoms include few to no students of color)? If yes, this program is designed to bring some healthy color to your department or your institutional racism back!

Step 1: Funding. Offer full or reasonable funding packages. Writers of color no longer want to be part of your debt plantation.

Step 2: Hire. Hire faculty of color (who should comprise at least half your faculty). Student writers need mentors who understand how to write about racialized experiences and how to survive and succeed as a writer of a color.

Step 3: Retire. Incentivize retirement for the mediocre white faculty that you hired 20 years ago, who are at best completely out of touch with multicultural literatures or, at worst, racist (you know who I'm talking about). If they refuse to retire, require "literary diversity training" under the guise of "mandatory faculty development."

Step 4: Require. Every MFA program should have at least one required literature course in "Multicultural and Indigenous literatures" and at least one required writing workshop in "Ethically Writing Race and Culture."

Step 5: Speak/Perform. Every MFA program should have at

---

73 Reprinted with author permission https://craigsantosperez.wordpress.com/2015/10/02/dr-craigs-11-step-program-to-curing-mainly-white-mfa-sickness/

least one required course in performance and spoken word, and should hire at least one Spoken Word and/or Performance faculty. You have ruined the literary reading by producing a surplus of writers who have no idea how to read their work aloud.

Step 6: Community. Every MFA program should have a community engagement requirement/component. Offer tuition remission or GAships for semester-long community engagement projects.

Step 7: Civics. Every MFA program should have a civic engagement requirement/component. Study protest literature and bring your students into the streets, into the legislature, into the public sphere. Offer tuition remission or GAships for semester-long for literary projects that engage political, social, or environmental justice issues.

Step 8: Invite. Half your reading series should feature emerging and established writers of color. I will give you a discount on my reading fee if you mention this program.

Step 9: Brochure. Be honest in your brochure. Don't put the only 2 people of color in your MFA program on every page of your brochure/website. Reveal the racial demographics of your faculty and student body. This will help you realize how much work you need to do.

Step 10: Partner. Partner with the many organizations that have a history of supporting writers of color, including Cave Canem, Kundiman, Kearney Street, Asian American Writers Workshop, VONA, Canto Mundo, IAIA, Pacific Tongues, Youth Speaks, Brave New Voices, Split this Rock, Urban Word, and more. Offer scholarships, featured readings, special issues in your program literary journals, etc.

Step 11: Accept. Accept the fact that you must change your program. Accept that you have not done enough to support writers of color. Accept that it will take time to rebrand and rebuild trust. Accept that you may not be ready for us. Accept that the passion, fire, and talent of writers of color might burn your program down. Accept that only we can help you rebuild this broken system.

Reprinted courtesy of Craig Santos Perez, 2015

Literary Activism At Its Best:
Craig Santos Perez's Anti-Racist MFA

Does this essay really need any commentary? The title of Craig Santos Perez's proposal for reforming, revolutionizing or saving MFA Programs reminds me of Co-founder of Black Arts Movement-West, Marvin X's *12 Step Program To Cure Yourself From The Disease of White Supremacy,* but while Marvin X is primarily writing to non-whites who have internalized this disease, Perez speaks to the professors like those I had as a student, and those I worked with (and probably was) when I taught in an MFA program: well-intentioned progressive teachers who have worked diligently and conscientiously to overcome their own upbringing and the personal prejudices their parents and teachers have had on an individual level, and who earnestly ask "How can I help?"—but who work in—and do not significantly challenge—what Ishmael Reed calls "the limited vision of American missionary education that's driving blacks and Hispanics (and I'd add whites) from the classroom." Like Reed, Perez wishes to "encourage others to join him in the reconstruction of American culture damaged by racism."

I'd like to make explicit an implied question: why would any white teacher or student disagree with any of his points? This is not a rhetorical question; I'm trying to understand, but I agree wholeheartedly with all of Perez's proposals, and wish such a program as he envisions would have been around when I was a student. Frankly, I'm surprised that there isn't more of a general outcry among white professors for such changes. Is what Nathan Hare wrote in 1968 still true, that "the average white doesn't want to drastically change the structure because the structure meets his needs?"

I must ask my white colleagues, does the current MFA structure *really* meet your needs? If so, how? And, if it doesn't, isn't it possible that the changes Perez suggests could meet them more?

Is it possible that the reason your degree is devalued in today's economic crisis is precisely because it's based on the white supremacist idea of exclusion that Perez, like Hare 48 years ago, is trying to eliminate? Or have you thoroughly internalized the "liberal arts approach" that, as Theodore Veblen showed, "grew out of the leisure class mentality, where it was prestigious to be nonproductive and to waste time in useless endeavor" and thus devised useless requirements "to serve the functions of exclusivity rather than recruitment?" (Hare, *Shut It Down!* 162)

You may agree with Perez that something needs to be done, but ask where, and how, are we going to get *funding*? Wouldn't such changes be a budget breaker? I think not—for though funding is high on Perez's proposal, it is not the only thing that is needed to cure institutional white supremacy; nor are quotas. It also involves curriculum changes: If Step 4, Step 5, Step 6, Step 7 and Step 10 were seriously proposed and executed, and required courses in Multi-cultural lit, Performance and Protest Literature were instituted, these could be much more attractive to more students and actually cost the colleges *less* in the long-term by bringing in funding from other sources.[74] I emphasize these points not because I don't think we should increase funding for diversity—we should—but because I firmly believe these plans would pay for themselves and help increase the value of writing in our society.

When CSP argues that half (50%) of the writers invited to read in the reading series should be writers of color, I can easily picture white folks objecting, "this is not fair. It's like an affirmative action quota that will sacrifice quality! Besides, POC don't yet make up 50% of the population. We might be willing to compromise and say 33%, but 50%, you have to be kidding me!" But, consider the fact that, in recorded and broadcast "en-

---

74 I explore a possible way this can happen in a little more depth in the chapter, "Community Outreach For Creative Writers." Chapter 13.

tertainment" media, it became clear by 1970 (if not before) that many more whites consumed music made by blacks than their percentage of the population.

White America, almost despite itself, was hungry for black wisdom, for black rhythm and deep thought. Roughly 12% of the population has created at least 40% of the wealth made by the music industry for a long time (not that they've ever received their fair share of the wealth they create), and have earned this wealth by actually creating a larger audience for mass-cultural electronic music; though this is not exactly integrated, the American education system (often labeled by detractors and proponents as more "liberal" than the corporate media is) is even less so.[75]

More mixing has been allowed to occur in the history of American music than has *ever* been achieved in Academia. Academia lags far behind; it had a chance and came closer in the late 1960s and early 1970s largely due to the efforts of the Black Panthers and others before reactive forces of Literary agoraphobia soon coopted it.

In 2015, Academia still has not had its 1920s "Charleston" moment, or its 50s rhythm and blues or 80s hip-hop movements.[76] We haven't seen the academic walls let down their guard enough so that blacks, and other POC, have the opportunity to seduce the white "gatekeepers" on their own terms. To ask for this is not to cry for a "hand-out," for I believe that

---

[75] This can be seen in the fact that the department I teach in is still called an *English*, rather than *American*, department; that is not a merely syntactic distinction, but explains the absence of required 'diversity' classes (for from the perspective of English, "American" means diversity, in the pejorative sense).

[76] For a more detailed account of the "Charleston Moment," see D. Scot Miller, "Finding Meaning In Dylann Roof," https://medium.com/@Afrosurreal/finding-meaning-in-dylan-roof-1282458c8430#.7ffor7hp4, and Ishmael Reed's *Mumbo Jumbo*.

if there were more non-white professors, more black (and even disenfranchised white) students would enroll. I have more faith that the discussions that can be aired out will provide a more equitable society (and help whites realize that what they thought they were protecting, what they had acclimated themselves to, if it's called "privilege," is also a "prison").

Although Perez doesn't propose such separatist ideas as an MFA Program in Creative Writing (with a concentration in Ethnic Studies) or an MFA Program in Ethnic Studies (with a concentration in Creative Writing), his proposal shares much with the more racially specific visionary ideas in Nathan Hare's "Conceptual Proposal For a Department in Black Studies" (1968). As architect—some say father—of Black Studies, Hare called for an "expressive and utilitarian" interdisciplinary curriculum primarily on an undergraduate level that would "wed and cement community and curriculum practicums and apprenticeships, in connection with course work…This would tend to increase the commitment of black students to the community while simultaneously permit them to 'learn to do by doing' and comprising a flow of volunteer assistance to cooperating functionaries in the community—i.e. businessmen, politicians, leaders, social workers, community organizers, teachers, preachers, educators, and the like."

Hare's important document rejects "individualistic" proposals for Black Studies programs for an "animated communalism" that stresses "the key component of community involvement and collective stimulation." (160) This would include initiatives in which "qualified black college students" will offer "intensive tutorial aid to K-12 dropouts" and "students in black history might be required to put on panel discussions for younger children in church basements" to show how education can be "made relevant to the student and his community while the community is, so to speak, made relevant to education." Another point Hare mentions that could be especially relevant to an

M(F)A program is the creation of a "community press" and a "textbook and syllabi writing corp."

Hare wishes to avoid "any (white) play to appease the black community while avoiding genuine solutions to the problem." He fears that most black studies programs will follow Yale's lead in omitting the key component of student field work as a part of course requirements. Unfortunately, many of Hare's warnings went unheeded, and his fears have proven all too true: in recent years, Black Studies (and Ethnic studies in general) have been under siege, and those that survive are rarely provided enough institutional support to foster this "animated communalism."

Half a century later, most MFA programs still resist incorporating a field work component, even if some other departments do, and in this context, Santos Perez's program is a brilliant, non-violent, effort to solve a grave crisis. The vigorous civic and community service component can help (re)ground education outside the ivory tower. It may even go toe-to-toe with Hollywood and Silicon Valley who have a head start on (mis)educating our youth under the more effective guise of mere entertainment. Is it possible than any "altruistic" reason for heeding Perez's anti-racist proposal would also be "enlightened self-interest" (selfish in a good way)? *Accept that only we can help you rebuild this broken system.* As I see it—by stressing a cure for "Mainly White MFA" sickness, Perez is actually giving us a gift, and we should work to make it a reality.

While I'm not aware of any schools who have adapted Perez's platform, Perez still hopefully has many years ahead of him, and I want to help him in any way I can. One way, perhaps, I can do that is to use my white privilege by trying to translate the spirit and thrust of what he says into more race-neutral terms that whites who believe in incrementalism more, and don't quite recognize this crisis, may understand. And this is one of the reasons I get to thinking, we need *An M(F)A In Non-Poetry*.

9. Notes To An M(F)A In Non-Poetry

In an essay in Jacket Magazine, Dale Smith writes, "Contemporary poets need to re-consider their roles in communication, exploring how language affects an audience, and how to make effective arguments that appeal more broadly to people whose situations in the world are different from our own."[77] In short, they need to consider the importance of writing "poetry for the non-poet." This is a matter of some urgency *in a land where so many who need poetry are rejected by it, at a time when so many "poets" are so busy being "poet's poets" that they forget—if they ever knew—to be poets.* While Smith recognizes the fact that today's "poetry"—for the most part—is only read by other poets as a crisis, many who are called poets don't seem especially bothered by this fact—if we judge by their actions (which I suppose could be called sublime inactions—insofar as "poetry makes nothing happen"). Apparently, many poets find some solace or comfort in assuming a specialized "audience predisposed to its [poetry's] shared goals and causes."

The implication that *poetry* itself is a shared goal or cause is rather common in poetry worlds (or scenes) as they are structured today, but although this may be useful in bringing some people together, [78] it tends to create very insular—or even gerrymandered—communities, even in the so-called non-academic institutions. For instance, the vast majority of poetry editors

---

77   http://jacketmagazine.com/30/smith-lyric.html. Smith doesn't specify "white poets," but it's implied by the mostly-white contexts his work circulates in

78   I can't begin to count the times, I've heard someone say things like "we may have our differences, but we're all poets" (or "Pound may have been a fascist, but look at those *iambs*). By contrast, I've heard writers like the great Brett Evans, say, with a healthy skepticism, "to rally behind the cause of 'poetry' is similar to deciding to shop at every store on 5th street, and not 6th st, because you found something you liked and needed on 5th st.)

and contest judges are themselves poets, so there's always the risk they're not judging the work on rather it's good, but on rather it's *good poetry,* regardless of their own particular definitions of poetry.[79]

One can detect in these writers' aesthetics and ethics a degree of contempt—or is it envy?—for any writer who manages to restore poetry to some of the functions it had in a less specialized time, and reach the "non-poet," whether they mouth the line that "a musician isn't really a poet," or that one of the best-selling books in recent years, Claudia Rankine's *Citizen: An American Lyric,* is "sociology, not poetry."[80] At root, such judgments are not simply due to personal aesthetic choices, but to the institutional definitions of what "poetry" is, or should be, and how the word "poetry"—and the objects recognized as a "poems"—circulates socially in our culture. These institutional definitions—whether explicitly or subliminally—make such a distinction between the "poet" and the "non-poet" that virtually renders writing "poetry for the non-poet" impossible unless also one writes "non-poetry."

You may ask why the term, "Non-Poetry?" I don't mean it as a pejorative or necessarily superior term to poetry; it's a descriptive term. *Non* implies a negation of the word poetry.[81] You

---

[79] See ch.7, the essay on Thomas Sayers Ellis' "Judges of Craft" for an expanded treatment of how this dynamic in the publishing world helps maintain institutional hierarchies, outside of the academy.

[80] http://www.theguardian.com/books/booksblog/2015/oct/23/claudia-rankine-citizen-poetry-defence

[81] And, by "Non-Poetry," I mean something different than what Oren Izenberg does (though there are some overlaps with Izenberg's definition, which could be the subject for another essay). My idea of Non-Poetry may ideally share much with the way poetry is defined in the Black Arts Movement, but as a white guy I don't want to be guilty of cultural misappropriation, and (academic) cooptation, by watering down that term, especially when I have to honor the Black need for a space where *no whites are allowed* (as the "invisible parties"

have to know something about what you're negating; you had to have done it. Since the word poetry is too often accompanied by a narrow exclusiveness that adheres to the demands of overspecialized society that thrives on social division—even if these exclusions are but defensive snobberies, attempted ethical transvaluations ("it's not worthless, it's priceless"), "non-poetry" strives to negate this, precisely by including it....alongside of other writings it currently excludes.

Poetry is usually thought of as a highly specialized, advanced, elite form of communication for the simple reason that most people aren't exposed to it, in any depth, until they reach college. Sure, before college, high-schools may offer their force-fed Frost and their common core curriculum, but these usually fail to seduce students away from the lyrical effusions known as song-lyrics, for instance—and certainly mass media is not very interested in making poetry cool for the skeptical youth. So, unless you're the rare child of literary parents, or the student who's privileged enough to have teachers like Kenneth Koch, Amiri Baraka or jessica Care moore come into your third grade classes and show how poetry can be fun,[82] you're probably not going to get some sense of poetry as a viable form of communication and expression until you make it to college—and in college you have to specialize more: you have to choose a major for a B.A., and a specialty for an M(F)A. Poetry—for all practical purposes—is placed inside English—which is placed inside college.[83]

As a teacher in an MFA program, in which I taught both graduate and undergraduate creative writing workshops in the

---

Hip Hop For Change holds), or in Thomas Sayers' Ellis "The Return of Coloreds Only") .

82   ...or many of the other young writer/teacher/activists in TheBreakBeat Poets, and (or various "School of Rock" programs like Deep Roots)

83   You may be able to take poetry out of college, but can you take the college out of poetry?

same semester, I saw a stark contrast: *the graduate students may be more advanced, but the undergraduate students are generally better at writing poetry for the non-poet!* They had almost opposite strengths and weaknesses. I admired my graduate students' intelligence, their acumen in close reading, and mastery of a sophisticated style that could be deemed publishable in fashionable presses, yet I felt sad as I watched them feel they had to beat the populist impulse out of them (not that every student necessarily had such an inclination in the first place). I began to ask to see their earlier poems (their juvenilia), and ask *how can you get some of that back into your writing?* I felt even sadder when I saw some of the most fascinating undergraduate student writers feeling turned away from the graduate program for either economic reasons or for aesthetic reasons—*because they wrote, and championed, poetry for the non-poet,* and I vowed that someday to try to do something to change that (once I pay the student loan back).

The more I thought about it, the more I realized that many of the differences between the student writing and in-class discussions in the undergraduate class and the graduate class were not just due to the wider diversity of students in the undergraduate classes, but also because the graduate classes were genre-specific while the undergraduate classes were multi-genre ones (in which students had to write plays and short-stories, whether fiction or non-fiction). So, I realized: If one is interested in *"poetry for the non-poet,"* a multi-genre creative writing workshop is more likely to create a context for this than a genre-specific "poetry" workshop. It would also make more room for the great undergraduate student writers who don't apply to M(F)A programs because they don't want or need to have to (overly)-specialize. And if MFA programs made as much room for such courses as they do for single-genre classes, it could help liberate poetry from its "poet's only club" confines, or fallback home-away-from home. If, in addition to all of **Craig Santos**

Perez's classes, we added at least one multi-genre course as a requirement of MFA programs (for all students, regardless of genre), we could create more inter-genre solidarity among our students, more possibilities for collaboration beyond the annual Fiction/Non-Fiction V. Poets softball game and picnic.

+++++

In the meantime, perhaps the best I can do—as a teacher—is to try not to perpetuate the assumptions of my training, and to encourage students to write poems for the non-poet, and to write poems *as* a non-poet: to realize that they don't have to call themselves poets (as a quasi-ontological category) in order to write poems while at the same time warning them that we live in a world, alas, in which your poetry very likely won't be taken seriously by the poetic gatekeepers and publishers should you embark on this path.

I have to be frank about the terrain: *these gatekeepers fancy themselves on top of a pyramid whose needle's eye you must pass through to get to the non-poets on the other side.* There's nothing necessarily bad about that, but if you really want your poems to reach non-poets—everyday people—that you have a much better chance doing that if you all got together and started your own press and multi-media outlet than wasting energy trying to win over these gatekeepers. I encourage students to explore other avenues, and though it's possible I couldn't be teaching this class had I not paid those dues, I like to believe that, together, we can come up with an alternative to it that could make it easier for you to do your difficult work.

Either the gatekeepers will come around, and meet you in the middle, or they won't. Yet boycotts and strikes may be effective. We'll have to see…In the meantime, I'll show you what they mean by poetry and why they may call what you do either bad poetry, or non-poetry.

Notes Toward An M(F)A In Non-Poetry

You can either fight for your right for your writing to be called "poetry" as many have done before—or you may feel free to consider letting "the judges of craft" have that word, and call what you write Non-Poetry (especially if it can't be called fiction, drama or creative non-fiction). This *new* genre may include many things that used to be called "poetry" (since, poetry, historically, was once a much wider genre). Just as narrative non-fiction and fiction have more in common with each other than either one does with poetry on an institutional level, *non-poetry* and poetry have more common ground in the emphasis of lyric, rhythm and argument. But when I say non-poetry, I'm not just encouraging you to write in, or invent, another genre that is separate—even if equal—to all other legitimate creative writing genres taught in college. I'm just asking you to consider the pre-genre commonalities that are too often edited out of our adult professional specialized genre commitments....at our peril![84]

+++++++++++++

I think of writers such as Laura (Riding) Jackson, Amiri Baraka, Leonard Cohen and John Yau. Each were important to me, in part because they had all begun their public(ation) journey with fine examples of gem-like lyric poetry, but soon broadened the range and scope of their work in defiance of the narrowness of genre conventions.[85] All 4 of these writers made collaboration (and not just with other writers but with musicians and painters) a central component to their work (and two even changed their names, and not just to problematize notions of single-au-

---

[84] Yes, your diaries and tweets and professional cover letters can be called creative writing, and workshopped in this class, but that doesn't mean we'll be easier on them.

[85] Regardless of whether you agree with their moral/aesthetic project...for instance, by this definition Ezra Pound's body of work could be called 'non-poetry.'

thorship). In their writing, all went beyond the "Perloff-Vendler" continuum, the parameters in which I safely operated in my 1996 *"Against Lineage"* essay, and even the "Raw Vs. The Cooked" debates of 1960 if updated and applied to the contemporary literary landscape at the turn of the 21st century. These writers even go beyond the wider narrowness of "literature" as we know it—most markedly in the case of Riding and Baraka.[86] All four writers grasp the essence of the difficult to define term, "non-poetry."

They all bring a wider sense of "the whole art" into the 20th century notion of poetry that threatens to be the 21st notion of poetry. Each of them resists the taboo against poetic telling, and provide models that, in their own ways, profoundly challenge the dogmatic adherence to lyric (even if it's in prose), and provide very useful tools to restore poetry to what it was in a less specialized era. But each of these writers—as well as many others—had to struggle mightily and repeatedly to free themselves from being confined or sucked back into what Riding calls "The Poet Role."

This struggle inevitably paves the way for a more engaged poetry. Baraka quotes Aime Cesaire saying: "Even tho I wanted to break with French Literary traditions, I did not actually free myself from them until the moment I turned my back on poetry. In fact, you could say I became a poet by renouncing poetry." And this also could describe the work, or project, of Baraka in renouncing the taboos of the white literary establishment. Aspiring to the hard-won freedom these writers achieved, *non-poetry*, unlike what's called poetry these days, is *not* the conditional love of a jealous god—but can make room for performance, politics, philosophy, drama, fiction, stand-up comedy, visual art, music, dance, culture criticism, and even revolution....

---

86 (By comparison with them, Cohen operated in a less inclusive Tower of Art; and by comparison with Baraka, Riding's work seems the opposite of a populist).

Notes Toward An M(F)A In Non-Poetry

Riding, Baraka, Cohen and Yau's projects could be called non-poetry because they include that which is currently called poetry and yet more, in contrast to, say, a famous prose writer who never even did a one-off book of poetry, in contrast to those who may work in every genre *except* what's called poetry today.

Yet, clearly, some poets, and especially Poets, fear that that already beleaguered, misunderstood, and underappreciated, art of poetry could be threatened by such a category of Non-Poetry. But that's not the intention here—if some value the current institutional definition of poetry based on exclusion, you may still have it. But for those who have read about how ancient poetry was less specialized, less disembodied, etc—than conventional 20th and 21st century conceptions of poetry, and who also feel a strong counter-tradition bubbling *beneath* these,[87] the term "Non-Poetry," in all playful seriousness may be a useful tool, especially if we can get institutional support, or a lone eccentric millionaire venture capitalist to fund a school that teaches it (whether in Academia, or outside it, more like, say, the church of St. John Coltrane still going strong after all these years).

Institutional support—that's the key. For I am not calling for a mere categorical designation, "Non-poetry," but an institutional designation: *An M(F)A Program In Non-Poetry*. Now is not the time for a business proposal, or a specific nuts-and-bolts Proposal for a Course of Study that speaks the language that College Administrators and Accreditation Committees can understand, but I hope to begin to weave a fertile trance of wonder so that the reader may ask "Oh, maybe we do need an MFA in Non-Poetry?" "What can I bring to it?" or even "Stroffolino's good on the diagnosis of the problem, but short on the solution or cure. I have a better idea, and a better name than 'M(F)A in

---

[87] Or even above these, as the *BreakBeatPoets* suggests (See Chapter 15)

Non-Poetry."[88]

In proposing such an *M(F)A In Non-Poetry* to supplement existing graduate programs, I must make it clear that the relationship between the poetry and non-poetry degree programs is not entirely analogous to the relationship between the fiction and non-fiction programs. Creating a separate, or additional, genre called "Non-Poetry" would just add to the mess and the muddle, and compound the crisis by feeding back into the economy of over-specialization with another layer of literary and academic bureaucracy.[89] For *non-poetry* would make room for all of those genres in its multi-genre emphasis—as poetry once did (for centuries), as well as making room for everything currently called poetry.

Since over-specialization caused this crisis, the M(F)A in Non-Poetry may have its primary value as a de-specialization—even a de-segregation (if not necessarily "integration") strategy, especially as it would be more eclectic and inclusive than the current M(F)A degrees. On the broadest level, the M(F)A in Non-Poetry, in contrast to the M(F)A in Poetry would not be institutionally subordinate to the English Department any more than graduate programs in Music, Drama, and the other arts. On the smaller scale of a single class, its workshops, for example, would place a higher value on appeals to common spoken English (while also making room for students' first languages if not English) like the multi-genre workshop does.

---

88 At the very least, as a precondition, it would strive to fulfill *all* of CSP's demands in the previous chapter.

89 Likewise, I'm careful to avoid referring to a writer *as a "non-poet:"* it's important to avoid this from becoming an ontological category as "poet," alas, is for too many.

b. A Defense of Multi-Genre Creative Writing Workshop

For centuries, poets have been claiming that their particular mode of poetry is much closer to the common (unspecialized) language than the previous fashion (even if they got their money from the patronage system which didn't require—or even encourage—such implied populism). The three—or six depending on how you count—Ws'—William Wordworth, Walt Whitman, and William Carlos Williams—all made such claims (roughly 60 years apart from each other). Today, we're much more likely to find that common language in the creative writing workshop than in the social conventions of the literary reading. In fact, poetry can come alive in classroom discussions much more than it comes alive in the vast majority of what's called 'poetry readings'!"

Now, I know that some consider creative writing workshops much more alienating than poetry-readings, probably because they had stiff hierarchical teachers. But in a classroom, I can—and, often, must—meet students on the level of common language much more than I do as a writer and reader swimming in the poet's only club like a drunken boat….At the core of the workshop is a polyvocal dialogue that is generally lacking at most poetry readings, even slams or "literary death matches" (except, perhaps, secretly in the wings, or in tweet form).

In the commodified conversation of the classroom—especially in a multi-genre course—I find a highly productive symbiotic relationship (or battle) between the more verbal common (s)languages and the more specialized written languages. I feel the most fertile ground to potentially create a new community that could revitalize the literary world from the ground up, and help liberate graduate creative writing programs from college English Departments.

In the workshop's learning community, these classroom conversations may become meta-conversations (as writing talks to talking, and talking writes to writing). Sure, these conversations may not be great artifacts or live up to the standards of the best Hollywood talk shows in front a live audience, but that may not be their highest function. Even though I do think it's important to let writing students know that you could get a great job as a great talker, I also honor and crave the presence of students who chose to be writers largely because they're *not* good talkers. We certainly need more spaces in which the introvert and extrovert can meet on equal footing.

In this workshop, we can investigate the discrepancy between the way we talk (while "workshopping") and the way we write (in solitude) our poems, plays, stories, essays (songs, sermons, or stand up monologues, etc)—to encourage that symbiosis (talking about the writing helps the writing, and writing about the talking helps the talking) so that by the end of the semester we're more comfortable with each other, and have come to understand more about each others writing projects, as well as the ways we talk, the perspectives from which we critique each others work. Many threads that got left dangling in one week's session could be picked up as a result of this; it would help create more continuity, and help forge communities that last longer than the "temporary autonomous zone" of the transient college classroom, while still leaving ample room for unprecedented sudden turns.

Since dialogue pieces are such an important part of this class (whether explicit or internal, or the kind of "interior" dialogue that poetry encourages), we may see in the class discussion the way verbal and textual exchanges can create relationships, and such relationships can create (and decreate) identities. Furthermore, because conversation is so important, it suggests a need to experiment more with collaborative writing (in a sense that goes beyond exquisite corpse), but closer to the way in which collaboration is the essence of musical *creation* than writing conventions would seem to dictate.

One of the advantages I found as a musician is the common recognition that artistic creation, in its essence, is collaborative. Poets may also claim this, but usually in a more abstract way, but generally it lacks the visceral call and response between musicians and audience, or musicians and dancers, as well as musicians with each other (if one isn't a "self-contained" DJ or one man singer-songwriter). The musician implies a different, more democratic, ontology than the poet role. For instance, one of the reasons poetry readings are so dense and hierarchical, is because the art was so slaved over in solitude that the performance is not seen as part of its creation; the performance is more like a cross between a marketplace and a courtroom, where few dare to say what they really think...for the sake of "community," but too often everybody thinks they're the best writer in the room. In music, by comparison, there's at least the recognition that one can be the best bassist in the room, and another the best drummer, and yet another the best pontificator. At best, it balances opposites, and is more likely to seduce non-musicians than poetry readings can seduce non-poets. And a workshop can be closer to this kind of collaborative conversation than a poetry reading is, even without music (though I encourage real music as well, as we shall see).

It could be an interesting experiment to record these conversations, and this could be a case where the new digital internet technology may actually help the learning process if it doesn't make students too self-conscious in a negative way. I let them vote on it.[90] I know the Kelly Writers House has had some suc-

---

90 But it's not so important that we create verbal artifacts that go viral on the web for this collaborative class project as long as we create something we can watch (or, better, listen to)—as a football team watches the film of last week's game to see what we could do better next time as the homework of revision, and beyond that check out films of other great performers as a team watches films of their next week's opponents.

cess with posting some of their class conversations on the web, and though I sincerely meant it when I wrote Al Filreis that these are better than 99% of "poetry readings" (give or take a few points), there's no reason why we couldn't do better (whether in an undergrad or a grad course).[91]

Alternative Paradigms For Performance And Collaboration

Since the circulation of poetry in America is often centered around the social medium of the "poetry reading," in preparing students for the "real world" of literary performances, I must invoke one of Amiri Baraka's greatest achievements, though it's oft unheralded by the white press: the monthly events he and Amina Baraka held in the basement of their Newark home, events which often spilled upward onto the first floor of their house, especially if she had cooked, say, a thanksgiving meal.

At these events, I feel Baraka came closest to unleashing his full repertoire of what could be called "performance art." As he and his wife combined the role of gracious host, nightclub MC (like what I loved about Ernie K-Doe in New Orleans; but that's another story), "Spoken-word" poet, often in conjunction with—as opposed to "accompanied by"—a musical ensemble, teacher (history, philosophy, etc), even preacher, and political activist presiding over organizational meetings with as much social acumen as he exhibited at the 1972 Gary Conference, and I'm sure I'm missing some roles. Perhaps most importantly, he listened and he dialogued; he was a master at goading hecklers to volley with him.

Thinking ahead, if collaborative writing/performance were

---

91 The Writing/Talk series surveyed in the book *Writing/Talks* also had benefits over the standard poetry reading, though see Leslie Scalapino (The Cannon (1999)", Wesleyan University Press) for a provocative outing of that scene's social exclusivity. "

more championed in the literary world, it could help rid of us of some of the elitist exclusionary individualism that dominates contemporary literature, and culture. Were I devising a creative writing program, I would also like to require one course in collaborative writing (even though I myself yet haven't done much of it) and strongly advocate for internships to create presses that would publish books written by more than one author. I'd advertise this as a selling point to help lure those who prefer to see writing be more like a team sport, a band, an arts ensemble, or a theatre troupe than a group of individual authors critiquing the individual or talking about how great "The death of the author" looks on paper.

10. A Yearly Anthology (Or Two)

Since there's a symbiotic relationship between the crisis in M(F)A programs and the crisis in community colleges, we need a clearer dialogue, or pipeline, between the two. On a community college level, there's a need for more creative writing course offerings, and visiting writers, but not enough funding. However, there could be more funding for these courses if we worked with MFA programs that provided internships for their students to provide us with an affordable labor force without putting any current faculty out of work.[92]

I believe the MFA students have something to teach the community college and high school students, but I also believe the opposite is true. For, if we send the M(F)A students (or, frankly, their published teachers) to the community college and read their wares to this audience, and these students say, "so, what's the point?" or "your meaning is not clear," etc., the grad student or published writer should be able to defend himself or herself in terms these students understand, even if they can't do it in writing and have to "resort" to talking.

You could say this inverts the hierarchy; I say it would help equalize it, especially if we remember that community college students could also teach others in teen afterschool programs, as well as provide a civic service to the community, and themselves gain important experience, as writers and conversationalists even if they don't choose English as a major. Since our students often need jobs more urgently than MFA students do,[93]

---

92 The lower pay could be exploitative if they weren't already students. But the MFA program could also provide more funding sources for these classes.

93 I'm told that roughly 15% of the students at the community college in which I teach are homeless, and know from experience that many more feel like they're hanging by a thread, and have struggled tremendously just to be able to attend this college in hopes that it can

I know we can teach students to become better writers if we can help create more contexts to (re)-establish College English as a vocational field at least as much as the Culinary, Cosmetology, and even theatre departments are understood as vocational.

There remains an institutional assumption that the English Department does not teach a "vocation." Though we are the biggest department on campus—in part because the state requires all majors to take our courses—we are viewed as serving the other departments which also require essay writing (For instance, everybody knows that even the best visual artist cannot get shown at a good gallery without distinguishing himself or herself in the fine art of writing artists' statements).

One way we can change this to both empower students and provide service to the community is to encourage students to publish their work (I was able to place some student papers in both *The Oakland Post* and Ishmael Reed's *Konch*, as well as our own school's newspaper, but I could do better)—for I've found that many of our students have important perspectives and innovative insights into solving many of the civic issues that plague our culture.

Sure, by the standards of more conventionally published Op-Eds, I generally find less stylistic fluency in my students' writing, but also many more deep analyses. And, if my students have to sit and listen to Op-Eds that often blow the smoke of clichés and "empty-words" just because they have better grammar, I also believe that the language police should have the decency as part of *their* civic responsibility to listen to our students' ideas.

---

benefit their economic and social conditions, and this pressure of necessity does not always provide the best learning environment. No wonder we have a high attrition rate. Over and over again, students have met with me, and ask me if I can help them find a job now.... or they will have to drop out. Sometimes I can offer them leads, but never enough.

Appeal To The Community (Insert City Here)

I believe that if we could (get funding to) publish a yearly anthology of my community college student writing (from both my creative writing and composition classes), we could create a far better book than many that are coming out of more advanced schools.[94]

As I envision this anthology, I imagine an exciting Oakland (insert city here) cultural magazine that could touch on every academic discipline and pressing civic issue, as well as the arts. The anthology would include writing from my composition/critical thinking classes as well as my Lit. and Creative Writing (themselves multi-genre) classes. That combination would give it its edge in a competitive market, as the interdisciplinary, inter-genre, sparks would fly to create room for a greater cultural dialogue than is usually allowed to exist in the professional over-specialized society. It would help make your town less of a cultural desert. To include "the arts" (including comedy and cartoons) we'd probably, more ambitiously, have to make room for audio and videos, but writing plays a role even in this (scripts, story-boards, song lyrics), and frankly, these days, more are likely to check out a well-constructed multi-media video of a poem than if it's merely on the page.

This anthology would be funded by the state or a "private foundation" (a corporation if they allowed freedom of expression), but I'd also be open to making it a more commercial for-profit enterprise (in conjunction with the Business department to help crunch the numbers and hustle some backers). Either way students could work in the art form, or literary genre of advertising. Advertising (or PSAs) in many ways is today's poetry (if poetry is the unacknowledged legislature of the world,

---

94 (and I could find a way to include every student I had that semester even if some would get more space than others).

advertising is often the unacknowledged poetry of the world).

Ideally, such advertisements would be commissioned by a critical mass of small locally-owned businesses, even, perhaps, the students' own businesses (Truong's restaurant for instance).

Even if the anthology were funded, we'd still encourage the *art form* of advertising, the mastery of the pithy sound bite. If nothing else, it can be at least as invigorating an exercise as a sonnet or sestina. It would help students to tweet better! The business community would do well to cock an ear in our direction because these students could be hired, upon graduation, much more cheaply than the over-priced ad firms that frankly make mediocre ad campaigns (like Kaiser Permanente's) that talk down to people and make them tune out.

If this talk of advertising mixes it up a little too much for some of the self-proclaimed guardians of our noble profession, we could also call this the art of the "bullet point" which could be used in a political manifesto by a revolutionary—or at least a reformist—organization. The same principle applies, regardless of which side of the political spectrum you're on, and this anthology will encourage diverse perspectives (no monopoly capitalist will be turned away, as long as they are duly enrolled students in these classes). This multi-media, interactive, series of yearly anthologies may be able to do more than anything to help create a community in, and around, this community college, and wouldn't exist in a vacuum.

Since I may have to appeal to other teacher/writers' self-interest and can't assume you're convinced this would help and that it's realistic, I need to stress that one of the main functions of this would be to help sell the idea of an English major beyond its traditional "job opportunities" it provides in journalism (another industry in crisis in the 21st century, as journalist/authors Alissa Quart and Scott Timberg point out) or in creative writing and teaching.

For though it may seem counter-intuitive to suggest that trying to create more venues for student writing wouldn't eat into the number of limited places to publish our own writing (or lead down a slippery slope to an ever more decreasing value of writing per se), I believe, on the contrary, that it would create more *readers* of writing, more people who have a stake in the cultural argument (it may even force our own writing to get its hands out of the clouds of utopian talk of 'sustainability" in the abstract).

If the multi-genre cultural anthology idea is needed on an undergraduate level, it may be even more needed on a graduate level (as part of the MFA In Non-Poetry) to help create a wider cultural dialogue, and create more opportunities for all students. Let the anthology created by the "basic writing" students and the anthology created by the graduate creative writing students compete with each other on equal footing; I believe both will be better as a result. If we create channels for a greater dialogue, even if hotly contentious, between these two groups, we may enliven the graduate programs (and the various literary scenes with which they are connected) and help enfranchise the community college students. This will not be enough to address the crisis, but at least it could be a start.

Sonnet With Commentary

"Our business is to protect your business"
is written on billboards across the town.
For a second, I misread the pronouns.
"Your business is to protect *our* business."
Who's protecting who? Depends who's talking.
And a phrase used to throw caution to the wind
"What have you got to lose?" could live again
thanks to the ad campaign's double meaning.
You *do* have something to lose. Buy a lock,
Invest, save; owe means own. Get tough on crime.

> My student's good at words, can sling a rhyme.
> Needs a job (time's run out on the loan clock).
> Can adverts be a possibility
> That can give words new practicality?

*In my lifetime, advertisers are more likely the "unacknowledged legislators of the world" than the poet is. Operating in anonymity, and working collectively, they come up with some of the most resonant pithy phrases. Poets may scorn this form, yet there is nothing categorically problematic it, even if the advertising industry as we know it in America in today could use a shot of democracy. And perhaps writing departments in colleges can play a role in making this a reality. We should, at the very least, consider lobbying local governments for economic stimulus funds that would provide mechanisms to connect community college students with small businesses—or non-profit organizations—looking for cheap (or even free, at first, in the spirit of a community outreach student internship) advertising or PSAS, which could help begin the long overdue process of leveling the playing field against the monopolies and duopolies of multi-million dollar capitalism, as a last ditch attempt to find a wider enfranchisement without demanding complete systematic overhaul. Otherwise, what do I think I'm doing teaching English at a community college? What do we have **to gain?** Protect students' business, but, first, stop calling their business mere play (or, worse, thuggery, personal expression or high art).*

11. Ebonics and College Radio

In 1996, the Oakland Unified School Distict recognized Ebonics (or black vernacular) as a language derived from West Africa. The school board wanted to "maintain the legitimacy and richness of such language" to "facilitate their acquisition and mastery of English Language skills." As Ibram X. Kendi, puts. "They wanted to make sure these students were bilingual, (471) just as ESL courses do for Chinese, or Spanish speakers.[95]

The corporate media, however, waged a savage attack misrepresenting the intent of OUSD's declaration, enlisting black spokesmen like Jesse Jackson to call Ebonics, "an unacceptable surrender. It's teaching down to our children." (472),while linguist John McWorther called it black "self-sabotage" and "anti-intellectualism." On the other hand, the Linguistic Society of America called such characterizations demeaning, as evidence shows that students could "be aided in their learning of the standard variety by pedagogical approaches which recognize the legitimacy of the other varieties of a language." Kendi believes that even defenses like this only went so far and did not "come around to discarding the racist hierarchy that places 'standard' or 'proper' English above Ebonics."

Kendi makes a persuasive case for why we should reject this hierarchy by showing an analogy with how the "English language" itself came about. "Ebonics had formed from the trees of African languages and modern English, just as modern English has formed Latin and Germanic languages. Ebonics was no more "broken" or "nonstardard" English than English was "broken" or "nonstandard German or Latin." What's called Ebonics, in fact, has helped transform British English into American English (ever notice why many southern whites speak more

---

95   Ibram X. Kendi, *Stamped From The Beginning: The Definitive History of Racist Ideas In America* (Perseus Books, 2016), pg. 471-72.

similar to many northern blacks?).

Though OUSD had to retract, and the controversy died down on an official level, 20 years later, I find the word, "Ebonics" still makes many academics as uncomfortable as the word "reparations" often does. Perhaps because of the stigma, the word may not come up much at English Department meetings of our diverse faculty (even though one of our faculty, David Mullen, was part of the team that designed it 20 years ago), yet the issues that underlie it often come up on a day-to-day basis in our work as teachers, as we seek to devise better ways to increase student success rates, especially given the disproportionately high drop out rates of our Black and/or African/American students.

One aspect of "Ebonics" is that it tends to emphasize oral forms of communication at least as much as written, and though racial generalizations are problematic, many other teachers have told me "in my years of experience, I have generally found Black students come into class with better conversational skills, while east Asian students are more likely to be better at writing than talking." Obviously, there are many exceptions to this, and I strive not to let such experience-derived generalizations pre-judice me to any individual student based on how they look, so it's safer, in departmental meetings, to skirt around it and express it non-racially: "Some students are better talkers, while some are better writers."

Yet, since the district has recognized that the high-drop out rates among African-American students is a large problem we need to address, and is discussing strategies on how to address this, it's hard to avoid the question: *is it possible that more black students are dropping out of our classes because we are not making enough room for oral forms of communication, as equally legitimate to written forms?* It would appear that this hypothesis should at least be tested. So I devote much time to class discussion as a well to help "sell" writing to these students (who, yes, are not just intimidated by the rigors of writing, but are in quite a few cases *skeptical* of it having any practical use) by telling them: *writing better can help make you a better talker.* (I scorn the snobbery that calls this phallogocentric)[96]

This translation from oral to written is as much at the core of "code-switching" as the transition of slang to standard English. For we're not just teaching College writing, but also Critical Thinking, and I find that many of these more verbal students have better "critical thinking" skills, even if they may sometimes, in the heat of a class conversation, want to talk over each other. I can usually mediate and moderate it, by slowing down the conversation, and underlining a point a student has made, and encouraging them to take notes on the conversation, but I try not to suck the energy out of the room by letting it speed up again to dramatize a collective brainstorm that could even lure in those reluctant to talk.

It never ceases to amaze me how, almost every semester, the classroom has a mind of its own, and how these talks can inspire students to write better than they ever have before. I can make no claims that the conversation-based strategy can decrease student drop-out rates and increase success as defined institutionally, but I do believe there are many other ways we can empower students by recognizing their verbal strengths, even if I sometimes need to translate their "ebonics" into what I call my "stupid white man vocabulary" so they can laugh with me; after all, I am the minority here.

---

96 This is one of the reasons I try to avoid teaching on-line classes, for I feel my particular strengths as a teacher mesh especially well with the more spoken word students—my fast talking east coast Italian American family stereotype—, without taking anything away from the more writing-centric students. I do not deny that on-line classes may work better for certain students, and I will gladly direct these students to those classes it may help, but please dear god, don't let them render the face-to-face classroom obsolete, we already could be on a slippery slope

When listening to my students' talk, I realize that many of them could be great teachers if they wanted to (some of them already are; some are mothers). I've also realized that it's far more interesting and engaging than much of what's on talk radio today (even much that airs on the alternative stations like KPFA). I need to let them know this is a legitimate skill. And just as I search for "extra-curricular" venues for my student writing (see previous chapter), I also realize that if I can find some extra-curricular venues for the great talkers we may also empower students so they feel they're *getting their money's worth*, and radio (or at least podcasts) inevitably come up.

I was talking with one of my star creative writing students, Chris Brown. Chris has a lot to say and excels at both written and oral forms of expression; he was an amazing presence in my multi-genre creative writing class, not just with his own writing, but also in his close, sympathetic, readings and analysis of other students' work.[97] I asked him if he would be interested in getting a graduate degree in Creative Writing, and he said he has to get his undergraduate degree first. In the meantime, I encouraged him to work for the tutoring center (which combines writing, reading, talking and listening, skills necessary for teaching in the pre-MOOC era), and asked him if he ever thought about being a talk-radio show host.

Laney College, after all, has electronic media outlets like PeraltaTV, and 9th Floor Radio, and it occurred to me that these are valuable resources students are paying for and that more could take advantage of. Many, alas, are not even aware of it. Although this radio station is located across the street from our campus, most of its current radio personalities are not students (though some are graduates), and it does seem that the station should do a better job of reaching out to students, especially given that many of the students most at risk of dropping out are precisely

---

97   https://a1abwriter.wordpress.com/

those who often excel at oral forms of communication.

So we managed to convince 9th Floor Radio to let us begin a radio show. We have a comfortable verbal volley in the few "pilot" shows we've done. We showcase his poems, but also his political and cultural analysis. He comes over-prepared, and could read a paragraph of Baldwin (like scripture) and then sermonize on it, connecting it to the latest police murder, or a recent suspension of Louisville's first black judge because he challenged the racial bias of an all-white jury pool in two cases with black defendants, or other stories that the corporate media will not report. And of course, we make ample room for the gentrification crisis.

We're hoping to make the show more interactive, and grounded in the local community. We've invited other students (such as Monae Dawson, Fred Rimpson) and members of the community to share their work[98] and join in on and extend the conversation and are lobbying the station to start a call-in (or request) line, which would be especially useful now that the station has got an LPFM license, and has a terrestrial presence (they still make cars with radios, right?).

Certainly appearing on a radio show will not replace the necessary written component of the English class, but just as recognizing Ebonics as a legitimate language was intended to "facilitate acquisition and mastery of English language skills," so can the radio (or at least podcast) option help students become more culturally bilingual, even if the FCC mandates that students are legally forbidden from using the kind of "cuss" words that may be part of Ebonics.

++++++++

I personally feel I have a long way to go, and much to learn,

---

98 http://www.9thfloorradio.com/yaketyyak/2015/5/28/05-28-15

before I can call myself a talk-radio professional (and whatever else one wants to say about Rush Limbaugh, there are things to be learned from his "aesthetic toolbox"), but one thing I've discovered is that working with a co-host gives me something to bounce off of, and I'm more than willing to play the role of the "straight man" to create engaging radio while learning by doing (just as I do in the classroom).

This space for trial-and-error, and learning by doing, is one of the highest functions of college community radio stations, as I learned when I worked as a DJ 30 years ago. And, of course, as a listener I preferred DJS on stations like WKDU over the more "professional" ones—just as KPOO remains, by far my favorite radio station today—so I suppose marketers will hardly consider me a reliable demographic target.

I'm a notoriously bad self-promoter, but I am much more comfortable promoting a show I co-host with Chris and other students and ex-students, just as I'm much more comfortable promoting a great band that lets me play with them than I am any lame solo-effort. And, once we get the call-in (request) line up and running, it will be much easier to make advertising fliers to blanket Oakland. "Check this out. It's on the web, as well as on FM-RADIO! We'll have events.[99] Come to the Laney-College teach in! Bring your friends and musical instruments.

Regardless of my particular show with Chris Brown (which I hope to continue as long as he wants, and can—hopefully I'm not just the "Black Man's Burdon"), I, as a radio activist, envision a station can someday make more room for more student and faculty co-hosted shows, and make ample room for music. Even if this station is legally forbidden to pay its DJS and solicit advertisements, this could create more opportunities for our students. KPOO, for instance, needs new blood.

---

99 As we shall see in Section 3 radio can create and nourish a community, especially if we add music to the mix.

Since this is an extra-curricular activity, this exercise in commodifying conversation may not need be a class requirement (but optional extra-credit). An English Department is not a communications department, but at least it's a useful option we can make available to our students (whether in Creative Writing or English classes). Perhaps there could be a way to make a Service Learning Course that would earn students' credit as at De Anza college.....

12. The Interdisciplinary Music Writing Class: An Appeal On Behalf Of Students Who Fall Through The Cracks

Although I work in a English Department with its institutional boundaries that keep it safely segregated from music, I have done my best to work within the confines of the requirements of the kind of analytical and argumentative essays in my undergraduate composition classes to make room for close analysis of song lyrics. Since students often have very passionate, personal, immediate and visceral responses to songs, I often let them choose one of the songs they will write about (even if I personally think it's terrible, whether musically or lyrically).

It's a way to transition from writing personal essays, in which students write about their experiences and aspirations (writing what you know with no need for academic research) into a more detached analysis of thoughts, and definitions of abstract words (how do they define love?). If the personal essay lets students know we care about their *feelings* and struggles, this paper shows we care about what they think, even if the lyrics they choose are just songs about feelings.

Yet, this assignment is also devised with the realization that most students are not themselves musicians—and haven't thought deeply yet about the difference between the ways musicians are able to use the non-verbal (musical) elements to be percussively persuasive, and the way college writers, abstracted from musical (and in many cases even verbal), forms of persuasion, do. This is one of the reasons I bring in a few excerpts from *Jay-Z's Decoded,* in which he "translates" some of his most famous rap-lyrics into the standard conventions of written English.[100]

---

100 For example, he writes: "The rhyme convinces you. The words connect. It was as persuasive as the hook of a hit song. That's the

I also ask students a variety of questions to consider in their essays: *What draws you to the song? Some people like songs more for the beat, or the sound of the instruments, or the sound of the singers' voice, or some like the songs more for the lyrics. Some like the* **chorus** *(of the song) which can hook you at first, but not the* **verses**. *Sometimes you can love a song even if you don't like the words, and sometimes you can hate a song even if you love the words. What is more important, the words or the music, for you? Does the song have a message? Is that message negative or uplifting? Can its words be interpreted more than one way, depending on your situation or mood? Is the song really about what you thought it was about when you first heard it? Is part of the reason you like a song knowing that others like it too?* (and this is just for starts....)

When asking these questions, I give examples of how I thought I loved some lyrics to songs when I was a kid, but then realized I really liked the songs in spite of the words, as I imagined someone actually saying in person what many of the songs say (for instance, some songs seem so gentle and vulnerable in their tone that they may be able to get misogynistic messages across). This leads to some amazing discussions, as they brainstorm for thesis topics. In contrast to writing about "official" literature, this assignment is a great way to teach the kind of close attention to worded-art that the academic study of literature demands, and also offers students room to juxtapose—through comparison and contrast—many elements of two different songs. I have had great papers comparing two songs from two different eras, two different genres and/or genders, contrasting a "positive" and a "negative" message, or how a song that might sound happy is really sad, while a song that might sound sad is really happy, etc.

But, even though this is a fascinating assignment, and helps

---

power of rhymes...but while it may seem like rhymes are tricking you into making connections that don't really exist...the truth is rhymes are just reminding you that everything's connected." (240)

whet the appetites of "beginning writers" for deeper analysis and even the professional genre of music criticism, it's not *really* a musical assignment (even if we may play some songs in class, to let students stretch, in part because it's been proven that rousing students' bodies as music does can aid in their ability to pay attention in the class much more than pharmaceuticals, or taking away their phones). It's not a musical assignment because students aren't forced to write or perform their own songs, though I did have a few who decided to compare a song *they* wrote with another song, and I encourage that, just as I encourage students to bring in raps or songs in other genres in my creative writing classes, and make it clear to the class that they are legitimate forms of poetry, in contrast to many of the teachers I've had, on both a graduate and undergraduate level.

One of my students who was a Music major (who wrote an analytical comparison of a famous contemporary hit to one of his own raps for the class) expressed some frustration that the music department was not really helping him with the task of more successfully integrating the *lyrical* aspects of his art with the *musical* (non-verbal) aspects of his art. As we spoke, I became once again very angry—not with the music department, but with the institutional segregation between the Music and English departments that, in many ways, are beyond both of our control. It made it clear to me that there is a definite need for an interdisciplinary class co-taught by a teacher in the English Department and a teacher in the Music Department.

The departments are separated because, centuries ago, it was seen as a sign of class privilege (and for some still is) to separate music and words—except in opera and religious librettos that built elaborate baroque bridges across the widening chasm between these genres. And, in the trickle-down academic and professional cultures, this separation has remained standard in the contemporary era. If anything, it has widened through all the sub-specializations. As a form of music and poetry, hip hop is probably still the most significant grassroots trickle up challenge to this specialization, but there have been, and can be, others.

The principle of conceptual juxtaposition that is necessary to critical thinking (seeing more than one side of an argument) as well as to creative writing (as beautiful as the chance meeting of a sewing machine and an umbrella on a dissecting table) needs to be applied to the institutional division between these two departments to emphasize the common roots of these disciplines. This interdisciplinary course could help meet the needs of students who "fall through the cracks, those who have been told, whether loudly or silently, "You're a jack of all trades, master of none, too poetic for the musicians, and too musical for the poets. You appeal to the lowest common denominator, the mushy middle of tepid compromise."

I believe that many people who have been accused of, and who have suffered because they've fallen through the cracks may be the ones who yet can create, or discover, the most profound—or natural—bridges between two distinct disciplines in our specialized society. In short, these are the people we need!

At the very least, observing what musical departments do may help us understand what we—as English teachers—do, for although music is often a non-verbal art, it is a language of communication and expression at least as profound as words. So I listen through the cracks in the walls between the English department and the Music department to feel, from within, the parallel struggles with generic limits that Music departments face.

There was a time when studying music in college only meant the "fine art" of music—what would be called "classical"—rather than popular music (say, The English Ballad, or The American blues). Yet, today, the 20th century form of jazz music is an accepted and encouraged part of many music departments' curriculums. I think it's great that many music departments are taking up the slack left by corporate culture by doing their damnedest to help keep jazz alive during a time when the commercial industry has largely abandoned it (with some notable exceptions, for instance if Sony is gearing up for a special 50 year anniversary box set of *Bitches' Brew* to coincide with the release of a Miles biopic, or if a watered-down Ken Burns PBS series on the history of jazz according to Wynton Marsalis appears).

This is one of the functions schools—especially community colleges—are forced to serve to help preserve what was great about American musical culture, tradition, and history—in increasingly hostile musical environments. Museums may also play a part, but schools are much more vitally dialogic compared to exhibitions, and if these schools were funded more, they could fill this need, this void, much better to help get "jazz" out of the ever decreasing corner it's been boxed into.

Jazz has a kind of "cred" among high-brow and middle-brow (often white) people who like classical music. In many music programs, equal attention is devoted to both. It has even been called "African American classical"—for better or worse, as this term has been abused by the kind of publically funded jazz stations that "promote" jazz as a cross between lounge music and "elevator" soft rock "easy listening" muzak (stripped not only of the vital essence of jazz, but even of the wildness of Euro-classical). As Amiri Baraka's seminal book of poetics, *Blues People* shows, the study of jazz is also central to the study of African-American history. But one risk of this "legitimation" is that it can fetishize the forms jazz has taken by abstracting them from the cultural conditions that made them possible and necessary. Nonetheless, the study of jazz has certainly opened up music programs to previously under-served musicians.

Recently, at Laney College, I saw three music students—a great trumpet player, a keyboard player and a human beatbox— combo perform on the campus quad. They also provided the soundtrack for Laney's Theatre Department's annual production of student-written plays, and have been invited to SF's Yerba Buena art center to perform. Indeed, the fusion of jazz with "hip hop" elements has been occurring at least since Herbie Hancock's "Rock It" and there are yet many untapped possibilities in such combinations. But jazz classes and programs are not for everybody interested in what could be called "Afrocentric" music (Black Music, or American music—as opposed to classical—if you will). Like classical, they are often mediated by paper. They often require mastery of difficult charts of the classics, and leave less room for the non-written intelligence that can come through in improvisation. They can leave less room for musicians who have a great ear, a great tone, but don't read sheet music (of course, quite a few great jazz musicians didn't read music either—for some it can get in the way).

"Jazz" implies blues, but you still can be "too blues for school" and, besides, Jimmy McCracklin and others have pointed out that, for a long time now, "black kids aren't as interested in the blues as white kids." But "rhythm and blues," in contrast to both jazz and blues, still has a degree of vital populist culture cred, and hasn't yet been as erased from mass culture—especially mass *youth* culture—as jazz has.[101] Still, its history is becoming increasingly murky, forgotten, aside from a few samples (or samples of samples) here and there. Many younger listeners of contemporary R&B don't even know it stands for "rhythm and blues." The time is now for schools—who have taken up the slack of jazz abandoned by commercial culture—to take up the slack of R&B, especially since so many young folks are interested in it, and would certainly prefer to study it than, say, algebra, if there were opportunities in that field. In fact, we can help

---

101 For instance, Beyonce's "Freedom" (featuring Kendrick Lamar), can please many old Aretha Franklin fans, even if the younger students who like it don't know who Arethra is, and think "At Last" is a Beyonce song.

create those opportunities.

If such college music programs—such as the one at Laney—were expanded to not only offer "jazz combos," but also "R&B combos" (R&B including soul, rock and roll, funk and of course hip hop), I believe these programs would draw more students, and also serve a cultural mission that could *supplement* what the existing jazz programs do. It would, in fact, help the established jazz classes and programs reach more people, create more alumni jobs, and benefit the larger community. Because it equally emphasizes instruments, vocals *and* worded art forms, R&B, like hip hop, would be central to any "interdisciplinary" team taught class between the music and English departments.

If music departments can't take it upon themselves to do this, perhaps English Departments can help (rather than usurp; that's the opposite of my intention here), or History departments, or AfrAm Departments. The fact that music, at its heart and soul, at its essence, can accommodate, and be accommodated by, any of these disparate programs (including Business programs) shows you how capacious it is. It also should show the necessity of an interdisciplinary approach, at least for a course or two. Beyond that, it could severely heighten student success if undertaken as a more systemic and structural re-imagining—and coordination—of the relationship between departments.

As an English teacher, I can use my skills in calling attention to the verbal aspects of songwriters' art, as well as the voluminous literary and theoretical accounts of music and its creation. I don't have to require students' to bring instruments into class, and create collaborative songs or grooves. This, however, could be the essence of a team-taught course with a music teacher, as we study the way in which the non-verbal musical elements and the verbal elements come together in American popular music of the Post-WW2 era to create a distinctly American culture that transcended the distinction between "Music Departments" and "English Departments" (to say nothing of dance).

So, I envision a hybrid course (with a writing seminar component as well as a music laboratory/practicum component)[102] in which music is required, and make it clear that one doesn't have to be a "musician" or play an "instrument" or know how to freestyle. Handclaps, choreography, vocal phoneme dances can be part of it. Furthermore, there will be a scholarship—or, better, a work/study community service—for drummers and bassists to build a sound around. These drummers and bassists, or DJs/Beat makers, could be called "guest lecturers," be my co-teachers, co-facilitators and organizers. Or you could call them the house band. I'd love to join on trumpet, backup vox, or even keyboard. They would only have to come once a week for the laboratory/practicum part of the class—a 3 hour rehearsal/performance—of music with the word people trying out their words—whether rapping, or just adopting a conversational ("spoken word") voice.

The issues that could arise from this laboratory/practicum in which the spoken word and music (especially dance music and/or shivers-down-your-spine music) come together could ideally help transform the ways our society thinks about the coordination of the communicative power of music and words, and, on the most basic, practical, level, provide great advertisements—to probably be coordinated with audio and video in another course, for a new small business being started by some of the women graduating from the cosmetology department.

By contrast, the weekly non-laboratory seminar class session would be much more traditionally academic. We will dramatize and theorize the different performance/creation styles that come out of the laboratory/practicum. Here, there would be at least one "paper" due, whether an analytical paper, or a traditional poem in the widest sense of the word, or manifesto, and

---

102 For a more detailed account of similar hybrid courses, see the next chapter "Community Outreach For Creative Writers"

we would study the history of American (mostly black) popular music of the second half of the 20th century in the class. I know my students who fall through the cracks would benefit from such a course.

The rough outlines of this class can be adjusted to be applied to both the undergraduate level as well to an M(F)A in Non-Poetry (for it may be harder to achieve on a graduate level in the current system because it's even more specialized than the undergraduate level is). It could also be applied to other disciplines; I've had student playwrights who would benefit from a team-taught class with professors in the theatre department, and it could be modified to include more white country artists depending on what school we're teaching at.

In order for any of this to happen, the existing accredited Music and English departments need to bury their hatchet (which they may not even know they're wielding) and work together to do away, or at least temporarily suspend, the force-fed Frost that tells us "good fences make good neighbors"—to help make culture more inclusive, and interactive and practical and, yes, even, healthy (We can't say religious or spiritual because of the separation of church and state, but feel free to apply this to your own institutional situations).

13. Community Outreach For Creative Writers

In the fall of 2009, during the height of the news media's coverage of the American economic crisis that we still haven't extricated ourselves from, I was happy to come across an advertisement for a job in a graduate creative writing MFA program in the Detroit area that included—at its heart—a required course that seemed designed to address this economic crisis as it effects the lives of creative writing students, and other culture workers in our society:[103]

CRTW 550, "Community Outreach for Creative Writers." is a hybrid course that expects students to engage in both the practicum of public projects in the arts and in the seminar that explores the significance of literary arts in community life.

While the department has worded this brief course description in a way that makes it seem that doing a poetry reading, or perhaps editing a community-based literary anthology would be enough to fulfill the "practicum" part of this requirement,[104] this hybrid course could also go beyond anthologies and group readings (and even community workshops for children and seniors, for instance) to lead to a much needed rethinking of the mission of creative writing programs to make them more relevant in this economic and cultural crisis.

You may ask "What is a *hybrid* course?" Although some schools use the term to refer to a course that is taught half online, and half in a classroom, in this proposal the word "hybrid" implies an interdisciplinary approach. As a hybrid text sur-

---

103 It can also help respond to the demands Craig Santos Perez makes to help cure "mainly white MFA sickness" in Chapter 8.

104   An anthology would certainly be a start, as I argue in a Chpater 10.

rounds the limits of genre, so does this hybrid course expand the limits of an interdisciplinary approach, in both the seminar's writing component and through the practicum, not only between academic departments, but also between academic theory and 'real world' practice. This "Hybrid Course" could also transcend the distinction between civic engagement, "community service," and an internship, but with the primary mission of serving *disadvantaged* individuals and communities with the purpose of helping create more opportunities in and audiences/markets for the arts.

On the most basic structural level, I envision a 6 credit-hour course, with one 3 hour seminar/workshop every week, and at least 3 hours of field work for the practicum.

The **seminar** that explores the significance of literary arts in the community would allow both "creative" and "argumentative" writing to, first, help define the scope of the practicum. The "**practicum** of public projects in the arts" can offer a visionary paradigm for other MFA programs to consider. It can seduce potential students who feel betrayed by conventional graduate programs that don't even encourage, let alone expect, such public projects. The tone is authoritarian enough to weed out the art-for-art-sake crowd, or even the theory-for-theory sake's niche. It also has a deeper understanding of "community outreach" than the way this term is often used.

"Community outreach" in literary and academic contexts still exists against the backdrop of the transience of the always already separate "ivory tower," as if the writers in the academic program aren't themselves actually part of the community they are supposed to reach out to. Sure, many students currently relocate to attend an M(F)A program, and feel no particular connection with the community in which it's located, but that doesn't mean that connections can't be created with community *inreach; inreach + outreach* equals *community engagement*. Otherwise "community outreach" means mere window dressing dangling on the cultural superstructure as "charity." Beyond charity, the phrase "public projects in the arts" implies, in a city with an almost 30% unemployment rate, there can be no community outreach that is not also a job opportunity, and not just for students.

"Public projects in the arts" recalls the Works Projects Administration instituted in the first Great Depression, although on a much smaller scale, as it starts from a university rather than from the federal government. The WPA was an ambitious program that employed millions to provide essential "nation building" services from material infrastructure to cultural superstructure, on both national and regional levels. Its policies resulted in the closest America ever came to full-employment.[105] All of CRTW550's public projects would fall under the umbrella of Federal Project Number One.[106] Most of these programs were very popular among both workers and audiences (or consumers if you must):

> In each state a Writer's Project non-relief staff of editors was formed, along with a much larger group of field workers drawn from local unemployment rolls. Many of these had never graduated high school, but most had formerly held white collar jobs of some sort. Most of the Writer's Project employees were relatively young in age, and many came from working-class back-

---

[105] Although criticized by the corporate media as an example of unwieldy bureaucracy, even at its height, WPA expenses were only 6.79% of the GDP, and most programs quickly paid for themselves.

[106] For instance, the Federal Theatre Project (FTP)'s primary goal was to employ out-of-work artists, writers, and directors, with "the secondary aim of entertaining poor families and creating relevant art." The Federal Writer's Project (FWP) employed writers, editors, historians, researchers, art critics, and others to compile local histories, oral histories, ethnographies, children's books and other works. The Federal Music Project (FMP) gave musicians in a wide range of genres employment and created entertainment that also educates.

grounds." This could describe many Creative Writing students. Today, college gives the *illusion* that the student's not really unemployed (or even working class), even as she's paying for the privilege of training for jobs that increasingly don't exist. Thus, the **seminar** aspect of CRTW550 can serve as a think tank to study, critique, and update FWP initiatives (*doing away with their racial bias*) with the aims of bringing employment, education, entertainment and art together to de-alienate labor and help repair America's ailing infrastructure.

Such a civic minded interpretation of the course description helps ground the literary arts more in local community life than they've been in the M(F)A era. But the meaning of the word "community" cannot be assumed, especially given the attenuated atomization of local communities in the 21st century tech economy.[107] What's important is the recognition that "community life" is inevitably *in* the literary arts (however sublime and ahistorical or merely personal and expressive in their generic strivings). Given the increased fragmentation of local communities since the New Deal, in which many more people's first sense of 'community' comes from commercial mass-culture, any new public arts project must acknowledge that it's not enough to create art objects anymore, unless we also create (or discover) contexts for that art. We can't assume a public context, especially as the current economic and cultural crisis may prove to be much worse than the Great Depression.[108] Our task is to help create it.

In an era in which Creative Writing programs are increasingly churning out too much supply for the kind of jobs there's

---

107   Also, the word "significance of" seems superfluous; one can too easily picture talking heads on "Face The Community" pondering and pontificating.

108   See Chapter 1 on *Culture Crash* for a fuller treatment of the crisis.

less and less of a demand (if not need) for, this course will explore what kind of social purpose art can, and/or should, have through the creation of, or the joining of forces with existing, arts organizations, media production companies, community centers, etc. We could bring community newspapers (for instance the San Quentin News) and other local wordsmiths and non-academic public intellectuals into these creative writing classes. This could conceivably open up channels for an equal and more comprehensive exchange between academia and the non-academic community in a given locale.

While some 'purists' claim such activities may compromise the abstract or expressive integrity of creative art, FDR's WPA initiatives set a precedent that if you pay your dues with mural arts, you'll get to be more abstract like DeKooning and Guston later—if that's what you need. And in this program you wouldn't be burdened by the Federal government's often clueless ideas of what populism is, because it would have a less mediated, more direct, relationship with the local community. You won't be "compromising" with the community, but conversing with them.

b. Detroit And The Ghost of Motown

As I write this, I'm picturing Detroit in which this school is located. Detroit has come to be the ultimate metonymy for "city in crisis" with its well-funded cheerleaders for "revitalization" or "urban removal." In the *Time Magazine* cover story, "The Tragedy of Detroit" *(10/5/09)*, Daniel Okrent offers a diagnosis of "Notown's" fall, and some prescriptions for its possible resurrection. He also claims that "Detroit is open to a new industry,"—and by this, he (predictably) means "21st Century technology." Yet, maybe what Detroit needs more than high-tech is the services this hybrid course could provide as a cultural and economic stimulus program.

Sure, a modest course in a M(F)A program won't be able to make much of a dent in a larger cultural crisis this city faces. But, even if the practicum aspect of the class could not truly revitalize this city, at least the attempt to do so could allow us to more thoroughly "explore the significance of literary arts in community life." In the seminar's "think tank," we can utilize our skills in creative writing to brainstorm and consider the question of what new industry could truly revitalize Detroit. Maybe what Detroit needs is *some of its old industries back*—specifically, for our context, its old *culture* industries that involve creative writing—and that an MFA in Creative Writing program could be especially well-equipped with the talent and enthusiasm (if not yet access to the cultural means of production) to help such recreation.

Perhaps Detroit's most veritable and beloved cultural institution is Motown Records. Motown was a cultural export at least as significant as the car (and the car radio) that helped make it possible. Motown Records could only come into being because of the industrial economy (hence its name), and today's "free market" conditions—with their de-industrialized America, to say nothing of today's monopoly mass-media, would probably prohibit this from occurring today. Yet if we want to understand the rich tradition of Detroit's *poetry*, we cannot ignore the role Motown plays. It certainly was my first poetry.

But Motown is important not merely for its historical aesthetic objects, but also the model of business and community outreach that, however capitalistic, may seem "too revolutionary" for today's civic leaders (while not revolutionary enough for the do-nothing left). During its heyday in its first decade,[109] before it left Detroit for LA, Motown excelled at community outreach and "market penetration": a home, a family, where you

---

109 During what *Culture Crash* calls "the Great Compression"

might see Bob Dylan's favorite contemporary poet, Smokey Robinson, cutting grass or Berry Gordy rounding up ladies from the beauty salon to get them to listen in on their quality control focus group where they get first listen of the new Velvelettes or Marvelettes single, and their vote counts as much as Smokey's. Much more of a bridge than a wall, it was able to do as much from its little "Hitsville USA" building as the major record conglomerates did from their skyscrapers. If only capitalism would have let it stay!

Even if the creation of a locally-based black-owned cultural organization as powerful as Motown was in its heyday is too ambitious and unrealistic, studying the factors that allowed it to succeed can provide a template for the collective of writers that makes up CRTW550 to collaborate with each other as well as with other departments and the larger community (working perhaps with such local writer/musician/activists as jessica Care moore). In a city with a 29 percent unemployment rate as well as a large population of talented high-school, and college-age artists, musicians, and entrepreneurs, any proposal to revive the local entertainment/art culture industries, as a revenue-creating "stimulus plan," to reduce unemployment, is worth considering.

Students in CRTW550 could imagine a project called MOTOWN 2.0, based on Motown during its first decade, before it left Detroit for LA. In the practicum, students will subject their own creative work to non-academic community "quality control" groups while also playing the role of "talent scouts" as much as "teachers." Each student will be encouraged to create a collaborative piece with someone in the community. There's at least as many talented artists in Detroit today as there were in Berry Gordy's day. What's lacking is an organizer who can bring them together so that the whole is more than the sum of its parts. I am not an organizer. I am much better as the person who sits beside one, whispering, or shouting, ideas. That's one of the reasons we're offering the Berry Gordy Fellowship to an organizer who will facilitate the practicum.

Despite this perhaps deceptive working title, one need not have any aesthetic interest in Motown, or American Post WW2 popular music in general, to thrive in this course. No one will be turned away because of pre-existing academic majors or disciplines or taste in music; no one will be turned away for engaging in the public/private "hybrid form" of commercial popular song, public service announcement or commercial jingle. In fact, this will be encouraged.

By "imagine a project," I must make it clear that I don't mean Motown 2.0 as a mere art gallery exhibition or installation piece in the sense of such "innovative" interactive pieces as the Oakland art museum's historical *Vinyl* exhibition (which included turntables and listening pillows, but, in its 1970s bias, it didn't even include 45RPMS). It wouldn't be merely historical and/or headphoned, but we could imagine it in terms of conceptual art.

Taking as a starting point, conceptual artist Christine Hill's Volksboutique *Pilot* Project (Ronald Feldman Gallery, NYC, 2000), this semester's final project will be the creation of a videotaped, and simulcast, variety show. Consider an interdisciplinary project, in conjunction with the theatre, dance, music, cosmetology, fashion departments—for starts. The goal of this coordinated effort is to create, by the end of the semester (or the school year, if the semester is too ambitious a time frame), an event that helps brand a local arts community with a ""unity in diversity" attitude. Let's call it a "Dance Craze" event.

You may ask what would a dance craze have to do with creative writing? For starts, it brings together people and helps build community more than any other form of expression and/or art, which is a central aspect to any "community life." Creative writing students could write poems, stories and essays about it ("I met my husband at that dance craze event" or "A dance craze is as beautiful as the chance meeting of an Italian or Nigerian laundrymat and TPP on a dissecting table.").

But beyond that, some poems could be used for the lyrics of the variety of songs the music department and folks from the community would create for the event (each with their own take on the dance craze theme). Some stories could be shaped into story boards for video-art, in conjunction with the theatre department and visual art ("new media") students. Other writers could write journalistic reviews or more scholarly critiques of the songs and dances.[110] Others could create multi-media visual projections of words behind the dancers (though this might end up being more "exploding plastic inevitable" than Motown). Others may create short skits working closely with choreographers.

If there's a three hour dance show in a small local club (or an on campus venue), the dancing will be so powerful a source of social integration in bringing a wide range of people together that there will be plenty of room for non-musical acts in between sets, or DJS. There's room for a dramatic monologue spoken by the Lobbyist for PetaKillsPets.Com and BlackJobsMatter.com, a Beckettian or Steinian dramatic dialogue, a poem painting being performed, as well a reading of a great poem in a monotone! There could even be room for a political discussion like the Barakas used to do during their Newark basement multi-genre events, or whatever else the students may collectively devise. It will be the essential supplement—if not necessarily culmination of—the weekly seminar sessions.....even if you personally don't like dancing (or a cripple like me, and can't anymore, though I'd advocate strongly for mattresses for us to horizontally dance).

What I just wrote here would be sent to students three months before the course begins, as an introduction. The assignment is to refine and better these ideas in a collective chat-room so that we can "hit the ground running" when the semester starts.

---

110   These could be collected in a multi-genre yearly anthology as mentioned in Chapter 10.

In conclusion, such a course both *goes out into* the community as a teacher, entertainer, or scribe recording oral histories, and *brings in* the community, in a variety of possible ways. Perhaps most importantly, it breaks down the artificially imposed boundary between "arts" and "entertainment," and a "fine arts" school and a "vocational" school and allows writers an opportunity to "put their money where their mouth is" if indeed we take seriously our desire to create more jobs, increase the quality of life, make city streets safer by bringing back more locally-owned nightclubs and theatres, increase a feeling of *enfranchisement*, a stake in the cultural life of the metropolitan area (and ideally create a more pro-active collaboration between city and suburb, poor and rich, white and black, etc).

2.

14. A Poem With Histories: Dudley Randall's "Booker T. And W.E.B."

Poem As Despecialization Strategy

Dudley Randall's "Booker T and W.E.B" is equally pedagogically useful in Creative Writing, Critical Thinking, and Foundational Skills classes for several reasons: 1) it provides an intimate look at the skeleton that undergirds the kind of skills required by comparison/contrast and argumentative papers as well as in creative dialogue in narrative fiction and nonfiction, by showing two sides of an argument without blatantly taking sides; 2) it's an introduction to a complex chapter in a history (with suggestions for further reading) that's too often erased unless the students have taken Afram courses or learned this on their own. 3) it's a good introduction to Post WW2 20th Century American Poetry, especially African-American poetry.

The poem's brilliant suggestive intelligence, which can tell, but also show, by showing the tellers, allows multiple perspectives and interpretations that forces the readers to draw their own conclusions and goads them to learn more about its subject matter. By packing so much into a one page poem of short lines, it also dramatizes poetic economy and condensation, which on a practical level, could be a very useful skill in various professional fields in search of "content providers," writers of ad copy, or the pithy sound bites that dramatize this tweet culture. In short, it generates students' own writing, inspires them to want to enter the debate, and show how it relates to their own struggle. It has never failed to yield excellent class discussions (even in a mostly white classroom). In a multi-genre creative writing class, it shows the common roots between poetry, drama, and (creative) non-fiction, and can thus be a useful de-specialization tool.

The dialogue/debate presented in Dudley Randall's 1965 poem has historical importance, and may serve to educate people into some central issues in the "war of words" between two powerful spokesmen that occurred a century ago during the height of the old Jim Crow.[111] Yet the debate was not just about two men, but about contrasting philosophies they represented: as essayist James Weldon Johnson wrote in 1933, "One not familiar with this phase in Negro life in the 12 or 14-year period following 1903…cannot imagine the bitterness or antagonism between the two wings."[112]

It may not be *necessary* to know any more about the debate aside from what is mentioned in the poem itself in order to appreciate what Randall is doing, but such knowledge can deepen the reader's understanding of the poem. The poem also invites the reader to ask: After reading this poem, do you identify and agree with one of the characters, both, or neither? Is the debate still relevant today, or would it need to be updated? Does Randall summarize and represent these two positions fairly? Does Randall purposely omit some information and leave the poem ambiguous?

One of the first things one may notice when reading this poem, especially if one reads it aloud, is that this poem uses rhyme and rhythm. Its rhythmic rhyming couplets may remind you of children's books like Dr. Seuss's *Green Eggs And Ham*.[113] When this poem was first published in 1965, many contemporary poets were abandoning traditional rhyme and rhythm schemes for "free verse" (or "blank verse"). To many of these poets, poems that relied on end-stopped rhymes were considered anachronistic, especially if they emphasize a sing-song

---

111   http://www.poetryfoundation.org/poems-and-poets/poems/detail/47690

112   George. 5

113   but I'm sure it could be set to better music

quality as Randall's poem does (as Ezra Pound put it, almost half a century before, a poem's 'music' should not sound like a metronome).

50 years later, such rhymes are still considered taboo amongst much sophisticated academic poetry. To many, this 20th century free-verse distinguished *American* writing from the traditional European formal rhyming poetry, and was considered a sign of American modern "freedom." Yet, Randall's use of these rhythmic rhymes make the poem more immediately accessible, and also much more easy to memorize, to a more general audience, like many of the popular songs of the time (as well as of today).

While some poets do not call song lyrics "poetry," in many ways song lyrics are much more like what was called poetry in America, and elsewhere, before Ezra Pound, and others made their poetic innovations that made poetry become less popular. Yet Randall's use of rhyme differs from the traditional European rhyming verse of the 17th, 18th, and 19th century by tapping into a more populist, less specialized, African-American (trans-literary) tradition in which abandoning rhyme was never a sign, or badge, of "modernism" as much as it was among the white-European literary tradition (which can also make the poem more accessible to a younger readership than a college student, even if it runs the risk of reducing these very serious, and powerful adult thinkers and activists, into cartoon characters).

For all of its sing-song accessibility and seeming simplicity, this poem becomes more and more complex upon repeated readings. The poem's masterful use of form, coupled with its poetic ambiguity and suggestiveness, come alive on the page as well as on the stage. Furthermore, its rhyme schemes and the length of each stanza help contribute to the meaning of the poem, driving home its main point of contrast between the two historical speakers: Booker T. Washington and W.E.B. Du Bois.

1st stanza   ABBCCDD
2nd Stanza ABBDDCCEE
3rd Stanza AFFGGHH
4th Stanza AIIJJKKLL (LL could be CC)
Coda/Envoi: AA

Randall's use of the rhyming names (or initials of their non-last names) is a musical *hook*, which frames the poem. They become rhyming *stage directions* in this dramatic-dialogue, signaling the stanza breaks. The stanza structure is also worth noting. This poem alternates between 2 stanzas of 7 lines (spoken by Booker T.) and 2 stanzas of 9 lines (spoken by W.E.B). W.E.B. Du Bois always gets 2 more lines, and there is clearly a thematic reason why Randall does this (even as his decision to do this can be interpreted more than one way).

Booker T. always speaks first, and W.E.B addresses his assertions point-by-point (even using the exact same end-rhymes in the first two stanzas). Why does Randall do that? Historically, Booker T. Washington came first, and was older than W.E.B Du Bois. But this device also seems to give W.E.B. the *last word*. The fact that W.E.B. gets the last word in this dialectic argument may suggest that the author Dudley Randall himself finds W.E.B's position more attractive, more empowering, and stronger than Booker T's. But the poem resists such an easy conclusion. Randall does an admirable job of stepping out of the way and presenting the argument without intrusive commentary that can prevent the reader from being empowered enough to make up his or her own mind. We must look more closely at the language and rhetoric the two historic characters in this poem use in order to understand exactly what the debate is about.

This poem is actually two distinct, if related, debates: 1) education and vocation; 2) civil rights. Contrasting the statements made in the first two stanzas, we may see that Booker T. believes that manual labor (whether hoeing, or cooking) is more valuable than intellectual labor (studying chemistry or Greek). W.E.B represents the antithesis to Booker T's thesis, arguing that "the right to cultivate the brain" is at the very least as important as rejoicing in manual labor ("skill of hand"). If looked at historically, one may understand that during the time this poem took place, whites put far more obstacles in the way for blacks working in white collar professions than they did for blue collar ones. Yet the contrast in these two stanzas (and the positions these two men take) is not simply *what* they argue, but how they argue.

Randall underscores the difference in their *manner* of speaking, first, by contrasting Booker T's use of the *passive* voice ("It seems to me") with W.E.B's use of the *active* voice ("I don't agree"). Regardless of whether the historical Booker T. actually spoke in the passive voice much more than W.E.B. did, the fact that Randall portrays the contrast this way, again, suggests that Randall considers W.E.B. to be a more attractive role model. This would make sense, given the fact that Randall himself was a writer and devout reader and thus more likely to identify with W.E.B. Du Bois, especially during this time in which African Americans were more encouraged to work in manual labor than be college educated (though that was starting to change).

Yet, however passive Booker T seems, he is also presented as a scold, chastising W.E.B. for "showing a mighty lot of cheek," and "sticking [his] nose" inside a book. He certainly is addressing W.E.B. in an aggressive condescending tone, as the historical Booker T. did. By contrast, W.E.B's language is more elevated and more respectful of Booker T. (at least at first). W.E.B is not saying that everyone has to agree with him that cultivation of the brain is better than cultivation of the land; he's acknowledging that both skills (manual and intellectual) can be useful, and important.

The second half of the poem changes the subject to the question of "Civil Rights." At the core of the debate in the second half of the poem is which strategy is better: can you buy your way out of racism or can you vote your way out of it? Here Booker T. tells his fellow blacks, "Just keep your mouths shut, do not grouse,/But work, and save, and buy a house." W.E.B counters, "Unless you help to make the laws/ They'll steal your house with trumped-up clause." These few lines get at the heart of division between these two factions within the African American community that these men represented. Washington wrote in the early 1900s in response to calls for civil-rights legislation, "The best course to pursue in regard to a civil rights bill in the South is to let it alone: let it alone and it will settle itself. Good school teachers and plenty of money to pay them will be more potent in settling the race question than any civil rights bill and investigative committees."[114]

While many African Americans sided with Booker T's position, and it did allow a large sector of the African American community to make economic gains within the segregated society of the early 20th century, by the time of the mid century Civil Rights movement, a young generation of blacks had painfully experienced over-and-over again the continued terror (lynching, burnings, real estate fraud) that W.E.B predicts in these poems, and came to reject what he calls Booker T's "little plan" of economic self-sufficiency. This doesn't necessarily mean that this poem is definitely siding with W.E.B. as a self evident truth.

Randall may *seem* to be siding with Du Bois in this poem. He certainly gives him more lines, more articulate and graceful speech, and one sees in miniature the same kind of verbal skewering in this poem that W.E.B. had made of Booker T's position in his *The Souls of Black Folks, yet* the coda of the poem ends with a tone of ambivalence that suggests a different reading Dudley Randall does purposely avoid commentary that says he agrees with one over the other. Even though W.E.B. is getting

---

114   quoted in Nelson George

the last word, from one perspective this could show that he is just a more effective *verbal warrior;* a better talker and writer. The repetition of their catch phrases ("It seems to me" and "I don't agree") suggests an argument at a stalemate, with neither man (or movement) able to convince the other of his point, and in this sense, the poem becomes more a lament for their argument never reaching a working relationship, and a very subtle plea for unity between these two positions and legacies.

Yet, the debates between Booker T. and W.E.B is not the only history we see in this poem. This poem may also be a comment on debates being waged in 1965, the year this poem was written (not long after W.E.B's death). When Randall published this poem in 1965, the Civil Rights movement was at its height. Many had fought for, and died, in the fight against segregation, to enforce laws already on the books and put pressure on Congress and the President to enact the Voting Rights Act of 1964. Yet, during this time, the mass media made much of the divide between Martin Luther King in the south and Malcolm X in the northern cities.

Because of this, some students have been tempted to see Dudley Randall's distinction here as a comment on the Martin/Malcolm debate within the black community. One student wrote that, in this poem, that Booker T. is more like Martin Luther King, while W.E.B. is like Malcolm X. And, indeed, these two debates have some things in common. If Booker T, seems more passive than Booker T in this poem, so was Martin Luther King seen as more passive than Malcolm X. It also must be said that Booker T. and MLK were both southerners (where the white power structure is made up of "political wolves"), while W.E.B. and Malcolm X were both northerners (where the white power structure is more like a "political fox"). And thus their different strategies and tactics can be explained by the different forms racism took in the south and north.

Yet, the analogy is of limited value, since Martin Luther King at the time was fighting, amongst other things, for the right to vote (which Booker T. disagrees with). If anything, Malcolm X was much more skeptical that gaining voting rights would change anything for the better. He was fighting less for Civil Rights than Human Rights, for economic self-determination, and in this sense shares more with Booker T. Furthermore, as both Malcolm and Martin's thinking matured, their positions came closer together, before they were assassinated.

In fact, by 1964, a year before Malcolm died, he spoke of how black people must come together in unity and overcome the tendency "we have to always be at each others' throats" (The Ballot or The Bullet), whether this is between the SCLC and the NOI in his day, or the Booker T/W.E.B. debate 50 years earlier. Malcolm was assassinated in early February 1965 before such accommodation between the two factions could be made.

Shortly after Malcolm's death, however, Congressmen Adam Clayton Powell Jr. introduced a seventeen-point program on March 28, 1965, "My Black Position Paper for America's 20 Million Negroes." This fused the ideas of Washington and Du Bois (or Malcolm and Martin) by demanding that the civil-rights movement "shift its emphasis to the-two-pronged thrust of the Black Revolution: economic self-sufficiency *and* political power" (emphasis added). He felt the legislation of Johnson, particularly the 1964 Civil Rights Act, meant nothing in the North without the economic contingent of 'black power' to support it. Martin Luther King soon came to express that *both* were needed to create unity beyond the stalemate presented in the poem.

Such unity is probably needed even more today. In 1965, when Dudley Randall wrote this poem, the choice of intellectual labor over manual labor—whether industrial or agricultural—was seen as a form of progress as it was when W.E.B. wrote. Higher education/white collar jobs were less available to blacks but were apparently on the verge of becoming more available, even as there was still the option of choosing a job in manual labor. It's doubtful Randall could have foreseen then the dismantling of these blue-collar manual labor jobs (the good union jobs) that has occurred in the subsequent 50 years. As a result of this, more kids felt *forced* to go to college in hopes of getting a job (even if they would have preferred working a blue collar job). Once again, history changes the meaning of the debate in the first two stanzas.

Today, the debate in the first two stanzas of this poem is simply not as relevant in the absence of these manual jobs, which has also served to lessen the value of the college degree. And the debate in the final half of the poem may also not be as relevant, as many have seen how the Voting Rights Act, and other Civil Rights Legislation, did not materially benefit most black folks. Black poverty has significantly increased and the murder and terror continues. In this light, I've found that many more college students these days are more inclined to take Booker T's side more than they did only twenty years ago when I first started teaching the poem.

Booker T. Washington may have been arrogant, as this poem and many others have argued, but his argument for economic self-determination, is not to be dismissed as the ravings of an "Uncle Tom" (or less of "a man") as it was to many during the Civil Rights movement. And W.E.B., during the time he was debating Booker T., was dependant on the patronage of northern whites—who later dumped him like a hot potato once he began questioning his earlier faith in the philosophy of integration. And, of course, as a writer and intellectual, as a philosopher and historian, W.E.B DuBois's own positions are much more complex than this debate shows. There's only so much you can put in a 35 line-poem, and this poem in suggesting hat both economic self-sufficiency and political power within existing structures are needed, at the very least can get students thinking of their own struggles in a different light, can make them feel less alone, a part of something larger, and plant some long term seeds.

15. The BreakBeat Poets

As a teacher, I get regularly bombarded or hounded by textbook publishers trying to get us to adopt their textbooks. Many of these books recognize that they must do a better job of seducing the skeptical student (and teacher) than they've done in the past, and it's somewhat standard to see such texts boast about how this new revised, expanded and updated version "extends our efforts to bring students to literature by including writing that speaks in voices more like theirs, to which they can connect," as the new edition of *Literature: The Human Experience* (Bedford St. Martin's) does. Yet such texts tend to merely repackage the same old "common core" or "canonical" work, while their contemporary offerings generally fit into a narrow range of de-politicized "personal experience" narrative genre and makes no room for "spoken word" poetry (with the possible exception of Timothy Yu's *100 Chinese Silences*) alongside of a broem like Joshua Clover. By contrast, the recent anthology, ***The Breakbeat Poets (New American Poetry in the Age of Hip Hop)*, edited by Kevin Coval, Quraysh Ali Lansana, and Nate Marshall**, is a corrective, and I can't wait to use it as a text in my next college literature or creative writing class.

Superficially, this could be called a "niche anthology," but after reading this collection of 78 poets, all born between 1961 and 1999, at least twice through, I can concur with the publishers' claim that this anthology offers "a fuller spectrum of experience of what it means to be alive in this moment" than any other anthology of contemporary poetry I've read in the past 30 years. "The BreakBeat poets are saving American poetry," Kevin Coval writes (xvii), and this is no idle boast.

The editors did an amazing job of creating an anthology that sets a standard for deep, difficult poetry that speaks a language, and shows the struggles, that younger people (of *any* race) can relate to. Its formal range makes room for some of the kind of poems the Bedford textbook would include, but it also goes beyond the mainstream Vs. "experimental" (say Vendler v. Perloff) continuum, as well as the mid 20th century battles between the "raw" and the "cooked" and helps create what Thomas Sayers Ellis calls "a path around both Academic and Slam Poetry, to eliminate the misconceptions between them."

The Breakbeat Poets makes me feel sane, more rational, less alone….not working in a lopsided vacuum of (mostly) white poetry communities or institutions…it gives confidence and maybe even the ability to confide…It may even restore my faith in the possibility that indeed poetry (even on the page) can do and say something that prose—or engaging conversation (whether commodified or not) cannot, as this work synthesizes my love of direct statement (that sometimes breaks the "show, don't tell" taboo) with a language play I always feel torn about having to edit out of my OP-ED like prose.

The *BreakBeat Poets* also sets a standard by gathering a community together by embodying the spirit of unity in diversity. This self-exceeding book is no dead artifact, but a social scene anyone who has read it can be a part of, like a cross between a sidewalk cipher and the best, most democratic, creative writing workshops. As hip hop broke with disco's whitewash to return to the un-coopted roots of funk, and claim the strategic separatism of a generational as well as racial identity as a power base, so does this anthology harbor the possibility of liberating us from the hierarchical ageist and Eurocentric conventions of literary and academic culture.

Sure, there are some writers who have first achieved notoriety through the white-mediated literary institutions, and who write in forms more accepted there—but there are also others who have first achieved notoriety on a grass roots level: in *The BreakBeat Poets,* the trickle down literary economy meets the trickle up, as these young (by poetry standards), gifted, and (mostly) black writers include much more existential wisdom (even about issues as grave as death) than the many collections dominated by older establishment stylists…

From 40 years hindsight, this anthology shows that even though hip hop may have at first been thought of as a youth culture phenomenon, even perhaps by some of its practitioners, it is increasingly becoming a multi-generational culture. The wide-range of aesthetics, perspectives and philosophies included in this multi-racial anthology nonetheless seem to present a unified front against a common enemy. This does not mean to suggest in any way that these writers don't honor their elders or their traditions, only that they weave the segregated threads of many traditions together in ways that could help heal America and show what a post-racial America could look like.

Two Legacy Poems:
Krista Franklin and Mariahadessa Ekere Tallie

There are an infinite number of portals through which one can enter the world created by *The Breakbeat Poets*. Thumbing through its pages, I notice more tributes to Black Arts Culture Worker Hero, Amiri Baraka, than to any of the hip hop artists celebrated (Biggie, Kendrick, Tupac, Sheik Spear, Ole Dirty Bastard, Kanye, and Nas for instance). Clearly many of the writers in *The Breakbeat Poets* are as influenced by Baraka as by hip hop culture (some even claim that Baraka helped open the door for hip hop culture), and when he passed away at the age of 79 in January 2014, 8 months before #HandsUpDon'tShoot and #BlackLivesMatter went viral, there was a palpable sense of loss, collective mourning and a more acutely urgent need to honor his legacy. His spirit, in death, goaded young and old, men and women, artists and activists, to do more, to do better, to grow and unite people in the struggle against white supremacy, capitalism and imperialism, and this sense of urgency for collective action informs *The Breakbeat Poets*.

Baraka's life achievement cannot be summed up in a paragraph, but he did more than perhaps any American writer of his generation to show the complex intersections between culture and economic/political issues and, through his insistent calls for collective action (especially after 1966) and refusal to shy away from (if not exactly court) controversy, helped create a coalition between the socialists and social justice folks, the cultural nationalists, artists and musicians, and those who value literature "as such," thus helping to "blow up bullshit distinctions between high and low, academic and popular, rap and poetry, page and stage" (as co-editor Kevin Coval puts it).

One of the goals of *The BreakBeat Poets*, according to Coval, is to "connect to a vastly disparate audience in order to bring awareness to the sanctity and humanity of the people and places at the center of the poem" (xx). And judging by the majority of the obituaries in the corporate press (as well as some comments on facebook), there are still many (whites) who doubt—or dismiss—the sanctity and humanity of Amiri Baraka (even if they liked Le Roi Jones).[115] Against this racist backdrop, the powerful tributes to Amiri Baraka by **Krista Franklin** (b.1970) and **Mariahadessa Ekere Tallie** (b.1973) each in their own way, help "set the record straight….or at least scratch it."

These two poems face different directions to explore similar themes and messages. Comparing these two tributes to Baraka, one may first feel the tonal difference: Tallie's poem reads more like an earnest—almost religious—praise poem, focusing on what she loves about Baraka with some aesthetic detachment, while Franklin's lament wields wit as a weapon against the same obstacles and foes Baraka fought against. Franklin focuses more on the cultural ground while Tallie focuses more on the hero-

---

115 http://chrisstroffolino.blogspot.com/2014/06/amiri-baraka-legacy-beyond-racist.html

ic figure(s); Franklin rope-a-dopes against the obstacles while Tallie refuses their right to exist. As Baraka knew, both strategies are necessary. Franklin expresses Baraka's anger and tough love while Tallie emphasizes the resilient workaholic gentleness which grounds that anger:

> *"insurrection of his tenderness*
> *surrender to the work*
> *of love....not just the romance"* (Tallie, "Possible")

Tallie's poem offers a way out that is also a way in, beyond the transience of "transcendence":

> *out of the box   they spring*
> *out of the narrowness of yesterday & some bleak projected tomorrow*
>
> *impossible men*
> *outlawed drum of their hearts*
> *our loving them is the forbidden religion....*

Tallie's "impossible men" can be actual just as Baraka was/is actual even if the white literary establishment said/says:

> **he's impossible**
> *exasperated arms fling*
> *shaking heads   closed doors establishment wallets shut*

Tallie's reference to Baraka's heroic ability to survive (and even triumph over) the white literary establishment's backlash and ostracization the more he came to spi(ri)t the truth and demand his people's right to the "outlawed drum of the heart" may contrast starkly with the reality Franklin finds in Baraka's absence, a reality conspiring once again to banish the drum, not through the blatant Nazi Music Regulations of Goebbels as much as by "market forces" (""and the drum got/pawn-shopped for a machine"). The drum machine is cheaper, and from Franklin's perspective the drum machine can be seen as one of the many "austerity measures" foisted on black folks more intensely since the 1970s (even if it was sold as progress).

Franklin drags us more through the contemporary hell that is trapped in this box from which Tallie's impossible heroes spring; this "box" of "hunched shoulders (where) McCay's call to arms/ is buried in the graveyard of the poet's imaginings." Feeling the bleakness of the contemporary world even more acutely after his death, Franklin takes up where Baraka left off in her description of the cultural decay, and backlash, that she has experienced ever since she was born in 1970:

> *America picks the lint from its navel, moonwalks*
> *Its way back to antebellum inertia, lulls itself*
> *To sleep with airwave regurgitations of 1970*
> *Before music sold its soul for a stripper's pole (66)*

In these last two lines, we see contemporary America stalemated between the *Scylla* and *Charybdis* of two equally destructive options, nostalgia and contemporary insipidness, both sponsored by the same corporate media. This impasse is similar to Tallie's "narrowness of yesterday & some bleak projected tomorrow," but for Franklin the bleakness is more *present*:

> "Meanwhile, while knee-grows still swallowing
> the jizz of the American dream....,
> we still ain't caught up where we need to be....
>   Who's gonna
> save us now that all the black heroes/
> Are....more concerned with erasing their records and record deals

> *Than delving into solving the algebra of black agony,*
> *Bolt-cutting the inextricable chains of imperialism*
> *That got everybody tied up in knots. Who's gonna*
> *Save us now that all the black heroes are making*
> *It rain in sweatshops where the heroines calculate*
> *Payouts in booty-bounce, and the drum got*
> *Pawn-shopped for a machine?*

Reading Franklin, one may wonder if Baraka, as Black Culture Worker Hero, would be able to achieve what he achieved had he been born 40 or 50 years later (in the 70s and 80s), in this more disillusioned era, when Black heroes are "more concerned/ with erasing their records and record deals" (both forms of exploitation, injustice and evidence of white colonization).[116] But while Franklin's poem may initially seem more despairing than Tallie's, the genuine cry to be saved (and to save...to catch up to *where we need to be*), nonetheless offers some hope for an answer, if not in the present (and its "impossible men") but in the future of a possible woman as her poem, lest it be forgot, begins with an image of passing on Baraka's wisdom to a younger woman (presumably, but not necessarily, black):

> *"Today I turned Transbluency over*
> *to the hands of a teenage tussling*
> *with her own words, still trying to decipher*
> *the difference between invention and insipidness"* (Franklin).

We also see a sign of hope in Franklin's title,[117] which sug-

---

116 Compare, for instance, the ethical standard implied in this poem to the younger **Aziza Barnes**' preference for "contemporaries who do not strive to manufacture a control over their own lives, but simply comment on their lack of it." (314)

117 "Preface to a Twenty Volume Homicide Note," which references one of Baraka's first poems; the pre-revolutionary "beat" Baraka when

gests that she, like Baraka, hopes to be able to write 20 volumes that will help answer the open question with which her poem ends, a question Baraka so consistently asked himself in his more than 20 volumes and lecture/performances ("Who will save us?)

It would be a mistake, therefore, to reduce Tallie to a romantic or optimist, and Franklin to a realist or cynic, in these poems. Both writers know that Baraka helped make a community possible (and a community helped make Baraka possible).

Neither Franklin's nor Tallie's poems position themselves as intimately and immanently within hip-hop culture as many of the other pieces in this hip-hop themed collection (perhaps because they were born in the early 1970s and thus see hip hop culture not as much of a universe or ecosystem as some of the younger writers born in the late 1980s like **Nate Marshall** and **Aziza Barnes**, who were baptized into hip-hop culture before they were old enough to think about it), but rather, as part of the Black Arts Tradition in general (a tradition which did not start with Baraka, even though he played a significant role in theorizing and codifying it), as they struggle to bring Baraka's revolutionary vision into the present, as it's clear both writers believe "A New Reality Is Better Than A New Movie."

Renegades Of Funk: John Murillo

Both Franklin and Tallie's poems also contrast with the perspective of some of their contemporaries. "Renegades of Funk" by **John Murillo** (b. 1971) places himself, as a 12 year old in

---

he still went by the name Le Roi Jones and his poems found more success in the mostly white literary world than among his black contemporaries like the Umbra poets. Franklin's remix of the title pays tribute to the more mature Baraka's Black Arts need for poems that turn their anger to the external oppressor rather than in on oneself.

1983, more intimately in the context of hip-hop culture, to flesh out the "they" Tallie celebrates and show some of the ways his generation managed to dig itself out of the rubble to bring the spirit of ancestors before Baraka back:

Reject the fetters, come together still—
Some call it *Capoeira*, call it *Street
Dance*. We say *culture*. Say *survival*.

Although this poem is not a blatant tribute to Amiri Baraka, this sonnet-sequence (whose formalism is worthy of Gwendolyn Brooks) is both a celebration of himself (and his hip hop culture homies) as a 12 year old in 1983, as well as a socio/cultural/analysis that is Baraka-esque in scope (cf. *Blues People* and *Whys/Wise*) whose rhetoric may have the power to educate young folks as well as persuade the whites who still unfairly dismiss or deride much of Baraka's post-Jones achievement as well as the sanctity and humanity of hip hop culture.

Set against the backdrop of the post-industrial small business urban decay in more straightforwardly physically descriptive ways than Franklin ("Strip-malls firmly now/ where haints once hung." And "the burnt out liquor stores and beauty shops,/ Mechanics' lots abandoned, boarded up/ Pastrami shacks"), Murillo traces the 12 year old's growing awareness of how contemporary reality conspired (and conspires) to erase black history, culture and even people: "the young, it seems, forget/ the drum and how it bled" in a world in which "The strip malls bleed/ The ghosts from banjos. Hollers caught in greed."

In this artful juxtaposition of his cultural present with history going back to the blues and spirituals,[118] his reference to the drum may recall the banned and pawned drums in Tallie's

---

118 A formal device Nate Marshall also uses to great effect in his poem "On Caskets" included in this volume.

and Franklin's poems, as the corporate takeover of the mid-20th century black music industry and culture Nelson George refers to as the "rhythm and blues world" during the 70s, left in its wake shuttered record stores, disenfranchised personality radio DJS, small black owned record labels; even the legendary Apollo had to shut down. Indeed, one of the points of this poem is to show the perennial love/hate relationship white America has had with black rhythm. This relationship is beautifully distilled into a single line in section II of this sequence (check out the use of the period and line-break):

Rhythm's why they keep us. Down.[119]

"Keep us" means chain us to them (whether through chattel slavery or through "market forces"). They feel a need to chain us, for the same reason they need to chain rhythm. One could write a long essay or 39 poems on this line (that's wider than a sentence). One could also compare it to a couplet in section IV:

The people shouting, singing in the fields
They lit the torches, compromised the yield.

In slavery times (but not just), slave owners feared black

---

119   You may contrast this with **Danez Smith's** "this land is afraid of the black mind." (258) Rhythm, contrary to Western dualisms, is not opposed to deep thought; it may be spatially figured as *down in the pocket* (the cave where the bass lives), but it helps Murillo and his homies *fly like thoughts* much more than the teacher who understands Isaac Newton's, but not Huey Newton's, theories of gravity. You may also compare this with **Thomas Sayers Ellis'** suggestion that the white media establishment was even more threatened by GoGo than it was by HipHop: "They did not brand Go Go violent to stop us from hurting ourselves, but to limit us to hurting and killing only ourselves and to prevent us from organizing our guns and fists into proper forms of community self-offense and community self-defense..."

music would get in the way of their profits. Murillo implies that maybe that was not a mere side effect of gospel praise, but one of the functions of it:

This earthly house is gonna soon decay
Said look like Massa's house 'gon' soon decay.
I got my castle. Where he plan to stay?

The "afterlife" in the black spiritual tradition is never just "otherworldly," but the medium is the message, the religion is only as good as the praise. And of course spirituals at their best always had a "secret" (to whites) message, as **Roger Bonair-Agard** reminds us:

The breakbeat is a direct descendent of the Negro spiritual, the wailing of the song to cross the river Jordan that tells you Mama Harriet is making a trip....it must show one message and interrupt it with another....it is also about a journey to be undertaken when we must cover our tracks or risk death." (321)[120]

In this light, the struggle for black freedom is precisely the *need* to compromise the white man's yield, to democratize, collectivize it, without being further punished or killed for it, as if he or she could actually teach the white man (specifically the massa here) that it would be in his own self-interest to free and decolonize the black man and woman. "I got my castle," but can this castle survive in what Barnes calls "the 9/11 era, the Trayvon era, the stop-and-frisk era, the supposedly 'post-racial era'?"

There's an (almost?) apocalyptic clash of world views here, that can be expressed in terms of hip hop as fully as in gospel, as **Patrick Rosal** shows:

---

[120] Other poems that explore the relation between hiphop and the spirituals include **Alysia Nicole Harris**, "**Praise**," and jessica Care more and Reed Bobroff.

> *When we think of a break in terms of business and industry, it's a period of time in which production stops. But on the dance floor, the break is when the crowd goes to work, movin' and groovin' and shakin' and winin'. While the work of business emphasizes efficiency, outcomes, regulation, and activity, work on the dance floor is about getting loose and getting lost."* (323-24).

In this passage, Rosal doesn't specifically racialize the distinction between business and dance, and, in Murillo's poem, this work must be (what European specialization would call) *interdisciplinary,* or multi-lingual, able to be expressed both in terms of high Euro-centric literature, as well as graffiti: "We studied master poets—Big Daddy Kane, not Keats....Instead of slanting rhymes/ We *gangsta leaned* them." And "We left/ Our names in citadels, sprayed hieroglyphs/ In church. Our rebel yells in aerosol—/We bomb therefore we are. We break therefore/ We are. We spit the gospel. Therefore, are."[121]

The "we" of this poem rejects the mind-body dualism of Descartes so essential to the Enlightenment tradition designed to justify slavery and today's racial inequalities.

Murillo's conclusion, as he looks back at the community he found as a 12 year old with 30 years hindsight, invokes the cultural unity and continuity of the black diasporic tradition, so desperately needed given the fragmentation white supremacy has inflicted on the black community:

> *The walls are sprayed in gospel. This is for*
> *The ones who never made the magazines....*
> *......We renegade in rhyme,*
> *In dance, on tains and walls. We renegade*

---

121 Compare his defense of graffiti with John Rodriquez's "Bronx Bombers,"

In lecture halls, the yes yes y'alls in suits,
   Construction boots, and aprons. Out of work
Or nine to five, still renegades.

The sparks Murillo's direct address to every day people (rather than the jealous gods of the literary world) sets flying allow him a song of praise of the survival of black spirit in the alien overspecialized society of America's official reality that is similar to what we see in Tallie's poem:

Impossible   Black & looking the world straight in its eyes
Not smiling/making mouths cushions for someone's fear to rest on/ not
     smiling

moving through streets   hills   universities   forests
like they gotta right

alchemy of voice   ideas & soul   taking up deserved space
creating it

Impossible   seducing language out of its corset
Into shimmy & groin   ("Possible" for Amiri Baraka).

Murillo's poem is called "Renegades of Funk," and it must be remembered (if it has been forgot) that funk *is* gospel (and vice versa), and as Patrick Rosal reminds us, the word "funk" comes from "an African word that refers to sweaty, musky smell of an elder, a stink which communities understand as a sign of wisdom." (324). Baraka had that funk, and, as the poems by Tallie, Franklin, and Murillo show, *The Breakbeat Poets* have got some young funky wisdom to pass on to those younger (or even older) than them.

Hip Hop Creation Myths:
Goodwin, Coval, Del Valle and Bobroff

"art that is born of the African and in the African diaspora is an art that takes the scraps of a culture that has been designed to allow it nothing..." Roger Bonair-Agard

Many of the thematic concerns and insights in Murillo's poem can be found throughout this anthology, especially in the generation of writers who were teens and tweens during the hip hop revolution in the 80s. These poems could be called "hip hop creation myths" (and by "myths" I don't mean that they're not also history lessons). **Idris Goodwin (b. 1977)**, who coined the phrase "The BreakBeat Poets," in "These Are The Breaks," the title poem to his essay collection, explores these myths and legends in a more general way.

Like Murillo, Goodwin reminds us that in order to fully understand the heroic grassroots rise, and block-by-block trickle up pushback, of hip hop culture in the 70s and 80s, one has to remember how the white corporate culture stole, distorted and cut the ground out from the mid-century blues, R&B and jazz cultures "like legislation imported. Stolen like real estate, inventions and credit. Broken like neighborhoods when interstates arrive."

It's against this backdrop of the Sisyphus syndrome that, "the children of the losing war...built a bridge again," even if the drum was pawnshopped and they had to use the cheaper "Asian technology that flooded the colony" to construct it with "so-called urban styling" when "finding new ways to stop the erasure of markings, finding new ways to break the laws of stolen land..." becomes a life-or-death imperative:

"Bring it back again. Edit. Gut. And tear new names up out of the wind... cause it's spreadin' like it always do." **Ishmael**

Reed would call this the same spirit of "Jes Grew" that rose through America in the 1920s. **Kevin Coval (b.1975)**, by contrast, in "crossover," gives a more personal account of how hip hop could rise like a phoenix from the ashes of 70s decay into which he was born:

it was the end of disco, all the jobs were moving or changing or drying up in the city like the river after a summer of no rain. The parents moved farther from the city or themselves or their families for those jobs. Hours in commute. We received a key to let ourselves in after school. They would not be home until late. Sometimes they would not be home at all. Sometimes the commute was too much.....

Though this account is more personalized, his use of the collective pronoun "we" here shows how this story is also representative of historical trends as this passage challenges and complicates a common, but reductive, myth that the black families who could afford it purposely left the ghettos during this time in order to disconnect and distance themselves from the blacks who didn't. Coval reminds us that it wasn't merely the assimilationist's dream of safer neighborhoods and better schools that caused "black flight" (or what some call the "brain drain"), but that it often occurred *for the jobs* that had relocated because the urban planners felt threatened by the compact black neighborhoods that had become a power-base in the previous generation.

Coval's creation myth goes on to show how hip-hop moved beyond "its genesis as a party music of the divested urban underclass" (**Marshall** 328), and grew to create more space for the more introverted, or bookish young philosophers/moralists and story tellers (word people in search of safe spaces to express their love and righteous anger) to allow a wider, more encompassing, aesthetic and community than the specialized confines of the white controlled educational and entertainment industries, in which education and entertainment (like words and music, body and mind) are more typically kept segregated.

It's from the perspective of a word-slinger that he recounts the early days of hip hop in "Moleman Beat Tapes:"

> *"when hip hop felt like a secret*
> *society of wizards and wordsmiths, magicians.*
> *You'd see a kid whisper to himself*
> *in the corner of a bus seat and you*
> *asked if he rhymed and traded a poem*
> *a verse like a fur pelt/ trapping*
> *some gold or food. The sustenance.*

Against the over-hyped distortions about the hyper-competitiveness of battle raps, Coval emphasizes the collaborative aspects of these competitions, and the democratic ethos that can radiate outward from a single meeting of minds that can *build* (Coval loves the word build) together. Scenes like these between "anonymous" rappers are even more the *essence* of what hip hop culture is than the litany of famous names. Even from my (admittedly white) distance, I saw scenes like this played out in the (pre-ipod) boombox era in subways, streets and parks in Philadelphia and NYC, and even in 21st century Oakland.

You could view Coval's as a more Apollonian creation myth that complements the more Dionysian creation(s) and re-creations (if you'll forgive my use of Nietzsche's terms) celebrated and evoked in **Mayda Del Valle's** (b. 1978), "It's Just Begun." Del Valle's poem gives voice to what the sacred non-verbal body says while dancing, as she pays homage to elemental/movement more original/than sin…." and offers "Blessings to those b-boys and girls/ Who lower their ears to listen to the earth's breath…" in lines that use the kind of markings that Etheridge Knight used to break the break (as Patrick Rosal puts it in his important essay included in this book):

"This is the resurrection of the real/
the rebirth of what they tried to kill/
this was captured from the youth and commercialized/
extracted from the ghetto exploited then despised

But this is history revisioned and revised/
The reprise/ they said it died in '84
But we're hear to show them
What ciphers were really created for[122] (Del Valle)

Reed Bobroff (b. 1993) also emphasizes the sacredness of dance-as-praise in "Four Elements of Ghost Dancing." Bobroff's culturally syncretic vision is all the more powerful because he shows the commonalities between the Five Elements of Hip Hop and the Four Elements of Ghost Dancing, or, more generally, between the only two still-surviving cultures indigenous to this continent: Native American and African-American...alliances that had to be forged over and over again (given the white man's repeated history of trying to play these two groups against each other). Yet his capacious syncretic vision also makes more room for the culture of the invader/colonizer/oppressor than the invader/colonizer/oppressor has made for his:

Natives don't gotta be the only ones who come back!

John Lennon, Robert Johnson, KeithMoon
Play Eagle bone
Whistles inside Bob Marley's Peyote clouds (283)

In addition to the centrality of dance, Bobroff's poem also

---

[122] An interesting comparison can be made with Del Valle's celebration of the dancers with **Aracelis** Girmay's "Break" (152)

celebrates graffiti:

They say Graffiti is/ a "stain"/ So, like Wounded Knee/ We sink in

The praise of graffiti is elaborated in one of the best graffiti culture poems I've ever had the pleasure to read: "Bronx Bombers" by **John Rodriquez (RIP)**, which starts with the criminalization of graffiti:

*The cops want us locked. Mayor Koch wants us blocked,
transit wants us stopped, their German Shepards want us chopped,
and that third-rail at night is like the Mason-Dixon line—
you can't really see it, but it's a problem nonetheless.*

You'd think with so many enemies writers would unite….." (98)

Instead, he shows graffiti writers competing with each other for limited space: (*you ain't going over my name/like B-52s over Vietnam, you toy-tagger*). Yet, despite this, his poem ends on a note or gesture of, or at least hope for, collective unity:

*A graffitied train is
no act of vandalism. Reading our names
when you won't even see us is a mercy, give thanks
you're not getting the bombs you deserve.* (98)

This poem, like graffiti, is able to make the sublime out of anger. A rawer expression of anger would be eminently justifiable, but these graffiti writers choose the path of mercy and beauty in hopes of a greater justice: art that is "louder than a bomb" indeed. Like Covall's celebration of himself, and other non-famous *creators* of hip hop culture (at least as much as consumers of the more famous artists the corporate version of history tries to sell us), Rodriquez's poem goes out to all the unsung graffiti artists without which the megastars would have never been possible.

DJ Tributes

Many of this anthology's best tributes are to the unsung, for instance the taken-for-granted club DJs just doing their job. **Joel Dias Porter (aka DJ Renegade)** (b. 1962) in "Turning the Tables" (a title which can be taken two ways), writes to, and on behalf of, DJS any and everywhere:

> *Laugh at folks*
>   *that make requests*
> *What chef would let*
>   *the diners determine*
> *Which entrees*
>   *Make up the menu*

This loving portrayal shows the DJs art is at least as rigorous as the old-school drummer's art, and is the lover's art. It's a pedagogical poem teaching "young boys" (and women) the art of "filling the floor/ with the manic/language of dance" and "knowing the beat/ of every record/ like a mama knows/her child's cry" with no need of "flashy flicks."

Patrick Rosal's "A Note To Thomas Alva" gives us more of a back-stage rehearsal room view of the DJ, a "behind the music" glimpse into the technical/mechanical and electronic ingenuity skills demanded to salvage beat-making machines from others' thrown-away equipment, and "jam econo." If DJ Renegade shows us the chef cooking, Rosal shows us the dumpster-diver famer bringing the raw ingredients to the kitchen, though he sounds like a damn good chef too: "Our hands could cut/ Back to Bambaataa and make a dance hall jump/ It was our job to keep one ear to the backbeat/ and the other to a music that no one else could hear."[123]

Hip-Hop Icons

Such tributes to the creative process and to the legions of nameless DJs, graffiti artists, and rappers share some similarities with the tributes for more famous hip hop icons, both living and prematurely dead, included in this collection. Many of these tributes are written by those born in the 80s/90s, such as **Safia Elhilo's** (b. 1990) moving polyvocal tribute to the late Ole' Dirty Bastard of the Wu-Tang Clan.

Elhilo's poem (or one may say "hybrid text") meshes music criticism, investigative journalism, the genre of the interview and poetry, to stir anger about the way ODB in particular, and musicians in general, are misunderstood, and their social function as healers are underappreciated in this culture, as this especially powerful passage spoken by ODB's mom, Cherry Jones, testifies

> *"he made a performance of his pathology/ rhymes his way out of his body genius/ is a carnivore you know a cannibal a fucking*

---

[123] See also **John Murillo's** "Ode To A Crossfader" on this theme (pg. 76), or in "1989," –a tribute to the late great MC Sheik Spear— where Murillo writes about *"Deejay Eddie Scizzorhandz—because he cuts/So nice—taps ashes into an empty pizza box,/Head nodding to his latest masterpiece:/Beethoven spliced with Mingus,/Mixed with Frankie Beverly, and laid/On Billy Squire's "Big Beat."* You could call this Afrosurreal in that it sounds like it could be more beautiful than the chance meeting of a laundrymat and an umbrella on a dissecting table. Of course, since we don't actually hear how this mix came out, our imaginations may wonder how good of a chef he was (shout out to **D. Scot Miller, author of the "Afrosurreal Manifesto"; gotta rep the underrepresented Bay!!)**

factory for martyrs he cried help/ you know but it rhymed so we applauded he/gutted himself into his own puppet."

In general, Elhilo's analysis and appreciation goes much deeper than standard music criticism (with the possible exception of some books in the 33 1/3 series).[124] In contrast, **Benjamin Alfaro's** (b. 1990) "What The Eyes Saw," is a lyric memory of what it felt like when he first heard that Tupac Shakur died at the age of 6: "I remember learning how death felt when it belonged to a stranger....before the anthem of adolescence would calcify these timid bones/ against any bad ethics that built them." Confrontation with death at such an early age may plunge one prematurely into "experience" out of "innocence" (to use those those canonical Blake terms), even if he didn't "know" Tupac.

Biggie, Kendrick & The Erasure

There are also two pieces with the Notorious B.I.G at the center. **Chinaka Hodge**[125] (b. 1984) uses form to code switch, translating Biggie's spirit in a feat of dramatic condensation in her series of 24 haiku (one for each year he lived), while **Aziza Barnes** (B. 1992) uses the poetic form of the "erasure" on Biggie's smash hit, "Juicy." For those who aren't familiar with the term, "an erasure...is a form of found poetry created by erasing words from an existing text and then framing the result of this effort as a poem."

Douglas Kearney (b. 1974) claims that one of the founding questions underlying hip hop (and by implication the entire

---

124 Formally, Elhilo's piece shares similarities with **Sarah Blake's** (b. 1984) series on the more recent, and still living, Kanye West, and Blake's attitutes toward Kanye could be usefully compared to that expressed in **t'ai freedom ford's** kanye poem.

125 Apparently the only writer in this Chicago-centric collection who still lives and works in the Bay Area; gotta rep the Bay!

African diasporic tradition) is "How do I ensure my presence against erasure?" Kearney sees the erasure as always already inherent in Hip-hop aesthetics/ethics. Kearney continues: "erasure puts pressure on presence—the wild style calls out at the same time that it encodes. Rappers warn you about danger even while they celebrate their place in it. The breaker's body is a explosion of presence, historically in public space; the DJ marks a track via his/her intervention, both inserting the DJS presence and suggesting the potential erasure of the track."[126]

For Barnes, the answer to Kearney's question of how to ensure presence against erasures is by writing erasures. She further defines erasures by explaining some of the difficulties she's encountered writing them: "The writer must go into the text with her own objective and carve out a poem from that which is probably inherently poetic.....In erasing "Juicy," I am excavating the song, digging for any deeper meaning behind Wallace's words...the erasure is about demanding a truth where there isn't one, or uncovering that which doesn't want to be found." (313/4).

Erasure is clearly not *negation*. An erasure may also compel the reader to go back to the original (especially if it's a famous original like "Juicy"), and look at/listen to it in a different light. The words Barnes decides to keep may tell us more about Biggie, and the words she chooses to erase may tell you more about her than her poem does. And, comparing the erasure with the original may ultimately tell you more about yourself than either of them.

I find Barnes' thoughts on the erasure a crucial addition to

---

[126] **Kevin Coval** refers to this as the necessity of a "legible/illegible read....that graffiti bequeathed to the page." And many of us more trained in the white late 20th century literary culture first became aware of such thoughts and gestures such as this through phrases like Ashbery's "shield of a greeting" in "Self-Portrait in a Convex Mirror." Yet the stakes are much higher in the Breakbeat Poets.

contemporary Poetics and Pedagogical theory as they thrust us into metacognitive reflection about what our motivations are in reading, writing and otherwise entering into a cultural discussion. I am compelled to take very seriously her bold claim that *erasure is a form of poetry most befitting to my generation….the act of creating one empowers the writer with ability to claim what is not exactly yours."* and consider making it a formal assignment in my class.

In her essay, Barnes also claims a preference for her contemporary Kendrick Lamar over Biggie because "The hip hop that speaks to me most clearly and acutely is the work of my contemporaries who do not strive to manufacture a control over their own lives, but simply comment on their lack of it." And, in this sense, her strong generational defense of Millennial disillusionment is an important response to the older generation who at times wax nostalgic for the 80s/90s golden age (in the music at least), like Kevin Powell and others.[127]

Barnes demands art that speaks the truth to her times ("the generation of kids who witnessed 9/11 from TVS and schoolyards—a war already happening to us—who came into the world on the heels of the crack epidemic—the dissolution of the Black home…the Trayvon Martin era, the stop-and-frisk era, a supposedly 'post-racial' era"). She grounds high conceptual art in an urgent passionate conviction in contrast to lesser, but overhyped, older conceptual writers such as **Kenneth Goldsmith** and **Vanessa Place**.

Interestingly enough, Barnes' erasure is placed next to another erasure, which also takes Kendrick Lamar as its found (or primary) text, "Badu Interviews Lamar (an erasure)," by **Camonghne Felix**, also born in 1992. I wonder if Felix writes erasures for similar reasons that Barnes does, and why she, too,

---

127 (**Denizen Kane's** (b. 1978) "Ciphers Pt.1" brilliantly satirizes this generation gap within hip hop without exactly taking sides)

chose Kendrick as a subject. Is it significant that both of these writers are women erasing men's words? Is Lamar's work especially conducive to erasures more than other rappers? Is there a significant difference between erasing a lyric or poem by a dead person and a living one with whom collaboration is still possible? Would Felix agree with Barnes' explanation/justification of her erasures? Are many other writers in their generation writing erasures of hip hop lyrics and interviews? Do men do it as well as women?[128] Are these pointless questions?

The Message

Dangling on the precipice of duende, "a poet is one who....breaks into language, i.e. puts himself at risk," (Tara Betts, Patrick Rosal)

Underlying Barnes' justification of her (generation's) need for erasures is the fact that "A fundamental aspect of black American culture, and it's outlook on life, is submitting oneself to the notion that one does not have control over one's life.....Never do I, a Black American, happen to something. Or, if I do, the result is ineffectual or ends with my demise. This point of view is particularly acute in Black America after 1968" (312). Barnes' suggests that Biggie's braggadocio might have lead to his demise more than had he not made such claims. Yet, beyond an attempt to manufacture control, even "the struggle for expression and communication is sometimes fatal," as **Tara Betts** (b. 1974) reminds us.[129] This doesn't stop these poets from risking it.

---

128   **Mahogany L. Browne's** (b. 1976) "upon viewing the death of basquiat" also uses some of the strategies of the erasure as Barnes and Kearney theorize it

129   Possible comparison topic: Compare what **Aziza Barnes** means by "control" (and the distinction between an "internal locus of control" and an "external locus of control") with what **Tara Betts** calls "expression and communication." How are they similar? Are they

In this light, consider this more conventional 14 line poem **Michael Cirelli's** (b. 1975) "The Message," as itself both creation myth and erasure. I'll quote it in full:

Malcolm was fed 16 bullets because of his. A slug kissed
the jaw of King Jr. and silenced him forever. Ghandi shriveled
like snakeskin, Joan of Arc became Joan of Ash—
So you can understand why Melle Mel was jittery scribbling it
all down, on a napkin, at Lucky's Noodle Shop in Harlem.
Sweat pearled into his green tea. He thought of Jesus
hanging from that dull wood. Heard about the poet Lorca
under an olive tree, shot in the back. Everyone has felt this way though,
he thought. Never could he have imagined what would happen
when he pressed his thumbprint into vinyl. Hip-hop was still
a tadpole. The DJ had just learned to scratch a record and make sounds
no ear had ever conjugated. How was he to know Tupac & Biggie
would follow his lead and get plugged with lead? So he wrote it down,
in big curling letters, emphatic: *don't push me.*

Cirelli's account of this momentous occasion in hip hop history dramatizes how a black man or woman in America can't help but risk his life to speak the truth, or assert his presence. There's the fear in any attempt to speak the truth that it may not only lead to the teller's death but also do more harm than good for the people he loves most. If Melle had known that Tupac and Biggie "would follow his lead and get plugged with lead," would he have risked being so bold? Reading Cirelli's poem, one can understand why Barnes defends erasures, and Kearney celebrates hip hop culture as much for what it conceals as what it reveals.

One may also come to a deeper appreciation of why **Roger Bonair-Agard** (b. 1968) writes, "the break beat...must show one

---

two ways of saying the same thing? How you would put this in "your own" words?

message and interrupt it with another," or in his poem, "In defense of the code-switch or why you talk like that or why you gotta always be cutting" writes:

shit. Stop trying to crack
the code and we'll stop (maybe)
inventing new syntaxes for
      survive......(37)

Bonair-Agard's use of the parenthetical "maybe" is brilliant because it acknowledges a realm in which the need to invent "new syntaxes for/ survive" is not a mere reaction to the massa's cracking of the previous code; the break may have to show one message and interrupt it with another even if blacks weren't subject to institutional racism.

Code-switching is a central strategy in this book, and **Patrick Rosal's** (b. 1969) essay, "The Art of the Mistake: Some Notes on Breaking as Making," is perhaps the most elaborated prose argument in the book that seeks to find the deepest commonalities between the best of the Euro-American "common core canon" and the best of the African-American tradition. Through a tremendous feat of code-switching, Rosal dramatizes the similarities between Emily Dickinson's "Tell the truth—but tell it slant," and how a b-boy's near-fatal mistake while dancing resulted in art high enough to cause a rival b-boy crew to back down, and how both these arts require:

Effort—fueled by surprise. And to be open to surprise is to yield some portion of one's will to what one does not know for certain by logic alone (negative capability) [break].....(325)

In Rosal's equanimous syncretic vision, the breakbeat break and Keats' ethical ideal of "negative capability" are one. Imagine if Rosal's essay (which also compares Dickinson to Etheridge Knight, certainly no hip hop artist) were taught to all K-12 teachers charged with teaching our students the common core? I wonder if he'd mind a job being hired to lecture to schools across the country to share his vision. Hell, from my experiences, many college teachers could learn from this.[130]

Throughout this essay, Rosal points to the possibility of what a true-post-racial society (and less segregated curriculum, and literary world) could be, with an acute double-consciousness of both *the black condition* and *the human condition*.[131] For the break (the breaking) is not only dance and literature, but it is also philosophy and politics, that is to say, religion. In any event, Rosal makes it clear that the need to "tell it slant" would

---

130   For instance, recently a well-known professor/poetic gatekeeper wrote: Yale students protest two-course requirement for English majors: "Geoffrey Chaucer, Edmund Spenser, William Shakespeare, and John Donne in the fall; John Milton, Alexander Pope, William Wordsworth, and TS Eliot or another modern poet in the spring." I, too, protest—the absence of Marvell, Coleridge, Blake, Byron, Keats, Shelley. Tennyson, Hopkins, Hardy, Yeats et al. (**David Lehman**, June 1st, 2016)

I say to this poet/critic/anthologist/ teacher: No, the Breakbeat poets aren't trying to take away (y)our Emily Dickinson (though they may ask that you stop trying to regularize her punctuation, and I mean you, Billy Collins). But they do show ample evidence for why students should be allowed to write papers that can show the formal ways in which an Etheridge Knight poem is better than Dickinson (even perhaps by her own standards). I'd even go so far as to argue that allowing breakdancing in a college writing course could help students produce better work!

131   **Ekere Tallie's** "Paper Bag Poems" (103) address this point by deconstructing a quote she finds offensive: "These poets use being black to write about larger subjects." For Tallie, and I believe for Rosal, there's nothing wrong with writing about "the human condition" if you don't claim that it's "a larger subject" than *the black condition*, (because when you're do, you often end up meaning the word "white" when you say "human" since that's this culture's fallback position.)

exist *even if racism didn't exist*, that *duende* is not just a matter of hiding from the massa who wants to kill you for it. It's not just a strategy to survive in a white world in which dissembling is necessary (yet still no guarantee of success). But a need to honor the mysteries of life that can't be controlled, or even expressed (not in any once-and-for-all commodified artifact kind of way)—as Africans knew centuries before the European invaded for the slave-trade, and as any preacher riffing off the Bible, or any DJ who experiments with mixing to get people (to not stop) dancing knows.

In terms of Rosal's essay, we can see Grandmaster Flash's beats and sounds in Michael Cirelli's poem as the "slant" way of telling, as a submission to the negative capability, and duende that is *not* white supremacy in disguise.

Show The Telling:
Paul Martinez Pompa and Lemon Anderson

While many of these writers (Barnes, Felix, Elhillo, Cirelli, Wicker, Rosal, Bonair-Agard, Kearney, **avery r. young**, **Paolo Javier** and **Marcus Wicker**) utilize various sophisticated and/or cutting edge literary technologies to "tell it slant," as it were, one of the great pleasures of this formally eclectic anthology is that it makes room for the more polemical or didactic poems that happily violate the "show, don't tell" taboo to help restore some fullness and balance to the range of American poetry which, on paper at least, has been lost since the mainstream anthologies purged much of the Black Arts Aesthetic during the 1980s.

In the 21st century, some colleges still teach such poems as historical documents, but one with very little contemporary clout compared to, say, the recently resuscitated sonnet. This became sadly evident when I co-edited an anthology in 1998, and more recently when I witnessed some younger contemporary white writers at the Occupy Oakland rallies in 2011 read

Allen Ginsberg's outdated "America" rather than venture their own public poems more in tune to contemporary reality. Yet, despite this taboo, Baraka's "Somebody Blew Up America" remains one of the most popular/populist—or some would say "notorious"—poems of the 21st Century).

It therefore gives me hope to see this anthology include work like "Beat Writers," by **Steven Willis (b. 1992)**. Despite the title's reference to the mid-20th century white San Francisco sacred cows, this poem soars as it finds its more contemporary idiom which the page cannot do justice to: "the gunshots from the block influence this poem's cadence

> The ethnography of poverty that we coat
> in metaphors and similes to help cope
> in beloved communities that are deficient of hope
> that's why the young and the music elope
> there's no way you can denote
> the syncopation that gave voice to the streets
> or blackball us from the poet elite.

Similarly, "I Have A Drone" (165) by **Paul Martinez Pompa (b. 1979)** and "The Future" by **Lemon Andersen (b. 1974)** are fine examples of contemporary poems that "break from the beats" (as Coval puts it in his introduction) and render Ginsberg's poem obsolete. I easily imagine these two public "catalogue-like" poems go over very well at reading/performances, and both present visions of the future and strong messages for the present, using humor (or sardonic wit) to get it across.

I have to admit I'm a sucker for angry poems like "I Have A Drone," even though some may call it heavy handed, or smart-ass in the way it rewrites Martin Luther King's "I Have A Dream" speech as an imagined speech by Barack Obama. At a formal dinner speech Obama joked about using his predator drones on the Jonas Brothers if they go near his daughters,[132] yet part of Pompa's joke (or "dramatic irony") is that despite Obama's silver tongue (which is still no match for Martin Luther King's), he would still never quite come out and *say* things like

I have a drone that one day the State of Mississippi, a desert state sweltering with the heat of injustice, will be transformed into an Oasis of neoliberalism that distracts poor black, brown, and white folks away from the root causes of their oppression......I have a drone today...."

Much less would he get more specific and say:

I have a drone that one day the city of Chicago whose great mayor is committed to disarming the common people, will be recognized as a model where little black boys and black girls will be able to join hands with little brown boys and brown girls and wilt together as their neighborhood schools are shut down..."

And ask us to join in with a shout of praise to the almighty:

Let capitalism reign from the curvaceous slopes of Cuba!
But not only that, let free-market capitalism reign from Indiana State Prison!
Let Capitalism reign from the American Cancer Society!

But even if Obama's words don't say this, actions speak louder than words, and Obama's actions are very much like his presidential predecessor George "W" Bush when it comes to the issues that concern Pompa. And, as Pompa drags us through the remains of those killed, crippled and/or refugeed by the cutting

---

132 https://www.youtube.com/watch?v=dMP7BQN2YBw

edge technology of this drone dream, his poem is no joke, or you could call it the kind of *gallow's humor* designed to make the listener/reader laugh *uncomfortably,* and consider the hopelessness of voting and discrepancy between words and actions, regardless of whether they are an apologist for, or "basher" of, Obama and Rahm Emmanuel (and the legions of neoliberal mayors doing the same thing in cities across the USA).

Pompa's critique of the present (disguised as a dystopic vision of the future) remains largely within the political sphere whereas **Lemon Andersen's** "The Future" focuses primarily on the "apolitical" politics of the entertainment industry ("The truth will go pop").[133] Anderson keeps the tone light, more high and dry (less bitter and angry) than Pompa:

The party people will strike
Against DJs, using MP3s....

I like the spirit, of "thinking outside the box," and the possibility of democratic action in a small dance club this image conjures up, even if I'm not totally sure this would be a better thing to enrich Apple at the expense of local DJS, but Andersen is not necessarily siding with the Big Tech here in order to put more DJs out of work. It's only a *strike*, and I picture beautiful democratic uprising of dancers demanding better performances from their DJs!

Elsewhere he clearly advocates for local community self-determination when it comes to music, and the entertainment and cultural industry in general:

Hollywood will move to Atlanta
For balance.

---

[133] Andersen's poem may recall, or be usefully compared to Lupe Fiasco's lengthier "All Black Everything."

Notes Toward An M(F)A In Non-Poetry

L.A. will celebrate their independence
From the entertainment industry

I love Andersen's forward-looking proactive vision, and it makes me happy when I hear that Anderson's struggles in the cultural superstructure have paid off, at least a little, and that by the age of 40, he has achieved cross over success on National Public Radio, the *New York Times,* NBC, and the *Wall Street Journal* and the *Nation* magazine, as if corporate mass culture (though racist itself) may be used against the equally racist literary establishment.

Perhaps, from Pompa's perspective, the revolutions predicted in Andersen's poem may seem trivial, if we assume that such changes on the cultural superstructure will do little to stop the drones of free-market capitalism. Yet, as Hollywood's power, in some ways, exceeds Washington's and Wall Street's, these two poems ultimately complement each other as necessary components of any anti-racist strategy or comprehensive critique of systemic equalities.

Putting "I Have A Drone" and "The Future" in dialogue with each other, we may ask: since the same forces that have centralized national culture in Hollywood (at the expense even of LA's own South Central) have also created and disseminated drones and other weapons of mass destruction, can we really do away with either of them unless we try to do away with both of them? Is it possible that if some of the revolutions predicted in Andersen's poem came true, would our government realize it needs less drones?

Andersen's poem also challenges the educational industry (even if more of us are educated by the entertainment industry than by the ostensible educational institutions): "Big L's rhyme book/Will be the basis/For all English majors..."

And, you might want to take a look at Big L's rhyme book before you accuse Andersen of any "reverse racism," if this may be accused of reverse racism America could use a little more...and Andersen seems more than willing to negotiate! America could also use more teachers like **Kristina Colon** (b. 1986), **Tara Betts (b. 1974) and DJ Renegade (b. 1962).**

Pedagogy

Dear students, Have you ever had a teacher who gave you permission to rebel against her authority and told you stuff like this:

"   …..you don't have to hold your breath
you don't have to behave. Stage your own rebellion
paint canvases with rage, and religion, and prayers for pilgrims
sleeping in the train cars at the border and their children….
Filibust the Senate and bust markers on the Pink Line
Stain the prosecution's case and force the judge to resign…
Speak away the limits to the heights of your existence…
Feed open mouths with the truth, the truth is we are famished."

Krtistiana Colon, "a remix for remembrence"[134]

In this era when statistic analysis of student and teacher success dominates pedagogical studies, **Colon** refreshingly foregrounds the human interaction involved. Similarly, **DJ Renegade** recounts the feelings of hopelessness and helplessness after showing up at his gig as a visiting writer at a high-school to find out one of his students has been shot. He walks in and a "Crisis Response team has the kids in a circle,/ and I've never seen them sit so quietly." Then the teacher, "Br. Bruno, asks if

---

[134] A remix, to pass on the tradition to the next generation, for as **Evie Schockley** (b. 1965), writes: "those who cannot forget the past are destined to remix it."

I still want to teach./ I open my folder of nature poems,/ then close the folder and slump in a chair./ What smile can heal a bullet wound? Which student could these pistils protect,/ here where it's natural to never see seventeen?" (4).

Incidents such as these can shake to the core any of your confidence about poetry (and its "the pen is mightier than the sword" or "pistil mightier than a pistol" pieties) or about your ability to do any good as a teacher, but **Tara Betts**, in her passionate defense of the personal essay, shows one strategy that can help students digest these traumatic experiences:

"At least three students died during my time as a teaching artist (at Westinghouse High School in Chicago): one was in a fire with her baby, one was shot, and another was hit by a drunk driver who dragged her body for blocks before he stopped.... The opportunity to write about loss and trauma affirmed that [my students] were survivors with capacity, talents and rights to survive and thrive."

Feminist Songs of Self-Defense, Self-Empowerment, and Community Empowerment

The "gender politics" (or "battle of the sexes") in this anthology, is complicated by racism, which has always been able to economically profit by separating black men and women from each other more than white men and white women are. One of the ways racism perpetuates this is with the myth that black men are more sexist than white men.[135] And, of course, hip hop culture is often cited or invoked as a main example, when it's clear that it's the white men who have systematically pushed the

---

135   In addition to the myths that black women are more domineering, or more highly sexualized, than white women; see Kendi, *Stamped From The Beginning* for instance.

gender violence and misogyny in rap as they have for centuries pushed it in their own poetry (and in the so-called "sensitive" musicians like wife-beaters Jackson Browne and Yanni). [136]

The 3 editors of *The Breakbeat Poets*, to their credit, are clearly aware of this problem, as **Nate Marshall** writes, "hip-hop, like the dominant world wide culture, is cis-male-hetero dominated. This is whack." (327). These editors (themselves cis-genderd, hetero men) strive to ameliorate this situation. This anthology almost achieves gender parity (41 male-identified to 37 female-identified writers), allowing significantly more room for women to express and represent themselves in hip hop than the corporate industry allows (even if these women sometimes challenge where the men are coming from, as in **t'ai freedom ford's** rebuke to some unnamed black men, "hip hop ain't your savior"). Thus, this book is as useful of an intervention into taking back hip-hop from the corporate industry as the Oakland-based **Hip-Hop For Change**, which also has much more gender parity than the national and global white corporate purveyors of hip hop.[137]

You could say that many of the women included in this book are talking back to the sexism in hip-hop culture, though some are clearly showing the anti-sexist aspects that have always existed *within* hip hop culture. There are certainly many "answer songs" to sexist sentiments and men of all races here. The form of the poem (lined as prose) "Pussy Monster," by **Franny Choi** (b. 1989), shares some similarities with Felix' and Barnes' erasures. Choi takes Lil Wayne's "Pussy Monster" as her found text, and arranges the lyrics in order of frequency, from the least frequent to the most frequent. This strategy yields amazing results.

---

136   The argument Belle Hooks' makes in her 1992 essay, "Who Takes The Rap," is still, alas, relevant today.

137   Gotta rep the Bay Area so underrepresented in this anthology: http://www.hiphopforchange.org

So, the poem starts with lines like:

"For flu food bowl stood no more soup remove spoon drink juice salt"
while ending with
"la la la la la la la la la pussy pussy pussy pussy pussy pussy pussy," etc

Ending her poem with such a mantra-like repetition of the word creates a catharsis beyond mere comedy. You may say she takes back the word "pussy" from Lil Wayne, and all other misogynistic uses of the word, giving it honor and dignity while also showing in the first lines what Lil Wayne is really saying about his life aside from his foregrounded claims about "pussy." The first line quoted here foregrounds the image of a poor person with the flu who needs soup, but all he gets is "salt juice."

Similarly, "Harbor," by **Alesha Harris** (b. 1981), is a strong feminist answer song to a man who says "you a pussy that pussy ass phone ain't workin tell alla dem bombaclat pussyhole fuh gawn!" "Pussy" and "harbor" can be synonymous, as Harris shows:

Here's what you say to Pussy:
"Hail Pussy, full of grace.
Blessed art thou among body parts
For the prophets cum through
And come through you
Forgive the forgetful foolish popes, poets, priests and MCS.
Amen"

She keeps her composure
But it's difficult when the classroom and the Congress
Are overrun with boys and girls who say they love

But act like they despise Pussy.
Pussy chuckles at the absurdity.
She knows that if it were white folks bashing black folks in verse
The way men bash women—I mean—pussy—in their songs
No one would dance along and say, "O but they're not talkin'
about me."
Or. "I just like the beat."

By calling out popes and Congress, Harris clearly shows that any misogyny that exists in hiphop is imported from the dominant white culture. Both Harris and Choi use deadly serious humor to challenge sexism disguised as "the male ego,"[138] and this collection also includes other poems that go on the offensive, poems of self-empowerment and self-praise that aren't concerned about whether they offend men, and/or know that they have to do that in order to get beyond it (as Baraka knew he had to offend whites to go beyond it). In "Let Me Handle My Business, Damn," **Morgan Parker** (b. 1987) writes, "I could scratch your eyes make hip hop die again. /I'm on that grown women shit....you are fallen."

LaTasha B. Nevada Diggs (b. 1970), also uses *braggadocio* full of highly energetic language in "who you callin a jynx" (*after mista popo*), another answer song to misogynistic sentiments, and **Fatimah Asghar (b. 1989)**, in "When Tip Drill Comes on at the Frat Party,/Or,/When Refusing To Twerk Is A Radical Form Of Self-Love," speaks against "the boys, howling/under the bright lights, who only see the dissected parts of you" by decid-

---

138 Here's another obvious contrast assignment: Compare "Pussy Monster" (245) with Alesha Harris's "Harbor." In order to successfully do this assignment you need to look closely at the lyrics to Lil Wayne's song of the same name. How does Choi's use of the formal device that rearranges the words of Lil Wayne's song from least frequently used to most frequently used change Lil Wayne's meaning? Does it illuminate a more subliminal message to the song? Could we call Choi's poem an answer song to Wayne?

ing to stand "still amid all the moving & heat & card/ & plastic& science & sway & say:/ No./ Today, this body/ is mine."[139] In this poem, as in her poem, "Unemployment," Asghar praises the power of the woman's body as a talisman that can be used to protect from exploitation! In this, this poem reminds me a lot of a poem whose name I forgot by **Phavia Kujichagulia** (gotta represent the Bay Area once again!).

The seemingly comical (and light) tone of these poems may undercut their serious, earnest, message. Although no scientific study has conclusively proven the male use of words like "pussy" or "bitch" in ways the women they're with (or would like to be with) find disrespectful has any necessary correlation to spousal abuse, sexual abuse, and rape (one of my black women students wrote a brilliant paper on how a particular song lyric that uses such words is ultimately much more respectful, mutual and even romantic than the "clean" smooth soul stylings of the classic R&B side by Marvin Gaye it samples), there are obviously cases when a man shouting *"bitch I need you"* accompanies an act of violence as in **Tarfia Faizullah's (b. 1980)** "Nocturne In Need Of A Bitch."

"How to get over (for my niggas)" by **t'ai freedom ford (b. 1973)** takes a different, more ambivalent, approach. Her first four couplet-length stanzas are full of praise for the men who are surviving and "getting over" in "a nation afraid of your brilliance," but when we reach the 5th couplet, she changes tone:

"slam dunk your way out/the projects…consider yourself post-racial facial hair/ and funk don't make you a man but it

---

139   "Tip Drill," by Nelly feat. St Lunatics, was a song from 2000 whose controversial video was pulled because it portrayed women as sexual objects—the term comes from a Basketball exercise in which players take turns to tip the basketball off the backboard consecutively without the ball touching the ground." Get it? It helps develop timing and jumping ability for rebounding…

might make you/ a punk/…hip hop ain't your savior….stop praising/ lil' wayne like jesus—nigga, please!/ that fog ain't the weather it's the weed bleed/ on the sidewalk and call it graffiti"

Though her harangue is harsh here ("Police know the sound/ of your stereo type"), it certainly wouldn't do the poem justice to reduce it to merely a criticism of these men (nor is it the place of a white critic like myself to use this to criticize a black woman for seeming to criticize a black man more than a white man).

If freedom ford's poem is both a praise and a criticism of black men, and the speaker's "take it or leave it" stance assumes a self-empowered moral authority, "mic check, 1-2," by **jessica Care moore (b.1971)**, dramatizes the woman's struggle to be accepted as that moral authority. Moore's poem is only a criticism of the men to the extent that these men get in the way of her ability to be and praise herself and her sisters. Moore speaks directly, and lovingly to these men:

I'm a hip hop cheerleader
I buy all your records despite the misogyny
not looking for the blonde in me

As cheerleader, "screaming from the sidelines of a stage/ I built," she literally tackles whatever is offensively sexist in hip hop which puts women on the defense, to defend the cheerleader's right to get off the sideline and be part of the *frontlines*, the trenches, and (even) while pregnant! She shows us a way beyond the reified gender duality of this culture (and along the way attacks other institutional and ideological dualisms).

Against the backdrop of a world in which "hip hop has turned pathological," and only men are allowed to call themselves prophets, Moore's poem sings for all the:

prophets who never get heard
because the microphone is just another phallic symbol
that allows jack to be nimble
jack to be quick
leaving jill with a man who can't climb
a hill and a bucket of spit
she can't drink or find her reflection inside....(71)

Moore's brilliant, and mordant, rewrite of the Jack and Jill nursery rhyme to describe gender inequality is much more personal and dramatic than freedom ford's, as she seizes the "phallic" microphone and puts herself on stage and shows her own personal strength, with a moral authority she clearly earns the right to brag about:

"took my poems and made food
put my baby in school
I'll be your Tubman compass so we can map out this land...
Self love freed me
Despite all your rhymes with bitches" (72)

This poem goes beyond self-empowerment to a praise of spirituality radiating from "beautiful black/ mothers with wishbone skeletons/ breakdancing into rock a fella/ prayer position poses" (70) and a vow for self-transcendence that honors the, "need to be/ plugged in an useful. Our lyrics/ and bodies so beautiful. Our roots sore/ the pain from pulling at earth's core/ our feet planted at our youth's door/ and life calling us to do more....."

Moore's poem is perhaps the most sustained and elaborated praise of black womanhood in this anthology, and ultimately this praise radiates to include the black men she began by criticizing, for yes one can be a goddess and still be a cheerleader—the two are not incompatible, and such goddess-cheerleaders can get the male team on the sidelines where they sometimes need to be whether they know it or not. In this sense, she moves beyond self-empowerment to community empowerment. Ultimately, she defends hip hop culture against "the duality of institutionalized academic wardens" (and what Kevin Coval calls the "bullshit distinctions between high and low," etc)—for her poem (which needs to be read in its entirety!) works well on the page and the stage.

It occurs to me that, if you're looking for a specific speaker and situation for this poem, that this is not merely a woman demanding to be heard at a patriarchical hip-hop mic check ("When you're a woman/ Sometimes all you got is a minute" or "we still wear the mask/ when the payback/ is the mic check"), but that this pregnant woman is also talking to her son in her womb: "I see you growing in me/ looking out from my belly."[140]

There are many ways **moore** backs up her message/vision with her own labor in the cultural superstructure. Not long after Amiri Baraka's death, she co-founded Radio Active, which as taken a heroic stand against Clearchannel Communications (which many of you know by the more benign, obfuscating name of #Iheartradio), one of the largest corporate conglomerates that wields tremendous cultural power (especially since Bill Clinton signed the Telecommunications Act of 1996) for the kind of music it censors and pushes, undemocratically, on its unsuspecting (and often young) listeners. Going far beyond **Lemon Andersen's** vision in which "party people will strike against DJS, using MP3s," Moore advocates more clearly for local control and self-determination of the radio conglomerates. Though obviously taking back (black) radio is a daunting task,

---

140 Or as readers/listeners perhaps we are all entering her womb (and the speaker takes on mythic proportions that contain multitudes at least as much as Whitman's "Song of Myself" or Nikki Giovanni's "Ego Tripping." *"Mic-Check, 1-2" is also a strong statement about why she can't resign herself to life on the page, because that writing "wasn't enuff/ to move/ you, and I am "looking" forward to listening to her album.*

Moore's example, as artist and activist, gives hope in an era in which many who feel the same way huddle in hopeless resignation contenting themselves that "poetry makes nothing happen." Through this, and her other activist interventions, More extends what's best in The Black Art Tradition.[141]

On the other hand, "Black Girl Art," by **Jamilla Woods** is both a tribute, and a kind of feminist rewrite (or erasure) of, Baraka's angry LOUD "Black Art" poem:

Poems are bullshit unless they are eyeglasses, honey
tea with lemon, hot water bottles on tummies. I want
poems my grandma wants to tell the ladies at church
About. I want orange potato words soaking in the pot
til their skins fall off, words for you to burn your tongue on,
words on sale two for one, words that keep my feet dry.
I want to hold a poem in my fist in the alley just in case.
I want a poem for the dude at the bus stop. *Oh you can't talk
Ma?* Words to make the body inside my body less invisible.
Words to teach my sister how to brew rememdies in her mouth.
Words that grow mama's hair back. Words to detangle the kitchen.
I won't write poems unless they are an instruction manual, a bus
Card, warm shea butter on elbows, water, a finger massage to the scalp,
A broomstick sometimes used for cleaning and sometimes

To soar." (261)

Aside from one reference to "the dude at the bus stop," men are not a presence in this poem. This feminine complement to Baraka is also an attempt to bridge the generation gap, and speak beyond the hip-hop idiom or code which her generation was born into to appeal to the grandmothers, just as the anthology's final poems, by its youngest writers, appeal to an even younger generation (who may or may not be fans of Amiri Baraka or

---

141   https://en.wikipedia.org/wiki/Jessica_Care_Moore

Etta James more than say Nikki Minaj): "My niece's hip-hop," by **E'mon McGee** (b. 1996) and "Lesson One," by **Nile Lansana** (1997) and **Onam Lansana** (1999).

+++++++

Epilogue: White People Denying Racism

Aziza Barnes writes, "Now more than ever, Black Americans question their power and continued lack of control over their lives in a society that has announced that the era of race as an identifier is over." (314). Such "post-racial" racism is especially evident today; while the traditional segregationist may proudly announce a lynching as a spectator sport, as in **Jason Carney's** "America's Pastime," today's assimilationists (like Martin Luther King's "white moderate") are more likely to call someone like Dylann Roof and George Zimmerman racist, while claiming post-racial "colorblindness" themselves, even as they judge black culture and people by standards most whites fail to measure up to rather than questioning those standards, or consider why abandoning systematic racism would be in their best interests.

In any event, while what Cornel West once wrote about black music is generally true of the *Breakbeat Poets* ("black music is paradigmatic of how black persons have best dealt with their humanity, their complexity—their good and bad, negative and positive aspects, without being obsessively preoccupied with whites"), at times it must recount numerous confrontations with whites that show how the era of race is an identifier is *not* over.

Lynn Procope's (b. 1969) "All Night," recounts a scene all too familiar to many black women:

> The white guy   sits across the bar
> He tells you how   he knows he is
>   Not racist   and
>
> No matter what you say he knows you are wrong
> About this
> Black thing   you are not dying inside"

And, to make it worse, the man is saying all this at the same time he's trying to pick her up (for the night at least).

Quraysh Ali Lansana (b. 1964) writes about how one of his "all white and pseudo-liberal....friends from high school.... maybe/ my closest oklahomey at the bar, assured me/ the residuals of chattel slavery no longer existed,/ while leaning against the door of a 100-year-old/family business....He will not remember/ this exchange/ any more than he will recall the night/ I was informed my blackness was a liability/ in his pursuit of teenage pussy. History will tell on you." (14). Quraysh writes how this incident *triggered* him to leave his town to study with Gwendolyn Brooks and embrace hip hop culture (even though Brooks herself didn't care for hip hop). This scene happened over 30 years ago, when some of the writers in this anthology weren't even born yet, but it happens today, whether you're a black person in a mostly white neighborhood, or classroom, or even in more "diverse" contexts. In both poems the white men may not even know their words are expressing a racist point of view, but for Lansana it was the "ah ha" (or fuck you) moment when one may realize "do I really want to integrate into a burning building?" or the proverbial straw that broke the camel's back....

"Gravity" by **Angel Nafis** (b. 1988) takes the phrase "the straw that broke the camel's back," and, eschewing the specific "speaker/situation" scenarios of Procope and Lansana, divides it into two contrasting prose poems: "the straw" (a variety of different white racist comments she's had to endure) and "the camel's back" (how she can arm herself against these comments through brilliantly theatrical language). Even more generally, In **Danez Smith's** "Dear White America," he writes "this land is scared of the black mind," and helps underline a central message of this anthology: it's not just "black bodies" that matter, but *black minds matter, black hearts matter, black culture matters* (and by implication black business, black self-determination, matters). Smith goes after both the assimilationist/integrationist as well as the segregationist: "I am equal parts sick of your 'go back to Africa' as I am to your 'I just don't see color." He holds out a dream similar to Martin Luther King's (or the Halie Selassie speech Bob Marley puts a groove to), but:

"until then I bid you well. I bid you war. I bid you our lives to gamble with no more. I have left Earth and I am touching everything you beg your telescopes to show you. I am giving the stars their right names & this life, this new story and history you cannot own or ruin."

Like a cross between Sun Ra and Malcolm X, he breathes new meaning, new life, into terms like "Strategic separatism" or "No Whites Allowed." But this anthology does allow a few poems by whites, like "If You Don't Know, *after* The Notorious B.I.G," *by* **Adam Faulkner** (b, 1984). This speaker of this poem is a 12 year-old white kid digging himself and his love of (what he thinks is) hip hop culture (but is really a misinterpretation and misappropriation pushed by the hip-hop industry):

Until finally, you reach the part of the song that is not Yours to say—even white boys like you who aren't Really white but for their ability to disappear, leap Into the wind, board a return flight when the clock Strikes homesick…"

Reminding me of Adam Mansbach's *Angry Black White Boy*, the 12-year old white speaker of this poem is trying to find a way to *earn* the right to say "the n word," the way Biggie does.[142] He doesn't actually say it in the poem itself, but obviously the editors appreciated Falkner's passionate sincerity: "how deep your hunger for a culture to weep for,/ a struggle to wrap your own two arms around, a roadmap to follow, another fire to hold" as the speaker realizes that he will never be able to undo the wound of racism. Falkner names this feeling "guilt." Does it end with resignation, or despair, or does this guilt lead him to become a better anti-racist and be more conscious of what some might call his cultural misappropriation, and consider using his white privilege to help get reparations for blacks, or at least to convince City Hall to help the shuttered local black-owned shops and defunded youth centers to reopen to help decolonize or convince other whites that they could actually benefit from this more than from the white-owned on-line dressing rooms that have replaced even the strip-malls?

The poem bows out before it lets itself get this heavy, but it makes me confront a feeling that could be called "White guilt" (and I'm still not sure if that's the right word for it), and mine often takes the form of fear of falling into a kind of racial essentialism (i.e. "Black people got more rhythm. I love rhythm," can be racist when it's used to criticize the black with a Ph.D. in Nuclear Physics who you can't convince to go out dancing with you....)

The thought/feelings Falkner's poem engenders inspired/challenged me to come clean and air some of my own racist dirty laundry in a sonnet form. I'm sure many black writers have said this better, but here goes:

---

142 Since the speaker of John Murillo's "Renegades of Funk" was also 12 years old, this might also be an interesting comparison/contrast topic.

By plucking the white meat out from your wing?
    "they love everything bout you/but you"—
    Paradise Da Poet (w/ the Black Arts Movement Arkestra,
Malcolm X Jazz Festival, Oakland, May 2014[143]

Oh no, here comes another white vulture
Circling, swooping, like he's doing favors
By introducing you to his neighbors.
Do I only love you for your culture
Or did (does) the radio have power
To lure white youth beyond segregation?
Could we ever say "my love is stronger
For you than for your music vocation?"
A doubt still arises. Old habits die
Hard. "I don't just love the Panthers because
They had the Lumpen and fought against the lie
Of mind-body dualism enshrined in the laws
And racist Hollywood. How can I earn
What John Brown earned? I got a lot/ to learn."

Michael Mlekoday (b. 1985), one of the other white boys included in this anthology, writes "I pray that, if my own words prove too weak or quiet or stale, the next kid in the cipher will save me," and I second that emotion…..to be saved by the next writer in the cypher…which is the same impulse that underlies **Krista Franklin's** handing *The Amiri Baraka Reader* to her student…and part of why I can't wait to use this book in my class next semester.

Conclusion: Extending The Cipher

Although The Breakbeat Poets is primarily a collection for

---

143 One more time, *I gotta try to represent (at least a little) the Bay Area!*

poetic specialists—neither including an accompanying CD (or download code) for the work here, nor the wider range of dramatic and prose works included alongside of poetry in *The Amiri Baraka Reader* compared to his more "poetry specific" collections, *Transbluency* or the updated, posthumous *S.O.S*, it's obvious that many of these writers share the need to de-specialize the narrow institutional confines of poetry, and be activists and public intellectuals in their art. In this light, I can imagine a sequel to this book that goes beyond the prose offerings included in this book's appendix to show the poets' writings that are not written to an audience for whom "poetry" is a primary concern. I could envision a great weekly show on a terrestrial radio station like KPOO, hosted by the editors, that would be much more engaging than what most college ("Community") stations are playing these days. Perhaps a grassroots movement that could help break a national hit (to help make Lemon Anderson's vision that "the truth will go pop" even more of a reality). In the meantime I'll try to sweet talk any library who doesn't have this book yet into ordering it and fight against more budget cuts, and look forward to see how students (and others) extend the cipher, and "pay the necessary titles" this book, and what it can stand for, demands.

And when I think of the amazing POC writers and activists of this generation who are excluded in this Chicago-centric book (especially those who make Oakland and the Bay Area their artistic home, shout out to D. Scot Miller, Jackie Graves, Paradise Da Poet Kwan Booth, uPhakamile uMaDhlamini, and numerous others), I see this book as a challenge: can I be part of a "We" than can do at least as good a job in organizing and popularizing work as this anthology is doing?

16. uPhakamile uMaDhlamini

For absolutely selfish reasons
I need to loudly proclaim
(with whatever megaphone that hasn't yet been taken away)
the brilliance, beauty and truth
of the writing of uPhakamile uMaDhlamini[144]

Officially, she was my student
but I know she taught me
more than I taught her
(for instance, that
sidlala emagroundini ngezinto esiithula esignangi
means "we play in the field with stuff from the dump")
She thought she was primarily a poet
when she entered this class,
But now she thinks she might be more of a story-writer
("Screw the narrow segregation of genres," I say,
"you're both!")

For absolutely selfish reasons
I must find a way to convince
the editors of, say, the,
the "revised and updated" 2016 edition
of *Literature: The Human Experience*,
an anthology the Bedford/St. Martin's imprint
is trying to push on college teachers throughout this land
that they need to include
the writing of uPhakamile uMaDhlamini
alongside its broets, beyond the slightly expanded
token corner.

---

144   http://ishmaelreedpub.com/Black-History-Manifesto-by-Tebogo-Motaba

Notes Toward An M(F)A In Non-Poetry

For absolutely selfish reasons
She should get free tuition, with room and board,
At a M(F)A in Creative Writing
or "Non-Poetry" in the best sense of the word—
if you can accept her on her own terms
(and what good is any creative writing teacher
if s/he can't help provide a forum
even if those who loved your apolitical/transpolitical
personal-is-the-political, show-don't-tell work
no longer publish you)

And for absolutely selfish reasons
"I feel so unnecessary!"
in the words of Rufus Thomas (as done by Rufus Harley)
for liberation reasons
but perhaps useful as a vessel
to not get in the way of her words:
and the process of discarding the lies,
learning and unlearning "truths," decolonizing,
liberating self against the watchful eye
of white supremacy is agonizing to say the least."

"Poverty is humorous," she writes,
and yes she's very good at mordant humor.
She says better what I can merely think
Backing it up with the blood, sweat and tears,
the love, pain and laughter, of lived experience
in a plain brown 8X11 envelope with her name on it,
a fuller-range of *the human experience*
than what the Bedford Editors call "literature."[145]

---

[145] and would inject more of that contemporary revolutionary fervor Tim Yu brings into those claustrophobia-inducing walls Billy Collins has apparently conned some people into thinking are win-

She cuts through the crap, the stuffy fat,
of those who say "We're in a Post-Black Arts Movement era"
or the black actors who *"failed to recognize*
the importance of the platform which should be used
for the advancement of the black struggle."[146]
Reading her, I recall how the OAU and the OAAU
Worked together! The necessary internationalism....

For absolutely selfish reasons,
I, as colonial framing device,
Stand opposed to the ongoing colonization
Being done by whites at home and abroad
and pray for the strength to combat
the West's *cultural misappropriation*
kept alive by our high levels of consumerism
which I fear I've been guilty of (as framing device)
and the strength not to water down, or clog up
her message and aesthetic
her work, her gift that must be shared (if she lets me)

For absolutely selfish reasons,
I ask you, oh Bedford Anthologists,
Richard Abcarian, Marvin Klotz,[147] and Samuel Cohen,
As well as the broets and women
Who lovingly wrestled with my work in the 90s
(if you haven't totally tuned out by now....it's okay, really....)
to stop "secretly" worrying about
being a traitor to your scene, your cause, and your race
if you included the work of uPhakamile uMaDhlamini

---

dows (on request, I'll send more detailed explanation, to "unpack" this reference)

146 This is *not* referring to Jesse Williams

147 RIP

beyond your "revised and expanded" gallimaufry
of diverse synecdoches, *The Immigrant Experience*.
(you can still have your broets!)

For my (absolutely selfish) taste,
she does a better job of making lemonade
than some I won't name—
And, for absolutely selfish reasons,
I'm trying to pay her back
For having stumbled on the good fortune
of being an early reader
And next time I submit to an editor,
I could say, "yes, I'd really like to publish another book,
But only if you publish a book
by uPhakamile uMaDhlamini first,"
And for absolutely selfish reasons,
Reading her, I am not envious of the facebook teachers
Exclaiming, "Yippee! The Semester is Over"
two weeks before ours.

17. The Two Underdogs: Sly Stone & The Great Fillmore Whitewash

We can use the past as shrines of our suffering, as a poeticizing beyond what we think the present (the "actual") has to offer. But that is true in the sense that any clear present must include as much of the past as it needs to clearly illuminate it.
Amiri Baraka, *The Changing Same*, 1966

People worldwide have this glassy-eyed memory of Bill Graham as being this wonderful godfather of all that was good about the summer of love and the psychedelic era. But nothing could be further from the truth. He struck me as this obssesive megalomaniac who wanted a monopoly on all live music in the Bay Area. Even a club as small as the Mabuhay or a hall like 330 Grove or 10th Street, it was unacceptable. It should not be allowed to exist.
Jello Biafra

In San Francisco, the spirit of what was best in punk began as a semi-organized reaction to what Bill Graham and his minions had done to the San Francisco/Bay Area music scene (in ways that strikingly parallel Mayor Feinstein's "redevelopment" plans). By the fall of 1979, Steve Tupper and others in the burgeoning punk scene had formed The New Youth Organization & secured The Clash to do a benefit for their non-profit performance space. Bill Graham tired to nix it; claiming The Clash was his band. But, as Ray Farrell says, "the demand was far greater than what could fit into Bill Graham's show. So a couple of nights later, there was this separate New Youth Organization show. The ticket price was less. The Clash did it."[148]

Instead of thanking, or wishing to continue a productive relationship with the new music scene, Graham vowed to de-

---

148 Boulware and Tudor: *Gimme Something Better,* 2009: pg. 61

stroy the NYO; storming out of the show as Jello Biafra's clothes got ripped off. Bill Graham was almost the only thing the fractious punk scene could agree about. Many people who became "punks" were disaffected, disenfranchised whites who hated the antiseptic impersonality of arena rock, but dug Lester Bangs' beautiful defense of the spirit of "Wild Thing" in 1966; whites who would have danced with blacks had their parents not been duped by white flight and moved to the more segregated suburbs.

Bangs, one of the first to prophesy, theorize and champion "punk rock" as both musical style and ethos (debatably even coining the term in 1972), traces the decline of rock and roll from the rise of FM-radio and bands like Cream to the "disco and jazz rock" of 1976.[149] If it weren't for the fact that Bangs, like most purveyors of 'punk,' was at least as hostile to contemporaneous arena rock and light rock, his *Summer of Sam* scorn of "disco and jazz rock," could be a coded, or unconscious, form of racism as in the parallel "disco sucks" movement sponsored by corporate "classic rock" stations around this time.

Punk, at least for Bangs, was not racist in its inception. The Clash songs about the white man in the otherwise all black Hammersmith Palais struck a chord for many. In fact, many of the white musicians who became 'punks' after 1976 were purposely trying to return, in the words of Steven Taylor, "to the most vital resource known to them: African American music... The distancing of rock music from its popular base in the 1970s sparked a renewed return to rock's marginal roots." (33) The punks, for the most part, did not return to African American *people*. Some jumped, but most were pushed. There were forces far bigger than Biafra or Bangs any in the punk or hip hop scenes at work that had already caused a re-segregation of SF

---

149   Bangs, *The Village Voice,* 1977

music.

To understand more deeply why Bill Graham was tied with Diane Feinstein as "Public Enemy #1" for most purveyors of early SF punk, I need to go back to what San Francisco music was like before Graham got his start: not to the Beat scene of the late 1950s, but that time historically in between the Beats and Hippies: In-betweeners, or as some like to say, mods. This fascinating chapter in the history of San Francisco culture is often erased in accounts of late 1950s Beats and late 1960s hippies; at its center was a young man named Sylvester Stewart.

Although there's no record of Stewart himself directly confronting Graham as Jello did 10 years later, in late 1969, Sly Stone was witnessed delivering a diatribe from the stage to a Bay Area audience. "You're over," he told the stunned crowd. "You thought you were cool, but your arrogance was your undoing, and San Francisco is now over, officially." He didn't explain it," noted spectator Joel Selvin. "He was just pissed off."[150]

To some, Sly's pronouncement, uttered only months after his iconic Woodstock triumph, and not long before recording the infectious country-funk of the international #1 smash, "Thank You (Falettin Me Be Mice Elf Agen)," may sound ungrateful, or drug-induced, or at the very least uncouth; yet in retrospect it's not only justified, but an accurate reflection of the rise and fall of the San Francisco rock and roll scene during the decade Sly had worked it, a fall it still hasn't recovered from 42 years later. So, even if we can't know the *immediate trigger* for this particular heat of the moment remark, we can at least attempt to understand why Sly would see San Francisco's music scene as undone by its own arrogance.

Sylvester Stewart was the major galvanizing force in creating and bringing a San Francisco rock sound & style into national prominence as a cultural export a few years before Bill Graham & Chet Helms dubbed "The San Francisco Sound." According

---

150   Kaliss, *I Want To Take You Higher* (2009): pg. 77

to Jeffrey Kaliss, San Francisco in 1961 was a "fortuitous time and place for Sly to be launching a career in popular music. He and the baby boomers, just a few years his junior, were listening to the radio, buying what they heard there, and going out to dance to the music...Sly could hardly wait to join this scene where blacks were hardly a minority." (20, 21)

Kaliss places the radio and records at the center of this scene along with live dancing, and for Sly, it certainly was. In 1961, top 40 radio was increasingly de-segregated (in part *because* r&b stations existed aside of pop ones; hence, the modicum of self-determination needed for "crossover"). The radio scene was more hospitable to Sly than what San Francisco would have been without it. In San Francisco proper; re-segregation (under the more 'benign' names of "Urban Renewal" and "Redevelopment") had been under way for over a decade; blacks were becoming increasingly a minority.

In 1954, the same year that Brown V. Board Of Education outlawed segregation in public schools, the term "urban renewal" was introduced, referring both to renovation and slum clearance (demolition).[151] The *de jure* ending of Jim Crow drove blatant racism underground to some degree, replacing it with the seemingly more benign and ultimately more effective tactic of increased economic segregation.

Meanwhile, longtime Western Addition residents, primarily white and Jewish, moved to the suburbs, while maintaining their Fillmore District shops and apartments. By 1960, 90% of Fillmore residents rented from these absentee landlords, whose tax base no longer poured back into the neighborhood. In fact, thanks to the Redevelopment Agency, more incentives were given to these landlords to keep these buildings empty and/or run-

---

151 Houses were being torn down as early as 1948; 75% of the people displaced nationwide was due to the urban renewal projects of the 20th century (PBS). http://www.pbs.org/kqed/fillmore/classroom/renewal.html

down rather than keep their costs affordable. In 1960, using the power of Eminent Domain, The San Francisco Redevelopment Agency claimed the Federlein home, forcing the family to move out of the house they owned for 90 years. The house was subsequently destroyed and made into a parking lot: 4,000 people were displaced by the Japanese Culture and Trade Center; and 2-lane Geary Street was widened into 4-lane Geary Blvd (effectively destroying many of the black-run businesses, and making Geary the "unwritten" financial dividing line). Even Justin Herman prophetically declares, "Without adequate housing for the poor, critics will rightly condemn urban renewal as a land-grab for the rich and a heartless push-out for the poor and non-whites."[152] Many more buildings were demolished than renovated by urban renewal, displacing thousands of residents.

Despite the urban decay brought on by white flight and redevelopment, the Fillmore neighborhood had had a vital music scene since 1946; most of these clubs (The New Orleans Swing Club, Club Alabam, Jackson's Nook and The California Theater Club, Bop City) specialized in jazz and blues, but by 1960 venues like Charles, "The Mayor Of Fillmore Street," Sullivan's Fillmore Auditorium had become a western anchor of the chitlin circuit, bringing in everyone from entertainers Redd Foxx, Bill Cosby and Sammy Davis to R&B luminaries James Brown, Big Mama Thornton and Joe Tex, the live music most appealing to the young Sylvester Stewart, but Sly was only 17 in 1961, underage for nightclubs. The secular music he loved he primarily got from recorded and broadcast media or from gigging around town with as many bands as possible. The radio was a haven, almost like the church, yet also a door to a wider world of possibility that need not be mere fantasy, but that could change the conditions of those who listened. The live scene is real, but the radio was no less real; at their best, they still could compliment

---

152   ibid.

each other, and Sly Stewart found some people who seemed to understand that.

Sly first became a "player" in this scene when KYA-AM, one of the most popular San Francisco rock stations, played Sly's then current, small-label limited run "Yellow Moon" single, with his band The Viscaynes, on their drive-time playlists (locally, it peaked at #16 in late 1961). This multi-racial high school band had recently won a contest on The *Dick Stewart Dance Party,* one of the most de-segregated local dance shows in the country, winning a management and recording deal; the band never saw a penny from the corrupt management deal, but radio was opening more doors. The KYA DJS who broke Sly's record locally, Tom Donahue and Bob Mitchell, became early converts. They also organized live rock shows at San Francisco's Cow Palace, hiring Sly to put together the house band.

Sly also took a prime-time gig on local soul & r&b radio station, KSOL after graduating from the Chris Borden School of Broadcasting in 1964. Targeting a primarily black demographic, but with some crossover to pop, KSOL hadn't been a popular "break station" (in contrast to KYA) until Sly took over the 7PM to Midnight slot. Sly's very innovative take on the "personality DJ" (he sang the news and weather forecasts, demanded requests and dedications and talked to kids on the phone on air, broke Ray Charles' "Let's Go Get Stoned" in the bay area, and much more) helped the station win over "youth of other ethnicities" not despite of, but rather because of, the fact that, unlike many of the older African American DJs at the time, Sly wasn't afraid to sound "too black."

As Greil Marcus puts it, during the heyday of Sly's career as a DJ, radio "changed every week, just like the world of work and family life, politics and war. As in the world of work, family, politics, and war, certain of the elements of the pop world—disc jockey patter and commercials, the rituals of contests and pranks—barely changed at all,[153] and other elements changed so radically they hijacked memory, to the point that whatever happened the week before could seem to have happened years ago. This was Top 40 radio: city by city, from one end of the country to the other, a true forum, in 1965 more open to anyone, known or unknown, black or white, northerner or southerner. American or foreigner, male of female, than any other culture medium—never mind business, religion, or college. (35)—for Sly it was all three.

While Marcus makes it sound too good to be true, Sly milked those potentials for all they're worth (which was not insubstantial from 64-67). Radio offered Sly an entry into the San Francisco scene as well as a finger on the pulse of what was going down nationally. Singles were still "king." Even Dylan was saying "people hang out on the radio" (not that they still didn't walk down the street, in 65 they did). Being a DJ allowed a more intimate, personal audience interaction and development than being tied to a touring band would, an ability to "be what you play" (as Bowie later put it), or at least provide witty voiceover if somewhat forced to play a hit you don't like, a place to check out the competition and bring people together; the kind of "eat where you shit" day-job that didn't have to get in the way of your longer-term night job (today much of what Sly did is "off limits" as 'conflict of interest,' even on non-professional community stations like KALX, but frankly anybody interested in revitalizing local music radio would do well to take a lesson from Mr. Stewart).

By 1964, Donahue and Mitchell founded Autumn Records, and hired Sly as the new label's in-house producer. Since the large California cities were still only starting to link up to the national mass-culture, at least as producers (think major league

---

153   Actually, Sly changed it up more than most DJS. See Kaliss, especially 28-32 for a good summary of the range of things that made such a uniquely expressive star on KSOL (and KDIA).

sports), there really hadn't been much of a record label in San Francisco before, at least with national pop hits. In the beginning, it appeared that Donahue and Mitchell's vision for Autumn Records, like their live package shows at the Cow Palace and the bands they broke as DJs, was both local and desegregated.

"Bob Mitchell had a heavy penchant for black music, and had a very strong feeling about Sly," remembers Autumn staffer Carl Scott. [154] They quickly signed SF R&B veteran Bobby "Do You Wanna Dance" Freeman to their label & to perform at their Cow Palace package shows, where Sly's house band was becoming a San Francisco version of Booker T & The MGs. Since Freeman didn't write his own songs, and hadn't had a national hit since 1958, Autumn put Sly in charge of coming up with a hit.

From his vantage point as a R&B DJ who loved The Kinks, Stones & Lord Buckley and had integrated his playlist, luring many young whites away from Donahue's own radio station, Sly knew what needed to be done to put Autumn on the map, and help give SF a more populist and integrated (and, in retrospect, more revolutionary) cultural export than the "Beat (Poetry) Craze" of the previous decade. Unlike today's multi-media conglomerates who got rid of their regional offices decades ago and are thus out of touch with what the new breed say, Sly didn't need a demographic focus group to, within months, come up with a national top ten hit that was also a dance craze.

After one show, Sly engaged Bobby about his onstage movements, likening them to a swimmer's. Sly, Bobby Freeman and North Beach dancer & businesswoman Carol Doda collaborated on a multi-media *event*. *The Swim*. The song, "C'mon & Swim," which was a #5 pop hit in the summer of 1964, ultimately cannot be separated from the dance-craze it spawned, as the two were conceived simultaneously, in a brilliant example of what is today called 360 degree cross-marketing.

---

154 Paleo, *Precious Stone: 6*

Legend has it: On June 19, 1964, SF's Condor Club became the first topless bar in the United States when Carol Doda stepped on stage to show off the new dance and song, the swim, wearing a bottom-only swimsuit designed by Rudi Gernreich: the *monokini*. Bobby Freeman debuted his dance with clothed dancers; and soon dancers did the swim while backing up The Kinks & other British invasion bands. Sly laid low in the background as "composer, producer, and, conductor," puckishly tickling the ivories: a brilliant meshing of three distinct sensibilities trying to out-Motown Motown, and during the summer of '64, pulling it off.

San Francisco had its first real rock/pop cultural export. Although it was Doda and Freeman's idea & talents that carried it across as much as Sly's, this collaboration is one of the highpoints of San Francisco music—even if the song itself, for many in this 'auto-tune' era, doesn't seem as fresh as the Family Stone does. The fact that the song doesn't sound particularly original is part of its point. In 1964, pop music was much more communal; much more embracing of what Rene Girard would call the cult of mimesis as opposed to the cult of originality that dominated the more elitist arts since the Enlightenment.

It may not be very original, but "Cmon And Swim" is highly *functional*. It's got a back-beat you can't lose it, a very visceral call and response aspect, and breaks that allow the dancers to mix up their moves—impressive, especially for a 21 year old. It's fun, easy and has attitude. Doda and Freeman can provide, and transcend, the originality. Nor is the song, as Sly knew, really separate from Freeman performing it, as attested by a youtube video where we see Freeman flanked by white and black women dancers very formally dancing until the end where they get down on the floor. It's fun, funny and harmless, but apparently freaked some folks out.

"The girls are frisky out in old frisco," from "California Sun," a garage-rock song from that same year[155], is clearly a tribute to Carol Doda; and Sly's fingerprints were all over that. How you like me now, Kirschner! Gordy! They didn't just have a hit; they put together things that often aren't put together—almost a perfect balance between individual and communal impulses that gave this "underdog" upstart label a fighting chance: that became a win/win situation for everyone, reviving Freeman's career as a performer, bringing money into Autumn Records as well as into San Francisco's "Barbary Coast" scene—and with reverberations for the cultural economic health of San Francisco more generally.

After the success of "Cmon & Swim," Sly's biggest success as producer was the locally-based white folk-rock pioneers Beau Brummels, whose "Laugh, Laugh" and "Just A Little" were both smashes. Although many of these Sly productions, in the words of Alec Palao, were "more vanilla than you'd expect," that, too, was part of Sly's point. Mods loved to dance to them as much as the hard-driving r&b of "Cmon & Swim."

Amiri Baraka writes: "so-called 'pop,' which is a citified version of Rock and Roll also sees to it that those TV jobs, indeed that dollar-popularity, remains white....White boys, in lieu of the initial passion, will always make it about funny hats...which be their constant minstrel need, the derogation of the real, come out again. Stealing Music...stealing energy (lives)....They steal, minstrelizes (but here a minstrelsy that "hippens" with cats like Stones and Beatles saying: "Yeh, I got everything I know from Chuck Berry," is a scream dropping the final..."But I got all the dough...") named Animals, Zombies, in imitation (minstrel-hip) of a life style as names which go to show just what they think we are...Animals, Zombies, or where they finally be, trying to be that; i.e. Animals, Zombies, Beatles or Stones or Sam

---

155 This version's a cover of an earlier Joe "You Talk Too Much" Jones track.

the Sham for that matter, and not ever Ravens, Orioles, Spaniels or the contemporary desired excellence of Supremes, Miracles, Impressions, Temptations, etc.,...get to them names....They take from us all the way up the line. Finally, what is the difference between Beatles, Stones, etc., and Minstrelsy. Minstrels never convinced anybody they were Black either." [156]

Sly's work with the Beau Brummels may very well invert the relationship. Though he "had been brought in to supervise the company's early R&B-slanted roster, Stewart's obvious talents led him to becoming the de facto producer for any act the duo chose;" as Sly put it, "producing the BB was no big thing to me; I just didn't know that *they* knew that. I was surprised that they could tell I could do that."

According to Justin Farrar, "throughout 1965, Donahue and Mitchell's showbiz chicanery helped sell the Brummels to a frenzied nation of wigged-out teeny-boppers craving the next big thing." Though they, too, were about 'funny hats' on an image-level, the fact that they were "ripping off" the British band almost brings it back full circle, similar to the more-hyped Columbia Records L.A. band, The Byrds (if not necessarily better than the less hyped Love).

While their name may fall short of the contemporary desired excellence of the Miracles, this young band was capable of more emotional content than many of their white American contemporaries, especially with Sly behind the boards. Nowhere is this more evident than on one of the last tracks they recorded for Autumn; a song which Sly wrote called "Underdog."

By October 1965, with Dylan's "Like A Rolling Stone" and The Rolling Stone's "Satisfaction" fueling the American white folk-rock and garage-rock crazes, The Beau Brummels were in

---

156 Baraka, The Changing Same, *Black Music:* 206/07 (1966). In the film *Cadillac Records,* when big-time "Break DJ" says "I'll make you famous," he looks at Chuck Berry, "and you rich," looking at Leonard Chess

danger of going the way of Freddie and The Dreamers if they didn't come up with an edgier song, and, that quickly, Sly was on it. Sly and The Brummels had already made a good chunk of change for the label, but Mitchell had left and Donahue wasn't reinvesting it in the musicians who had started creating a brand for him as an up-and-coming mod label. It is against this backdrop that Sly and The Beau Brummels recorded "Underdog" as a possible single and/or album track for the third Beau Brummels album in late 1965:

"The Brummels didn't care about anybody else producing them. They liked me, man. I was running from the control room to the floor, I put all my heart into that. I like the way Sal sings "I'm a man" on "Underdog." Go on, Sal. I like that groove they got too. Yeah, that's the Dylan influence. I loved Dylan, man. He can't sing, but who cares? He's got a sound, and I love it"—-Sly (Listen To The Voices, 7)

What may seem like "nonsense lyrics," like many Dylan parodies and/or tributes being released that year, gain depth on each listen. The Beau Brummels' version of "Underdog" is lyrically an answer song to "Like a Rolling Stone." In Dylan's song the repeated chorus of "How Does It Feel," is primarily directed to a sheltered white woman who now is confronted with the difficulties of the real world (with implications of racial fear); but in late 1965, it spawned answer songs like Curtis Knight's "How Would You Feel," featuring the guitar work of Jimi Hendrix. Knight's song took Dylan's question and threw it back at him and his audience.

To many African-Americans, the "socially conscious" lyrics of much of the "folk-rock" now fashionable among the "more adventurous bohemian white groups" came off as just "white kids playing around....The 'protest' is not new. Black people's songs have carried the fire and struggle of their lives since they first opened their mouths in this part of the world.... With secular music, integration (meaning the harnessing of Black energy for dollars by white folks, in this case the music business) spilled the content open to a generalizing that took the bite of specific protest out ("You know you cain't sell that to white folks)."[157]

Sure enough, the specific protest, palpable in Curtis Knight's "How Would You Feel," ensured it wasn't a success in 1965. Even when Hendrix became an international superstar less than two years later, he had to cover Dylan's song rather than the Curtis Knight song. The lyrics that Sly wrote for The Beau Brummel's version of "Underdog," with their repeated *"I know how it feels,"* lyrical hook, are similarly influenced by "Like A Rolling Stone," but the blatant racial signifiers are ambiguous or even edited out. Had the song been released in late 1965, it's doubtful most people would have realized it was written by a black man any more than other Dylan-influenced hits of that year (i.e. Los Hombres "Let It All Hang Out"); the anger is there, but also humor and a sense of fun; it can "pass" for white boys playing around.

The song combines other fashionable influences from the pop culture of 1965. Sociologists often claim the "underdog" is a particularly American myth, even in 2011 when the American Dream of "upward mobility" that seemed available during The Great Society (LBJ not the band) has been replaced by the most rigid class structure in the post-industrialized world. In 1964/65, the TV cartoon series, *Underdog,* was as popular as The Swim was, and many young people were gearing up for a new season (before he needed his super-energy pills).

The main 12-string guitar riff hook "out-Byrds the Byrds," the heavy tambourine, hand claps and floor tom, are like Sly's lower-fi take on Motown's funk brothers meets "Peggy Sue," and Sal Valentino's high-pitched but snarly lead vocals are delivered with a passion more like Them's Van Morrison than the earlier Beau Brummel hits. The hurt and anger in the song is Sly's,

---

157   ibid.

but when the young urban working class Italian American Sal Valentino begins by singing the fast internal rhymes, a "Dylan device" that should at least be traced back to Chuck Berry's "Too Much Monkey Business," the anger seems like it's one he and Sly shared:

> *I know how it feels*
> *when you know you're real*
> *but every other time, you get a raw deal*
> *coz you're the underdawg*
> *I know how it feels*
> *when people stop, turn around and around*
> *stare and signify a little bit—low rate me*

Valentino could be referring to some "youth culture" badge of honor, or proto-freak flag like long hair, and Sly himself was "a very flashy black man, dressed in Beatles suits and this weird pompadour." [158] But in The Beau Brummels' version, the anger is about class as much as it is about youth culture. In 1964/65, the perspective of working class youth culture was making a comeback on top 40 radio and "Underdog" is addressed to a big boss man who gives you a "raw deal" when you want a "fair shake" at least as much as it is to people making fun of your funny hat like Sonny Bono's "Laugh At Me."

In this sense Sal & Sly's collaboration is analogous to the kind of integration Jazz had allowed in the 20s and 30s. As Le Roi Jones wrote in 1963: "The young white jazz musician (in contrast to the white liberal and sensual *dilettante* and the communist party during the Harlem Renaissance and Depression)

---

158 If the word "mod" was in the dictionary, and had a picture beside it. 1964/5 Sly would be as good as any—but it would have to be a moving picture, singing, playing, and talking and jumping around. According to singer Catherine Kerr, "He was strange! But he was always very sweet to us, always very protective."

at least had to face black Americans head-on...and they could not help but do this without some sense of rebellion or separateness from the rest of white America."[159] Likewise, The Beau Brummels (in contrast to the white Pete Seeger folkies, Berkeley Nimbys, and the hippies of the Haight), at least seemed to understand that R&B "had created a music that offered such a profound reflection of America that it could attract white musicians...It made a common cultural ground where black and white America seemed only day and night in the same city and at their most disparate, proved only to result in different *styles*." (38)

Structurally and thematically, the lyrics of "Underdog" are more like the early Dylan of "A Hard Rain's A Gonna-Fall." After the litany of social horrors in "Hard Rain," the singer ends by standing on the water until he starts sinking. "Underdog" is also a song of working class perseverance and resolve; however comically portrayed (like the cartoon), it also *means it*. Super! Lines like "super free" cater to Valentino's vocal and expressive strengths. "Sometimes I think I'm losin' it but I can make it because I'm made of some kind of super special stuff!" and "First honesty, then destiny, then you can't believe that I've done in my life just what I was supposed to." As Sly predicts the reactions he's gotten 40 and 50 years later as a "retired" musician, I can hear Sly's joy in verbal articulation he had kept mostly musical (or on the level of DJ patter) before; in the last verse especially, the palpable excitement in being able to honestly express his purpose, even though he's "hiding behind" (shining through) Valentino's voice.

In the second and third verses, the criticism is much more specific. Listen to Valentino sing, "too many people they get together go up one side and down they other, they try to make it sooo tough" against the backdrop of what was happening with

---

159   Jones, *Blues People*, 40

Autumn Records and the San Francisco scene at the end of 1965, and its "I'm Not Your Stepping Stone" passion, garage-rock sound and proto-punk "Dylanesque" vocal phrasing, become a perfect description of their prodigal boss, Tom Donahue. Donahue was jumping ship, whether or not he could admit it to himself, let alone his employees including Sly & The Brummels.

Donahue had only come to the Bay Area a few years before Sly and The Brummels appeared on the scene, to escape a payola scandal in Pittsburgh. By the end of 1965, his lack of commitment to the established R&B/Mod scene in San Francisco, was revealing itself to the younger Bay Area raised Sly and Sal. Donahue stopped listening to Sly's suggestions (for instance, to lure Billy Preston to the label) and kept deferring the live-album of Sly's Cow Palace show. Instead, in late [November] '65, with the Brummels' hit records and incessant touring bringing money into Autumn, Donahue expanded [his] local roster, adding three new groups from the budding Haight-Ashbury scene." [160]

Sly dutifully tried to lend his talents and experience as producer, arranger and songwriter to create hit singles, but the new bands Donahue was bringing in, however popular live to a different (and apparently more *lucrative*) audience, were not studio-ready. It took over 45 takes to get a passable version of the Great Society's first single, "Somebody To Love." Sly's exasperation is evident on the masters Alec Palao unearthed from the Autumn vaults. "As far as Sly was concerned, they were amateurs, and as far as they were concerned, he was Mr. Plastic-Hey-Baby-Soul."(26) You can see the seeds of the resegregation that overtook the country a few years later in this little quip.

As Donahue's attention started drifting to the beatnik/folk-music/performance art/jazz and hippie scene and the upper middle class youths from the northern suburbs, resorts and the

---

[160] Justin Farrar, "O Pioneers," *SF Weekly*, March 1, 2006 (The Charlatans, The Warlocks, and Great Society)

midwest migrating to the Haight, this reawakened the working class chip on both Sly and Sal's shoulder, as Donahue had gone up on their side and was now trying to come down the other. Yet, they're (hilariously) defiant and stand their ground:

But understand...I know what to do.
You look down on me, and IIIIIIII.....look down on you

I guess I'd rather be the underdog
than to be in a fog sittin on a log
going down the river by the go nowhere...
no matter what you do to me, or try to make me be
I'm in contact with something sup-er free-ee...
Coz I understand....your mind is small...
no understanding...and that ain't all...

In this working class mod anti-flake song, Sly has it both ways—bonding with Italian Sal against the fickle Irishman, and enjoying a little joke at the expense of the white protest song movement. Like The Thirteenth Floor Elevators or The Sonics, 15 years later it would be called punk (change it only slightly, thicken the guitar on the choruses, and it's The Descendants or...). By the end, the song's able to cathartically work out the hurt, the anger, the justified feeling of abandonment, with the realization that you can't count on anyone, but you still got your sense of destiny and purpose; if anything, you're more driven than ever to make it on your own, since now you're left with no other choice.[161] Well, almost. In the song's last line, intended to be sung during the fade-out ending, Sal Sings: "leave it up to the human race, for destroying one of the human race, you ought to

---

161 I bet if Hollywood did this story, they'd side with Donahue and render his rejection into the tough love Sly needed to rise to new heights (like the moment where the cymbal hits the young Charlie Parker on the head in Clint Eastwood's *Bird*).

be ashamed of yourself." It works both racially and non-racially.

"Are You Sure? (Life Of Fortune And Fame)," the proposed flipside (or even A-side) for "Underdog," is a beautifully haunting introspective, or even despondent, folk-rock piece, like Love's "A Message To Pretty." The two songs complement each other in the spirit of the best double-sided singles of that era.[162] Sung to an upper-class (presumably white) woman who the male singer fears is treating him like a "specimen," "Are You Sure," in Sly's words: was inspired by the real. Some party, some girl, back in Vallejo. The homecoming queen. Her parents were rich and she liked me alot. I didn't understand it. It always happened like that, too. Yeah, I was her specimen. It's important to whisper lyrics. Without knowing it, people hear the words better." A Specimen, like Clay in *The Dutchman* (1964).

Both these songs were breakthroughs for Sly, and he returned to both of them with The Family Stone. Now very popular among retro-mods (many of whom don't even know it's a Sly Stone side), and record collector geeks in The Bay Area, "Underdog" remained unreleased; Donahue never even paid to get the tapes back from the studio, claiming financial difficulties, even as he was taking the money Sly and The Beau Brummels had brought into Autumn and pouring it into "The Great Society."

Instead, for the next Beau Brummels single, Autumn chose the much less distinctive, but already in the can, cover of the Lovin Spoonful's "Good Time Music," blowing an opportunity to cash in on the folk-rock/garage rock craze, and show off Sly's songwriting rather than New Yorker John Sebastian in helping the Beau Brummels transition (as bands like The Kinks were, single by single). "Good Time Music" bombed, a fitting swan song to Autumn Records, while other potential hits, like Billy

---

162 In its own right, "Are You Sure?" could have been the A-side; as it builds on the slower, lusher, sadder direction of the third and fourth Elliot-penned BB singles (which were not as popular as their more up-tempo first two national smashes).

Preston's Sly-produced "Can't You Tell" and "I Remember," lie in hock.[163]

By the end of 1965, it was starting to seem that Donahue was doing everything he could, however indirectly, to subvert Sly. This didn't really make sense, unless maybe they really didn't want to be a successful nationally-known label in the first place. After all, they only released "C'mon And Swim" after L.A. based Warner Brothers rejected it. By April 1966, only four months later, Donahue sold the label, and The Beau Brummels, to Warner Brothers as a tax-write-off. Like the label that had signed the Viscaynes five years earlier, Autumn was never as important for Donahue as their live shows and management deals. No wonder Sly felt "demoted," even though Sly could now buy his parents a house in a middle class black SF neighborhood and Donahue bought him a Cadillac and ostensibly "promoted" him. He might have been moving up just a little too fast!

Sly, through no fault of his own, found himself stuck in a historical moment when mass-culture was starting to become less local, less working class and more racially segregated than the local-based mass culture he entered only 5 years earlier. A musical chameleon, Sly helped enliven the music-centric culture of San Francisco more than any of his contemporaries. He offered a multi-dimensional community through records and the radio, as well as through small clubs with topless entrepreneurs, but when Bill Graham muscled his way into the scene, it had the almost immediate effect of cutting out the very ground of the cultural coalition Sly was putting together to create a context in

---

163 In the late 1965-Autumn sessions with Preston, you can hear Sly, apologetically (and perhaps passive aggressively), saying "another demo, another demo," as if Donahue, far from being supportive, was treating Sly's final sessions with the Brummels and Preston like a dad (on a log in a fog) catching his kid in the cookie jar; a cookie jar Sly had built and was now being farmed out to Grace Slick; not that property is theft or anything.

which he, and his music, could be more free. The culmination of years of struggle was slipping away...

When SF Mime Troupe founder, R.G. Davis, was arrested on charges of public obscenity for a performance in Golden Gate Park, self-made millionaire Charles Sullivan allowed Graham to use his dance hall license at his Fillmore Auditorium so that Graham could hold a benefit on December 10, 1965. The benefit was so successful that Graham asked if he could book additional concerts. Sullivan offered Graham his "off" nights.... Graham secured a contract from Sullivan for the open dates at the Fillmore in 1966 *and a four-year lease option on the Auditorium if anything unforeseeable happened to Sullivan.* Sly was too busy with his radio gig and live engagements to make that scene much, but he promoted The Fillmore shows on KSOL; through Sullivan, Sly helped get R&B/Gospel singer, Gloria Scott, who he had produced at Autumn, a job as an Ikette.

Sullivan, still the largest promoter of African American music west of the Mississippi, continued to book R&B headliners, such as Ike & Tina Turner, on Wednesday February 2, 1966 (featuring Jimi Hendrix on guitar). Later that month, Chet Helms, a white "counterculture" entrepreneur, who had made his initial seed money from the growing marijuana business, formally founded Family Dog Productions to begin promoting concerts at The Fillmore, alternating weekends with Graham. As the concerts became more popular, inevitable "conflicts" arose between the two promoters, based in part on the notion that intra-hippie public conflict and controversy could generate free publicity. Meanwhile, Sullivan was trying to appease the Redevelopment Authority by working with these white outsiders in hopes of saving the nightclub, as well as the neighborhood for which it was named. The San Francisco black community was torn over whether this was a smart move.

Sly tried to stay out of this debate, especially now that he was scrambling for a new boss who would pay him, or at least not charge him, for regular studio access; neither Sullivan nor Graham were looking to fill the vacuum left by Autumn, much less hire Sly. With no regular studio gig in the Bay Area, in April of 1966, Sly went to LA to record Billy Preston's Steve Douglas produced Capitol album, *The Wildest Organ In Town,* and the amazing "Can't She Tell I Love Her" single. His band, The Stoners, gigged with Freddie's band, The Stone Souls, at Bo Peep's in The Mission/Excelsior. Freddie's career as band-leader and guitar stylist was taking off in its own right. The Stone Souls had formed in September of 65 after Sly used his radio show to say "he starting a band, and he's looking for musicians." Freddie reminisces: "we were smoking Sly's band" when they shared bills at Bo Peeps, and Sly was the second to admit it.

In April 1966, Graham and Sullivan booked The Stone Souls to play at the Fillmore, but Graham and Helms showed little interest in integrating with Sullivan's existing scene. By the end of 1966, Graham had branched out to promoting, managing and branding a new crop of live bands who he'd help get signed to national labels (not based in the Bay Area). Since Tom Donahue was a radio person first and foremost (having started in 1949), Graham convinced him to take advantage of the newly opened FM band as an outlet for the acts and shows he promoted.

By 1967, "Donahue, that savvy, sharp-dressed Top 40 DJ, was sporting gaudy tie-dye fashions, transforming San Francisco's KMPX and then KSAN into two of America's earliest underground stations, and declaring in the pages of *Rolling Stone* that 'AM radio is dead and its rotting corpse is stinking up the airwaves," as Sly was still broadcasting on KSOL-AM. Donahue's now one of the few DJS enshrined in the rock and roll hall of fame.[164]

---

[164] Sly, at the height of his celebrity, could put it behind him, and graciously reached out to Donahue, who was dying at the time, in letting him work on *Fresh* (Kaliss). Here's a link to the only example of Sly's DJing I've been able to find: http://airchexx.com/2005/01/11/

Sly was writing his best songs ever, but was at an impasse. Once again, Billy Preston tried to send help from LA. In August, Sly recorded a Four Tops song for Freddie's group as part of a talent cattle call that Capitol A&R man Herb Hendler organized at the tiny Commercial Recorders in SF. On the Stone Souls' songs Sly produced, you can hear them forging a distinct mid-60s Bay Area soul sound, halfway between Gordy and Toussaint (with a pinch of Stax). But Capitol was on the verge of letting Preston himself go, let alone take on R&B acts from the bay area.

Something unforeseeable happened: Charles Sullivan was found murdered on August 2, 1966, south of Market Street in San Francisco. Luckily for Bill Graham, to this day, the murder remains unsolved, and "The Fillmore Sound," which became synonymous with the Summer of Love, was born. With Sullivan out of the way, acts who had headlined for Sullivan such as Howling Wolf or Otis Redding were now relegated, under Graham and/or Helms, to opening for The Jefferson Airplane, Big Brother and The Holding Company, the Grateful Dead, Country Joe and the Fish. There was no room for white bands like The Beau Brummels here; as Valentino puts it, "I remember going to the Fillmore from time to time. I was envious of it. But it wasn't us at all." Nor was it Sly, at least not in 1966/1967. Love fashion is in, but so is clueless paternalism that makes the word "redevelopment" practically a synonym for Jim Crow segregation, or, worse, "ethnic cleansing." This was Graham's bag, and he wasn't alone.

As predicted in Malcolm X's "The Ballot Or The Bullet," The Republicans swept the majority in congress for the first time since 1948, largely in reaction to LBJ's policies of racial desegregation. After Malcolm's murder in 1965, the war against the inner city African American community and culture accelerated. For all the white media's trying, what was happening in San

archives-sly-stone-on-ksol-san-francisco-1967-828-scoped/

Francisco and other cities could not be swept under the rug so easily. In 1966 Los Angeles, the Sunset strip live-club scene over which Arthur Lee's Love presided is under seige. In 1966 San Francisco, there's a riot going on in Hunter's Point. The Western Addition Community Organization is formed to fight against the displacement of the Fillmore residents by Redevelopment. Frustrated by the ongoing demolition, WACO takes direct action by picketing and filing a major lawsuit. More "abstractly," FM dials are placed *above* AM dials, anticipating the "disco sucks" racism of a decade later, like it was the new dawning of an era of systematic re-segregation (after the briefest whiff of de-segregation: Reconstruction II).

During the three-month fall of 1966, as Huey Newton and Bobby Seal, who had met in a class at Merritt College, were forming The Black Panther Party For Self Defense in Oakland, Sly finally found a band that allowed him to combine the range of his talents that had previously been professionally and institutionally separated. Like The Panthers (with their Maoist rules), Sly and Family Stone were a highly disciplined outfit: "If we rehearse every day, we will be better than everybody else...I think we did it. Sometimes we wouldn't play as good as I thought we should, so I didn't care what people said; we had to have a rehearsal after the gig, and that was all there was to it...." [165]Maybe you don't need to work for the man, if you can work *with* your brother and sister. Much has been said about the fact that they just so happened to be 4 blacks and 2 whites; or two women and four men, flaunting the idea(l) of a youth family band as the hippest thing you could be—but less is said about the musical relationship between Freddie and Sly.

Take your tandems—Reed/Sterling; Lee/Echols; Berman/Mallkmus, and The Kinks' The Brothers Davies, and put the sonic spotlight on Freddie and Sly. Sly, like the older Ray Da-

---

[165] Sly, quoted in Palao, *Voices*: 13

vies, was the solitary songwriting and studio workaholic/genius, Freddie, like the younger Davies brother, was more the extrovert rocker, but not the songwriter Sly was. They checked each other; Sly had been such a musical chameleon (the occupational hazard of both studio and DJ) while Freddie was much more at home with straight R&B.

Together, Sly's creative restlessness and Freddie's need for a band with a constant line-up and pocket rhythm-section solidity were an explosive combination; an elastic, fluid, capacious band. Larry Graham's slap bass helped Sly crawl out of his shell, while Cynthia Robinson and Jerry Martini's horn tandem opened up space so that the middle ranges were never clogged as many of the hippy-psychedelic bands were so you could never forget they were a soul band.

On December 16, 1966, Sly And The Family Stone played their debut gig at Rich Romanello's new Winchester Cathedral. The Cathedral "was not a hippie place; if you look at photographs... kids dancing, you can see how appropriately dressed they are for the time." In contrast to the burgeoning hippie counterculture scene, from the upper-middle class Northern suburbs and, increasingly, the Haight and Fillmore, the scene Sly worked was mostly working class kids from the southern suburbs on the Peninsula; mostly white (mod) kids who dug r&b. Because of Sly's popularity as a radio disk jockey, the event had to turn people away.

When The Family Stone quickly outgrew The Cathedral, this almost forced them to win over Graham's scene if they were to have continued success in their home town, but Graham expressed little interest in the band's dance-inducing appeal (or Sly's studio prowess and the R&B audience he could lure through his radio show), despite his previous year's booking of Freddie's band before Sullivan was murdered. Romanello tried in vain to convince Graham, "Bill, you probably have one of the best dance floors in all of Northern California. But you've got all the hippies in their Indian squats, sitting on that floor like a bunch of vegetables. Do you think you ever want to get these people up and dancing?"

When Romanello told Sly about Graham's rejection, Sly said "I'll change the music." Romanello urged him to stick to his guns, "Fuck Graham and his psychedelic heads, we're on this path and we're staying on this path." Sly may not have changed the music for Graham, but shortly after Romanello invited the local promotion manager for Columbia Records, Chuck Gregory, to check out the band in March, 1967, the band did change their *look:* "They came out looking like fucking clowns. Jerry with his polka-dot shirt and Sly with his knickers...but Sly was right, I was wrong. They were gonna be unique, their music was different, they were on their way. (45)

Though Romanello stuck by the band, by 1967 as dance-oriented local scene Sly had helped put together had mostly been swallowed up by Graham's increasing monopoly (by the summer of 1968, Romanello's club had been burnt down).

Radio was still proving itself more integrated (eclectic) than any real-life scene allowed him to be; so Sly stayed on KSOL. Being that AM-radio and the Black community were so important to Sly's entree in the music business, he simply could not follow the reigning ideology of "San Francisco Sound" architects like Graham, and the recently re-invented Donahue, that FM, album tracks, were the new thing (and that horns, dancing, and tightly-structured songs were out, so-called aesthetic standards that may ultimately just express an "anti-black music" ethos, since the vast majority of soul stations remained on the AM-dial).[166]

Since no other local promoter or record label had the industry muscle to provide an alternative to Graham's empire, New York-based Columbia's David Kapralik essentially rescued The

---

166 http://en.wikipedia.org/wiki/San_Francisco_Sound

Family Stone from its very precarious position in the Bay Area scene. By the time Sly and The Family Stone recorded their debut album in June and July at Columbia's LA studios, the "Summer of Love" was in full swing, and the band recorded their version of "Underdog" as a single and the opening track of their first album. The new version of "Underdog" is like the "After" picture of the radical transformation redevelopment had brought to San Francisco and its music since The Brummels' "before picture" in October, 1965

A whole new underdog

In *Blues People*, Le Roi Jones points out that Louis Armstrong's departure from the Oliver Creole Jazz Band in 1927 is a "musical and socio-cultural event of the highest significance" as it signified the "ascendency of the soloist" in jazz:

"The development of the soloist is probably connected to the fact that about this time in the development of jazz, many of the "hot" musicians had to seek employment with larger dance bands of usually dubious quality. The communal, collective improvisatory style of early jazz was impossible in this context.... The move North, for instance, had broken down the old communities (the house parties were one manifestation of a regrouping of the newer communities: the Harlems and South Chicagos).... The dance bands or society orchestras of the North replaced the plot of land, for they were the musician's only means of existence, and the solo, like the holler, was the only link with an earlier, more intense sense of self in its most vital relationship to the world. The solo spoke singly of a collective music...[167]

40 years later, 1967 signifies a similar socio-cultural event in the fields of rock/pop: redevelopment was rendering the r&b communities of the Fillmore (like the Harlems & South Chica-

---

167   Blues People, 44

gos) into yet another "post-communal black society." AM Radio, in Sly Stone's DJ hands, was at least as "collective and communal" as any house party blues, but it too was being broken up by the same forces that broke up Autumn records. Columbia records was the "plot of land" (if not the reparations or the mule) offered to Sly—as his only means of existence. While Columbia, to their credit and in contrast with Atlantic, did not try to break up the Family Stone and force Sly into a dance band of dubious quality, there was still a price; Sly was willing to pay it, but not to deny it. Sly's vocals on "Underdog," like the jazz holler, *spoke singly of a collective music.*"

If the Brummels' 1965 "Underdog" is a serious, danceable, joke, the version of "Underdog" that opened The Family Stone's debut *A Whole New Thing* is straight-on soul earnestness. It's like before Sly felt he had to guard his misery, and now he could flaunt it. Sly himself, joined by Freddie and Bill, never sang so expressively and passionately, or unleashed his church upbringing so fully (and sounded so "black") as on this song. Although now in a minor key, it's got a driven groove and, in contrast to the sunny summer single ear candy of the 12 string guitar, defiant horns: the sounds of struggle: "'Radical' within the context of mainstream America...The New Thing beginning by being free...freed of American white cocktail droop, tinkle, etc. The straitjacket of American expression *sans* blackness...It screams. It yearns. It pleads. It breaks out (the best of it). But its practitioners sometimes do not. But then the vibrations of a feeling, of a particular place, a conjunction of world spirit, some of everybody can pick up on." [168]

Even this version is not without some ingenuous "Black Humor" as it's framed with a minor key version of "Frere Jacques."

---

168   Black Music, 208. Although Baraka was not a particular fan of Sly And The Family Stone, he does prophecize a "unity music. Which is New Thing and Rhythm and Blues. The consciousness of social re-evaluation and rise, a social spiritualism."

Less than a month before the recording of "Underdog," The Beatles released *Sgt. Pepper* and the "All You Need Is Love" single; the latter famously begins with a horn section playing The French National Anthem.[169] By contrast to this major key war song, Sly's quoting of a minor version of a song about someone named John who's sleeping through the morning bells seems directed at "Brother" Lennon in his "dream weaver" phase, at least as a metonymy (synecdoche) of The Summer Of Love. Sly's 'joke' is a musical version of now absent lyrics about the guy *on a log in a fog going down the river by the go nowhere*—fine for the millionaire to complain about being taxed 95%. Even Dylan hated *Sgt. Pepper*...

This little joke actually enhances the feeling of *reality* in this song. If Donahue was going to be such an FM-Radio turncoat, it seems to reason, we might as well go even more soul, more black, and see if the older soul people can get down with this prog-soul thing we got. AM isn't dead. Separatism was in the air; and so was re-segregation. "Underdog" violates every Motown rule of what the pop-hook should be, as if in defiance. When I imagine a video for this song, I see the ghettoes of Oakland the Panthers were starting to patrol, and the Hunter's Point of the late 66 riots.

Though about half the lyrics are retained from the 1965 version, the Family Stone version is about as race-conscious as one can be without saying "black" or "white" (let alone "Mighty, Mighty, Spade and Whitey").[170] As an indictment of Bay Area Summer of Love racism, *"Underdog"* rivals Otis Redding's *"(Sittin On) The Dock Of The Bay."* While the despondency of Otis's song contrasts sharply with the myth of his triumphant

---

169   The Rutles featuring Eric Idle & Neil Innes, recorded a parody called "Love Life," which uses The Battle Hymn Of The Republic in lieu of the French National Anthem.

170   The Impressions, *The Young Mod's Forgotten Story* (1968), "your black and white power is gonna be a crumblin' tower."

performance for the hippie Monterey Pop crowd, "Underdog" is more blatant and assertive. It's at least as working class as the Beau Brummels version, but it does away with the "youth culture" signifiers their version relied on. It sounds more adult; more *experienced* than Jimi Hendrix at the time, in part because the words are sung slower and can sink in more.

Compare, for instance:

I know how it feels to get demoted
When it comes time you got promoted
But you might be movin' up too fast, yeah (Yeah, yeah)

to a verse in the 1965 version it replaces:

Leave it up to the human race,
what a big disgrace, for destroying one of the human race,
you ought to be ashamed of yourself

On the page, the word "demoted" doesn't seem as desperate as "destroy," but the vocal and musical delivery tells a different story.[171] It could still allude to Donahue's abandonment: the Brummels "promotion" to Warners wasn't working out so well, and Sly wasn't sure if signing with Columbia/Epic was really a promotion. More broadly, it can recall reconstruction, the "promotion" from 3/5ths of a person, or the ruse of the urban north revealing its ugly side more nakedly in the two years since the earlier version; politicians telling you to "go slow," walls and cops closing in. Almost any example of the man's double-speak could apply; especially when you know how "inflation" is just a device to make you think you're getting a pay-raise when you're really getting a pay cut; and the street in Oakland you

---

171 When he sings "my own beliefs are in my songs," he doesn't just mean the *words*.

used to gig at with Larry Graham is now being "promoted" and renamed Martin Luther King, now that they're tearing down the nightclubs and the small singles-only r&b labels are going out of business.

The other new lines should be self-explanatory:

If you ever loved somebody of a different set
I bet the set didn't let you forget
That it just don't go like that (Yeah, yeah)
I know how it feels when you're feelin' down
And you wanna come up but you realize
You're in the wrong part of town, yeah (Yeah, yeah)

I know how it feels to have to go along
With people you don't even know
Simply because there happens to be
A whole lot more of them, (Yeah, yeah)
You're the underdog, and you gotta be twice as good (yeah, yeah)

While the 1965 version was an answer song to Dylan, this version comes from musically such a different place that it seems prior to the Dylan song, like Sly had successfully exorcised the white influences (at the risk of sounding racially essentialist). You can compare Dylan's line about the mystery tramp who's not selling any alibis when you stare into the vacuum of his eyes with this man in the wrong part of town (that might have been the right part of town only two years earlier), being "racially persecuted" because he's with a woman from a different set, like the woman in "Are You Sure?" This version could be sung to a rich white woman, but with a vulnerable empathy & tenderness lacking in Dylan's; when I listen to *the way he sings*, "but you realize you're in the wrong part of town," I hear him talking to the white woman who also has to deal with the black family's disapproval ("Don't call me whitey").

If one doubts that you don't have to be at least "twice as good" in America 2011, just look at the media's treatment of half-white President Obama. Of course it doesn't have to just refer to race. "Underdog" is itself twice as good (with the "white" and "black" versions existing separately, and not blended together into some universal humdrum fusion or blinged-out black power fist). "They get uptight if you get too bright:"

Say, I'm the underdog
I'm the underdog I don't mind, 'cause I can handle it
Underdog, it's gonna be alright I'm the underdog

While Sly always claimed, "the intelligence in my music comes from David Froelich" (his early mentor, a white musicologist at Vallejo Junior College), the Family Stone's "Underdog" was "straight on and from straight back out of traditional Black spirit feeling," (with the possible exception of "Frere Jacques").[172]

Columbia gave him access to the wider national context, as Autumn had a few years earlier, but at first no one at Columbia knew how to market Sly. He "fell through the cracks." Although *A Whole New Thing* was a critical success and their live shows won over New York audiences, both the single and the album for Columbia (Epic) were commercial failures. The mistake: Sly took the "utopian" notions of underground FM free format at their word as more open to the "progressive" elements of the first album, as well as honest lyrics of social protest. Clive Davis, then President of Columbia Records, told Sly: "I'm concerned that the serious radio stations [the underground FM stations that his former colleague and boss Tom Donahue had bolted

---

172 Voices, 9.

toward], that might be willing to play you, will be put off by the costuming, the hairstyles." "Underdog" may have been a hit had Columbia pushed it more to soul & R&B stations. Sly, however, was determined not to make this "mistake" next time.

Given Sly's willingness to "change the sound," the radio & recording studio were ways to integrate and still maintain autonomy, as the live shows, the bigger they got, were not. In moments of musical introspection, Sly was as *far away* from "black" as from "white." That far away place was the key, the weapon even, the divining rod—for any real integration, especially since the possibility of this happening at home was being destroyed. Columbia was originally trying to get Sly Stone to fit in with the AM-singles-oriented (and more 'black music friendly') format, like Fifth Dimension or Peaches and Herb, which may have come closer to Sly's "costuming" but no closer to his sound than The Grateful Dead were.

Krapalik, who had a close bond with Sly, however, and understood what he had achieved at Autumn more than Donahue did, gave better advice: "Sly, you gotta make a hit single. And you have to have a dum-dum-repeat lyric. And in between all those dum-dum repeats, you put all your *schticklach*." (53) Sly remembers Krapalik telling him the first album was 'too funky:' "He didn't know what funky was, but I knew what he meant: that it was too complex. I had tried to make sure, I didn't want any feeling to get away. But, because I had to sell records, he said 'Make it simple, you know how to do it.' OK, what's simple? Dance to the music...just dance...to the music. If you think about it, that's the simplest thing in the world. I didn't believe 'Dance To The Music' was funky at all. To this day I don't think it's funky, but I know what it is. I know people can understand it, quickly, and they can dance to it."

The result was the international top ten smash. Sly broke nationally on the AM-format that his former mentor had declared dead less than a year earlier. In 1965, Greil Marcus noted, "Top

40 radio was a mystery; it was up to the artist to solve it;" [173]Sly proved this could still be done in 1968, and without "selling out." Rather, Sly realized he could sing a simple song, and it wouldn't be alienating, especially if it could allow him to get what he calls his "funkier" stuff out there (whether "Underdog," which is now much more known in retrospect because of the success of Sly's other chart toppers, or the later *There's A Riot Going On* and *Fresh*). As we can see in the brilliant and subtle code-switching in songs like "Hot Fun In The Summertime," (in which he sings both "them summer days" and "those summer days" as well as mixing "black" and "white" musical elements), Sly was a master at transcending the choice between AM and FM, and their racialized connotations, on a larger scale than he had achieved in San Francisco, in the reified world of pop music at least.

Despite Bill Graham, Sly and The Family Stone, by leaving San Francisco, ended up selling much more than any of the "San Francisco Sound" bands (with the possible exception of the Jefferson Airplane Conglomerate). Krapalik and Epic's Al De Marino proved themselves much more open to Sly's populist, integrative, band, than the locals did. No wonder Sly didn't really want to return, and, for awhile at least, thrived on the increased pressure (and opportunity) his new bosses demanded; at least they wouldn't flake.

The radio could still reach "everyday people" more than overpriced arena shows. In songs like "Everyday People" and "Don't Call Me Nigger, Whitey" he even went so far as to bite his own (angry) tongue in a way by pointing out that "reverse racism" might be a problem too. In the process, he helped usher in a new heyday (68-72) of black music on top 40 radio in part *because* of the white flight away to "serious" and underground FM, while kids of all races could still buy cheaper singles. When

---

173   Greil Marcus, *Like A Rolling Stone*, 45

they took many of the brightest whiteys along with them to FM, for a little while there it opened up AM to more expansively experimental (and "raw") black music (even Sun Ra's Arkestra had a top 40 hit!). You couldn't kill AM, at least as quickly as you could the Fillmore.

By the time Bill Graham was finally persuaded to put Sly on a double-bill with Jimi Hendrix (who also had to leave his home town, and the United States, to break big) in 1968, he had moved from the building at 1805 Geary Blvd in The Fillmore neighborhood after only two years, citing the "deteriorating neighborhood and the modest capacity of the Hall (1199 capacity)." Leaving in his wake a community he helped devastate, Graham relocated to the Carousel Ballroom at 10 South Van Ness, at the corner of market." Now outside of the black neighborhood, and very close to the spot where Charles Sullivan was murdered, literally and symbolically; as a final insult, he kept the name "Fillmore" for the new venue.

Nonetheless, it is during this period that Sly made perhaps his best music (we don't know enough about the hours of unreleased music he's done in the past several decades). As Sly's hits became anthems on the AM radio the new Culture Tzars hated, and managed to cross over into FM in some markets, Sly and the Family Stone influenced everybody from Stevie Wonder, Norman Whitfield at Motown to Miles Davis and Prince.[174] After 4 albums with the classic Sly & The Family Stone lineup, it's fitting that their swansong was also one of the last great double-sided non album-track 45RPM autonomous singles, "Thank You Faletting Be Mice Elf" b/w "Everybody Is A Star" in 1970. It was the end of an era, in more ways than one, as the increasingly centralized, consolidated and corporate music industry had

---

174 Betty Davis, Gil Scott Heron, Santana, Chicago Transit Authority, KC& The Sunshine Band, Earth Wind and Fire, etc. Even Genesis's "Misunderstanding" steals, to lesser effect, the main riff of "Hot Fun In The Summer Time."

virtually mandated that 1970 be the start of a new age. [175]

Sly fits that script, even as he flips it, and while 1971's *There's A Riot Going On* was credited as the long awaited next Sly And The Family Stone album, it was much more like a solo album. Upon its release the white critical establishment—like Greil Marcus and Robert Christgau—was somewhat puzzled and ambivalent. Was it a primarily a "deeply personal" introspective singer/songwriter album as was in fashion at the time (*Tapestry, Sweet Baby James, Plastic Ono Band, Curtis, What's Going On,* and soon *Talking Book* and *Innervisions*) helping to usher in and legitimize the "me decade," as we witness Sly slowing down his last big hit to thank Africa for talking to him as if it were a priest in a confessional booth? Or was the album 'socially significant' as a sign of racial anger and black defiance of the man, even if he was black like Berry Gordy in the case of Wonder and Gaye (Gordy, too, had followed the corporate script by breaking up The Supremes to elevate Diana Ross as solo superstar, and breaking up the local Detroit scene by relocating operations in LA).

Yes, Sly had created that classic work so deeply evocative and suggestive that it could allow, and baffle, both interpretations, but we can't overemphasize that the industry-imposed mandate to create the "serious" album was heavy in the air in 1970, even as many lamented the loss of that good time party band waving its communal freak flag, suggesting a new post-segregated—and even post-patriarchal—America, which flattered the mostly white hippies, to whom Sly was speaking when he said, "thank you for the party, I could never stay." I'm not going to weigh in on whether *Riot*—as an album—is better than *Stand!* (though it's a fascinating argument one can get entangled in while dancing and debating). But the hurt you can hear more

---

175   It affected musicians as diverse as Neil Diamond: http://chris-stroffolino.blogspot.com/2013/04/part-7-i-am-i-said-neil-diamond.html

clearly on *Riot* than on *Stand!* is the same hurt expressed in the two "Underdogs" about what San Francisco could've been ("Luv N' Haight" for instance), and the same hurt that you hear in his diatribe about the arrogance of the Bay Area in his late 1969 concert; it's a return to that "funkier" feeling he edited out of "Dance To The Music" and his other major hits.

Meanwhile, Bill Graham, revealing the extent of his deep-rooted love and commitment to "the San Francisco sound" and its musical culture, closed the Van Ness Fillmore in 1971, going to "find himself" in a Greek Island. Like many, Graham blamed Woodstock for destroying the promise of the 1960s: A couple of years ago, a couple of geniuses put on something called the Woodstock Festival. It was a tragedy. Groups recognized that they could go into larger cattle markets, play less time and make more dollars. What they've done is to destroy the rock industry." But Graham had set the ball rolling in this direction to begin with.[176]

From the perspective of 40 years later, it's amazing that one could turn on national TV, and witness Sly join Mohammed Ali in lobbying a congressman to "take your face and your complexion to the white-house, and tell them to repay the black people for all the work that they've done,"[177] but by the time

---

176   Given the way Graham treated Sly in his hometown, it's quite possible Graham's problem with Woodstock was precisely that The Family Stone stole the show! He soon returned and tried in vain to rekindle his former glories because he was upset that no one on the otherwise paradisal Greek island knew who he was. Graham, never known for his "ear," later died in a plane crash on the way home from a Huey Lewis and The News show not long after Nirvana ushered in what Thurston Moore, with tongue-in-cheek, called "the year punk broke," a rich, but bitter man. Today, Si Perloff of Outside Lands ensures that Graham's legacy of killing local music by speaking for it is alive and well.

177   Mike Douglass Show July 17, 1974 https://www.youtube.com/watch?v=vBFAHd189V8

of *Fresh* (1973), arguably an even better album than *Riot*, Sly's sales were starting to decline; part of this is because Columbia didn't need him as much as it did before it commissioned the Harvard Report in 1972. As Nelson George shows in *The Death of Rhythm and Blues*, The Harvard Report (—"A Study Of The Soul Music Environment Prepared for The Columbia Records Group, submitted by Harvard University Business School On May 11, 1972)" was commissioned by Columbia to increase "market penetration" in the "soul market." [178]

Columbia had lagged behind such black owned "independent" labels like Motown and Stax in signing black talent and seducing consumers. It also lagged behind Atlantic, though Atlantic had already transitioned from an R&B label to the label of Led Zeppelin and Yes and—like Autumn Records 7 years earlier, but on a much larger scale—was abandoning the R&B acts—even the blue-eyed soul acts like The Rascals—that had allowed it to succeed in the first place. Columbia's two pronged attack would be to sign more black artists while also breaking up what remained of an autonomous black music community, the network of black DJS, label-owners, promoters, retailers and listeners who hadn't been as seduced by Columbia's product (with the exception of Sly and a few other "specimens")—even with payola—as they had by the independent labels based across this country (from James Brown's King in Cincinnati to Allen Toussaint's Minit in New Orleans).

Sly and The Family Stone had helped Columbia gain such market penetration, but they could do much more after the Harvard Report with the signing of Gamble and Huff's Philadelphia International records (The O'Jays, Harold Melvin, etc). During this time, Sly had achieved everything he had set out to do in the public sphere of the mass cultural musical industry, as the first "Underdog" predicts ("first honesty, then destiny, then you

---

178 Nelson George, *The Death Of Rhythm & Blues (1988)*, pg. 136

can't believe I've done in my life just what I was supposed to"), in his pact—I won't say compromise—with mass culture mega-stardum. But by the time of Sly's last major national hit, in 1974—whether Sly was pushed or whether he jumped—there could be no turning back.[179]

Throughout what Nelson George calls "the rhythm and blues world" in 1974, shockwaves were being felt; even The Godfather of Soul, James Brown, felt them. Commenting on the structural changes occurring in the American musical industry during the 1970s, Brown writes "most of my music right on through the mid-seventies did...well on the pop charts. But," he adds, "a funny thing was happening to music on the radio then. It was starting to get segregated again, not just by black and white, but by *kinds*: country, pop, hard rock, soft rock, every kind you could name. Radio formats became very rigid." (225)[180]

This re-segregation happened because radio stations were being consolidated by corporations. Personality DJS like Sly were increasingly a thing of the past, as it was cheaper to have automated formats than to pay individual DJS. Since this cost-cutting device also allowed the corporations more control in what was played, it had the effect of making music less democratic than it had been previously. It wasn't just radio that was being taken over by conglomerates, it was the record labels, and this also affected James Brown, as well as many other musicians during this time. As Brown puts it, "the government hurt my business a lot, a *whole* lot. But they didn't destroy me. Polydor did that."(238).

Polydor's roots in telecommunications and electronics ominously foreshadow the direction the music industry has gone into in the past 40 years, especially since the Telecom Act of

---

179   I personally don't think he was really *trying* to make a comeback with the album titled, *Heard Ya Missed Me, Well, I'm Back* (1976)

180   James Brown, *The Godfather Of Soul* (1985)

1996. It effected the distribution of music, but it also affected the *sound:* "The company didn't want the funk in there too heavy. They'd take the feeling out of the record. They didn't want James Brown to be raw. Eventually, they destroyed my sound." (239-240) Polydor rode Brown in order to gain a foothold in the American music industry, and "once the door was open to them in the American market, they had no more need of me." (240). Polydor, it turns out, ended up pouring most of its effort into pushing electronic disco acts. As Brown puts it:

"By the middle of 1975, Disco had broken big. Disco is a simplifications of a lot of what I was doing....Disco is a very small part of funk...the difference is that in funk you dig into a groove, you don't stay on the surface. Disco stays on the surface....*It was all electronic sequences and beats per minutes—it was done with machines* (emphasis added)...It destroyed the musical basis that so many people worked hard to build up in the sixties. The record companies loved disco because it was producer's music. You really don't need artists to make disco. They didn't have to worry about artists not cooperating: machines can't talk back and, unlike artists, they don't have to be paid. What disco became was a lawyer's recording; the attorneys were making records." (242).

It also affected live music:

"By this time the Apollo was in trouble. A lot of the big acts wouldn't play it anymore because it wasn't profitable enough. I could see it wasn't going to make it, and I said that this show might mark the end of an era in black music. Mick Jagger and Ahmet Eretgun showed up for the Friday show; they knew what was happening. Not too long after that, the theatre closed. (242)...."The black concert business was already hurting. Whites wouldn't come even if the black artist had big record sales. Black America was in a serious recession; there was just no money in the black community. Later on, that situation hurt record sales too. For everybody." (243).

The seeds for all these developments that eventually trickled up to "white America" can be traced back to the great Fillmore whitewash. Indeed, San Francisco's arrogance—and Bill Graham's arrogance in particular—undid it, as it would have undid Sly had he stayed. Now some may argue that it helped undo Sly anyway, as the "drug addiction" narrative has tremendous clout in this society, but I think the "drug addiction" narrative is purposely used to obscure the changes in the music industry, the corporate machinations, that are usually much closer to the real "behind the music" stories, just like it is in biopics of Gil Scott Heron and James Brown.

Sly, like many mega-stars who rose up through the older, more democratic system, saw what was happening to the business and the culture, but like the family watching the wrecking ball destroy downtown in Gary Adelstein's *Reading 1974: Portrait of a City*, was helpless to do anything about it. Yet Sly was smart enough to know that the San Francisco—and the locally-based national music culture he had thrived in was on its last legs in 1967, and he couldn't return to it in 1975 if he wanted to. 40 years later, the murderer, like the murderer of Charles Sullivan, has still not been prosecuted, or even brought to trial (and may even be the judge), but it's clear that Bill Graham (and Rock and Roll Hall-of-Fame inductee Tom Donahue) had a large hand in it.

18. "Rich:" Beme The Rapper in Oakland (December 2010)

"Obesity is the only epidemic that you can cure by keeping your mouth shut."
Richard Berman, The Center For Consumer Freedom

"Women have babies; men have shit"
Joan Fisher

Genre Preference, Prejudice, Envy or Racism?

I was working the door at our Oakland warehouse space on San Pablo one night when we had a last minute change in plans. A show at The Stork Club, one of the few legal music venues left in Oakland, had been double-booked apparently. The booker wanted to know if we could combine it with our regularly scheduled show. It was a low-fi hip-hop show (old school, just a DJ and 3 MCS), and we jumped on the chance to do it. I was suspicious that the Stork Club was really double-booked, as the manager had his share of white supremacist tendencies, and had already alienated much of the black community in a recent incident), but their loss could be our gain.

When we told the already booked bands about it, they got uptight. We reached a compromise; the rappers (Beme, Grl Abstrakt, and Pill Kosby) could play, but only if they don't get paid. BeMe said that was fine with him, and I told him we'd book a show soon in which he could get paid. Still, the already-booked white bands were less than thrilled. During the first, very short, hip hop set, a guy from one of the bands came up to me with blood in his eyes, "How the fuck are we supposed to follow that?!" I could've regaled him with tales of Jerry Lee Lewis and

Chuck Berry, to enjoin him to take it as a challenge—but instead I just gave him a "dude, get over it" look and went upstairs to get a more physically imposing doorman to back me up, just in case....

Meanwhile, the women got the dancing going, and many of us were won over by the low-budget beats of Pill Kozby and the charisma of BeMe. Beme got progressively more comfortable as he performed, falling into a touring band's drum kit that had been set exactly between the stage area and the audience. The tour-manager freaked out; she went up stairs and started shouting, "this is unacceptable" and such. He certainly wasn't trying to be violent; it was more like moshing; besides, why did they chose that particular spot to set up the drums?[181]

We tried to calm her down; "it's just like punk" Matt & Evan reminded her, yet the night made it clear to me how much prejudice and latent racism exists in "our" scene—not any more than at SMC, but not really better either. Frankly, what Beme was doing was even more 'punk' than what these bands were doing. No wonder they didn't want to share the bill with him. None of them got people dancing or even bobbing their heads as much as he did. I got so swept up in the spectacle, and trying to dance with my bad leg, that I had very little sense of his words (probably for the same reason I suck at free-styling; I get distracted by the beat especially on first listen) aside from the chorus:

Five in my pocket just spent two skinny jeans own the ain't new
I can't wait till I'm rich rich Imma buy a whole lotta shit

When I posted the video and learned the song was called "Rich," I wondered if it was typical of most corporate commer-

---

181 http://www.youtube.com/watch?v=tQmMwiwGSgw

cial hip hop in glorifying consumerism and personal wealth,[182] though later Paddy was pontificating about BeMe's lyrics. "Oh, he's *conscious* hip hop. Only clueless folks who know nothing about rap are into that." I was just happy to be a part of the event. How important is the overplayed difference between "conscious" and "gangsta" anyway? I am more than willing to admit I'm clueless about hip hop in general, but when I finally heard all the lyrics, they cut as deep as any page-based poet as well as any of the more known 'poetic' white bands I've worked with.

A month or so later, we invited BeMe back to the warehouse for what I had hoped would be a paying gig. My new band was playing as was a new band featuring ex-members of The Cuts and Detroit's The Go, but there had been a big December rain storm and the slum-lord, one Mr. Thomas Leung, had still failed to come through on his promise, and legal obligation, to fix the leaks. I discovered the warehouse was flooded, puddles everywhere. Wading in ankle-deep water with a flashlight, we discovered the PA was destroyed.

We went through with the show, but even the people who lived in the warehouse were so pissed off they had left to crash on other people's couches. Thus, there was no one to work the door, and hardly any one came (I had largely become a shut-in). I felt terrible after what had happened to BeMe at his first show, and started suspecting that the flood was just an excuse for the other guys in our so-called "collective" to screw him again—but I have no proof of that, as I tried to stay focused on the common enemy, Mr. Leung and the City of Oakland's crackdown on live

---

182   As in this critique of contemporary hip hop, "We don't need Marx to see that the result of selling the world ghetto raps was not an improvement in conditions for those living in the ghetto, but instead, a means of production was developed to sell the condition of the ghetto by simultaneously sustaining those conditions...." (Republicans).

local nightilfe culture. All of the plans Nehemiah, Matt and I had for the warehouse seemed to be going down in this flood.

Still, BeMe was much more into performing even to the audience of 20 at best, even though he had found out his drum machine wasn't working. I asked him if he'd be up for us backing him up. We could do one of our instrumental two chord jams and he could do one of his raps—what do we have to lose? He was into it. It took a little arm-twisting; Jed was intimidated and preferred to do the set we had rehearsed, and of course funk was out of the question for him. Eric was into it, but didn't want Nick Allen to join us on guitar. I thought that would be amazing, but I saw Eric's point: BeMe's raps and my piano playing are both rhythmic and melodic, and it could be too busy with the guitarist on the fly, especially for a bassist who doesn't like being treated like "glue," but who also wouldn't lead with a groove we could've followed (ah, if only I had brought my trumpet). We could do it next time (or so I thought...).[183]

BeMe chose to do the same song, "Rich," he had performed at the first show. The band was sloppy as hell, but grooving and fun. And the words were perhaps the deepest words I ever had the honor to back up live (though some could claim Leonard Cohen and Silver Jews are deeper). So we decided to record it at The Creamery.

Eating Disorders & The Childhood Obesity Epidemic

In the studio, I realized the song was primarily about his eating disorder, and this personal testimony can suggest a way out of both our culture's "obesity crisis" as well as the *energy* crisis. Once I heard all the words, the chorus becomes deeper and more complex than a mere ode to salvation through con-

---

183   http://www.youtube.com/watch?v=ILOuDLD7UmQ

sumerism. The song starts:

> Grew up on the floor wishing i had more\
> Chillin with my sister waiting by that door
> Wishin bought something from the liquor store
> She threw down in the kitchen "can i have more"
> Maybe over did it got too chubby
> Cookies and cream ice cream was my buddy
> One of the only way she could show that she loved me

The first verse portrays an inner-city food desert. The speaker has special powers, as his wishin' can get him food, but limited horizons. Notice how the verbs chart a progression from *chillin'* to *waitin'* to *wishin'* and *dreamin'* to *workin.*" As the nouns move from "more" to "door" to "store," to "poor," his horizons expand; he becomes aware of the stigma of poverty, *working poverty.* "She," as we soon discover, is his mother. One of the hardest things about being a parent is saying "No." As a kid, my mom used to pour milk and loads of sugar onto a bowl of strawberries. I loved it, or thought I did. It took me years to realize that strawberries were actually sweet without all that, and that there's many rich and powerful people who don't want us to know that.

Though we didn't have to rely on the liquor store for food, we were also nutritionally challenged. "You look sad; you want a sandwich?" Of course I did; it tastes good. You certainly aren't going to hear too many 5 year olds complaining that pizza is not a vegetable. He's sympathetic to his mom, and can't blame her for living in a culture in which "food" becomes the main way to show love. As post-industrial America became increasingly alienated from the body; this was sold as "progress" to the first generation under this new food regime, and increasingly the "norm" to Beme & my mother's generation.[184] Yet Beme's song goes deeper into the roots of the problem.

Digression On The Center For Consumer Freedom
(for David Berman)

One of the richest and most powerful men in America today (in many ways more powerful than the President) is Richard Berman. He gets paid millions by multi-national corporate fast-food chains and beverage (soda, alcohol) conglomerates to do public relations (propaganda) work to prevent any government regulation of his clients, and his work goes much deeper than merely lobbying against a soda-tax or minimum wage raise.[185]

For decades, he's been honing his rhetorical messaging skills to discredit the opposition and persuade people that the poison he pushes is, in fact, healthy. When he says, "Obesity is the only epidemic that you can cure by keeping your mouth shut," he sounds reasonable enough, as he preaches "personal responsibility" and moderation; he himself is not the skinniest man in the world, and his paunch gives him a kind of charming cred that the skinny Cosmopolitan cover models placed next to a picture of a big fat cake lack. You can see his id-appealing hedonist wink, if not quite the celebrated twinkle of Coca-Cola spokesman Santa Claus, as if he's the voice of "fun." Surely, it's

---

184 When TV came out in the 50s, my grandmother war warned by a friend: "it might make you fat!" so she decided to start smoking to prevent that, after all she was a working mother.

185 As his son, David Berman (of the Silver Jews) puts it, "my father is a sort of human molestor. An exploiter. A scoundrel...He props up fast food/soda/factory farming/childhood obesity and diabetes/drunk driving... if you eat food or have a job, he is reaching you." *My Father, My Attack Dog*, http://www.prwatch.org/news/2009/01/8168/front-group-king-rick-berman-gets-blasted-his-son-david-berman

okay to have a little fun, and devil's food cake can taste just as good even after his clients replaced sugar with corn syrup and other polysyllabic ingredients you can't pronounce (like doctor and lawyer speak, such food industry obfuscation-speak can render even those with Ph.Ds illiterate). [186]

Berman does his job very well, appealing on a "subliminal" level in the fine tradition of Sigmund Freud's American nephew Alfred Bernays.[187] Of course, his job in pushing his clients' products is made easier by the fact that they're omnipresent in supermarkets, mini-marts, gas stations and liquor stores throughout this country. Yes, he preaches personal responsibility and moderation even as he knows damn well that they are addictive substances that may require superhuman strength and wisdom for any toddler, let alone a poor one in a food desert, to overcome.

Despite the millions these companies spend on advertising, soda, starch, sugar and salt may not even *need* advertising anymore. The fact that these manufacturers are able to distribute them everywhere, and disproportionately in poor neighborhoods, for the last 60 or so years as America became less rural and the split between urban and rural became greater ("we used to be a producer, but now we're a consumer" as Gil Scott Heron put it back in 1981) has become so ingrained as the assumed norm in this culture that community gardens and public water fountains are now as rare as mail-boxes or phone booths (besides the soda-companies now make even more money off of water than off of soda): for many, these corporate junk-food products are almost the only game in town.

Yet the advertisements do serve a function in reminding us who is in control, and flooding the Clearchannel-owned radio

---

186 Yet Berman's quote reveals that he wants our mouths closed unless we're eating, and buying, his shit. We're only "free," in his definition, *as consumers*, not as producers.

187 For those who do not yet know about Alfred Bernays, see Adam Curtis' BBC Documentary *The Century Of The Self*.

stations and billboards with these messages brings in so much money to the media-outlets that it's rare that any journalistic muckraker will be allowed to criticize, or even call much attention to "the man behind the curtain" even if Rachel Maddow and others have dubbed Berman, "Dr. Evil," an appellation he wears with a kind of devious pride to the extent he consents to step out of the shadows where he does his most sinister work. [188]And he ain't working alone; there are others like him (When he dies, they'll find someone else).

Regardless of whether the corporations are purposely trying to poison us, or are merely trying to increase their profits by lowering the quality of their ingredients, and making sure they're addictive enough so we keep coming back to this *soda-to-hospital pipeline*, they certainly fear that we "small people" will collectively rebel like in the movie *Network* when a renegade/rogue newscaster tells his viewers to smash their TVS yelling "I'm mad as hell and can't take it anymore" (if not quite like when the Epsilon semi-morons in *Brave New World* hold a strike for soma).

Yet, they need not fear this as long as vegans, vegetarians and healthy-living spokespeople for alternatives, continue to lose this propaganda battle. They have not done a very good job of seducing people away from the CCF ideology: their tendency to preachinesss is often off-putting to kids, and overworked adults who believe a Big Mac will give them a much-deserved "break today." And Berman and Company over-emphasizes, and milks this moral smugness tendency in some of his opposition for all it's worth, just like the lobbyist in *Thank You For Smoking*, which some say is based on Berman, did when he exposed the self-interest in the hypocritical democratic "Vermont Senator." (for those of you who "feel the Bern").

Living near Berkeley, with more than its share of hypocritical

---

188   http://www.dailykos.com/story/2009/10/7/790619/-

no-fun culture police ("do as we say, not as we did"), I can understand Berman's appeal.[189] And, too often, in these cultural debates there's little middle ground between Dr. Evil on one hand, and the No-Fun police on the other (despite the initiatives of Michelle Obama and the NFL's "play 60" campaign designed to address childhood obesity, sponsored by Pepsi and Doritos, etc). Yet Beme's rap not only reveals the human toll of Berman and the Center For Consumer Freedom's policies,[190] but provides that middle ground by showing that he, too, used to believe that these junk-food companies were actually selling "fun" or even a kind of "upward mobility" through "consumer freedom." This makes Beme's overcoming of his obesity/diabetes school training all the more heroic, and even potentially useful in the propaganda battle.

Foodaholics & The Food-To-Hospital Pipeline

When I told Beme I could immediately relate to the psychological and cultural truths here, he told me that as a teenager he had actually weighed over 300 pounds. This admission blew me away, as one who has struggled with food all my life, the fact that he was able to lose all this weight, and write a song about it, was impressive. The song may not be as "universal" as songs about love, death and friendship, but it can be an anthem. There just aren't that many songs in any genre these days with lyrics this blatant about dieting.

There are more songs about other addictions: alcohol, heroin, crack. But one reason I consider his song deeper than songs

---

189 I, too, as a kid, thought it was cool that B.B. King did ads for Burger King....

190 Which are also a contributing factor to the *Culture Crash* analyzed in chapter one.

dealing with these other addictions is because these other addictions usually occur much later in life than the childhood addictions to diabetes and obesity-inducing processed foods. Understanding this, it's reasonable to suggest that these perfectly legal drugs of sugar, and soda are the ultimate *gateway drugs* and at least as harmful as some of the other "adult-addictions" they lead to.

There is evidence to support the conspiracy that one of the main reasons they're slowly letting marijuana become more legal is because the makers of corporate "snax"—a.k.a. "munchies"—have done studies to show how marijuana use increases consumption of *their* products (though I don't know if Richard Berman is specifically involved in that; his alcohol clients could get offended. And, though, as far as I know, Berman is not working for Big Pharma, his policies certainly benefit it).

Thus, if we as a country were really serious about waging "a war on drugs," we follow it to these roots in poverty and toddler "consumer freedom." I know some parents who have complained that Clearchannel pushes songs like "I'm In Love With The Coco," to purposely send negative messages to kids, to make it seem cool to do and sell coke, while censoring other songs with more positive messages like Beme's rap. Yet, if "Coco" pushes a negative message, what about songs like "Sugar, Sugar" or, earlier, "My Baby Calls Me Candy" (is there a catchy anthem song out there that calls his boyfriend, *Corn Syrup*)?

Before Beme can tell us about his hard-won triumph over obesity, he must first give us a "before" picture that many of us can relate to so we may understand the social conditions that were especially vulnerable to attack by the addiction-pushing "consumer freedom" army:

We couldn't go to Disney land
we was livin with Mickey's fam
Sometimes even seen roaches

> Thats the life that you live when your po kids
> Dreaming of the promise land like Moses
> But didn't make it "sorry coaches"
> Mama said you gone buy me a house boy
> I'm still workin on it mama no doubt boy

The resounding implication is that if these social conditions didn't exist (if, for instance, they hadn't defunded the playgrounds which aren't even that safe in the first place with the police drive-by shootings of 11 year olds playing with toy guns), he and many others wouldn't have destroyed their health with junkfood. As a poor kid, it's hard not to hear that subliminal message tickle-whispering in your ear: here, eat this *rich* food (the unhealthiest food is often sold as rich). It might have even been healthier had he been *eating* "Mickey's fam."

When the chorus returns, it now has deeper significance:

> Five in my pocket just spent two
> Skinny jeans on they ain't new
> I can't wait till I'm rich rich Imma buy a whole lotta shit

First, the contagious *carpe diem* catharsis of "I can't wait" shows how working for a better future can be an adequate excuse for living most fully in the present (and, as we shall see, "shit" turns out to be more of a verb than a noun). He seems very happy that he's still got $5 left, perhaps because he didn't waste it on all that rich, fattening food, and is wearing old clothes—skinny jeans. The second verse fleshes out the "before and after" picture. It starts with a list of the food-like things he could be buying with that $5 in the skinny jeans—but if he did, he would have no money to buy the Fat Pants he'd have to get. A "while back" he was just a consumer, now he's working his butt off, and loving it:

What you know about dollar cup breakfast
3 dollar Loko's livin reckless had that on my 7/11 checklist
Next to oatmeal raisin cookies and chips
And next to that a sandwich
    looking up at the owner like dude I'm famished
that was a while back...

Then a resolve:

Livin clean and sober bout to get my money right
Working out daily bout to get the honeys right
Did you see my video yeah i got my tummy tight
Floyd Mayweather shit a big money fight
Fightin for my life and i don't fight fair
Nigga stand when i rap i don't like chairs
How you actin bored and i featured
How you actin poor and you ain't paid to be here

When dieting is fighting for your life, $5 in your pocket goes much further if you don't have to spend it to feed the belly beast in the belly of the beast. The American dream of getting rich may be quixotic, but certainly no more toxic than the more 'modest' gratifications of junk food, as it embraces the emptiness rather than trying to fill it with food. As he works out daily, he *spends* the fat, and realizes it can actually *buy* him time to work on his music (and "make shit"). In this sense, he's subverting this "American dream" by glamorizing a more econo (if not "Spartan") lifestyle, as he turns his focus like a sanctified preacher to address the worst possible audience he can imagine: a *sedentary* one.

    Since I'm paid to be here, and you're not, why stand there bored dreaming of the Oatmeal Raisin and chips you'll have when you get home?[191] He's not just singing for his supper but also a video or a gym membership. These things cost money, but are much less than expensive than inadequate health insurance needed to navigate the food-to-hospital pipeline. He says "I don't fight fair," but everything he mentions here seems pretty fair to me. As Beme comes to reject Berman's poison, he realizes he can not only "have" more fun, but also *be* more fun, more productive, help bring people together, help them dance while testifying his own personal credo against the Center For Consumer Freedom (to help transform a temporary triumph into something more communal and lasting).

Refusing To Keep His Mouth Shut

You could say Beme both *is* and *isn't* taking Berman's advice. Yes, he achieved a "normal, healthy" weight by eating less food, but he didn't exactly keep his mouth shut. For rapping, and letting the rhythmic word energy flow more freely through his entire body, his entire being, with the help of a DJ (whose got "the best tracks") and an audience of con-conspirators (at the shows I saw him, mostly female) is what allowed him to lose weight. If you're spitting rhymes, it's kind of hard to shove food in your mouth.

It's a work out that can make you less hungry. As a mural from the Oakland-based Community Rejuvenation Project suggests: there'd be less eating disorders and drug addictions if people were allowed to talk more, if public word-jazz and sing-

---

191   When he performed at Copland [The unfortunate name of our Warehouse space before it became Qilombo], many of the white guys were clearly *acting* bored, in their defensive hipster coolness, neither would they pay him. The girls weren't acting bored, as he claimed space like a one-man army against The Center For Consumer Freedom, and the food-to-hospital pipeline.

ing were more acceptable. And there'd be a lot less childhood Attention Deficit Disorder to usher kids into the arms of Big Pharma. It's not really a coincidence that the rise in junk-food and drug, both legal and illegal, addictions (among both blacks and whites) in the last 30 years parallels the loss of street-music culture and the increased tension of *silence* in the streets.[192] And Beme's song suggests there would also be fewer guns if the cops didn't crack down on street musicians.[193] In this sense, Richard Berman is wrong: it's harder to solve the obesity crisis by keeping your mouth closed. The extra energy you get from dieting has to go somewhere. And, in this song, rapping is also what allows him to *spend less money* on food and that, in effect, makes his tongue richer.[194]

Labor, Shit and Healing[195]

In 21st century Bay Area culture, where self-proclaimed "foodies" have a loud voice in determining cultural policy,

---

192 At the risk of sounding like Bill Hicks or Greg Ashley, and on the side of Richard Berman, I also think the demonization of cigarettes contributed to the rise in these other addictions and health problems.

193 They've also been trying to take away the drums since Congo Square, and computer technology has helped with that, as recent noise bans of the Pleasant Grove Baptist Church and the Sambafunk drummers in Oakland attest.

194 And isn't that the more real meaning to the miracle of the multiplied fish and loaves, that less can become more, and I bet the devil that tempted Jesus in the desert during those 40 day fasts acts a lot like Richard Berman.

195 If these rudimentary tropings on the word "shit" in this section is offensive to you, you could translate "shit" to "spit" (as in "spit a rap"). Or should we attempt to translate back to the cleaner, more acceptable, terms of business and finance?

there's a lot of denial over the fact that there never was a foodie who wasn't also a *shitty,* but shit produces, gives back, and can get you off the floor that too much food put you on. As the Oakland graffiti puts it, *"stop buying/ shit, shit shit."*[196] Shit, at least human shit, is largely outside commodity. But just as that war between "the world of industry and business" and "the dancefloor" is waged in the connotations of the word "break" (see Patrick Rosal essay discussed in Chapter 15), so is it raged in the connotations of the word "shit." And, on the dance floor, what Beme calls "shit" is much more like "sweat," or labor.

In this song, Beme becomes a transformative recycling *factory,* changing the shit you call food into the food you call shit to critique the food/shit dualism that is so central to this consumer society. This is not mere inversion, but balance. In this anti-labor, trickle-down society, laborers, insofar as we are spoken of, are not presented as doers, or makers, but rather treated "like shit." No, we're told that the *real* makers are not the Chinese slave labor making your computer, but the Job Creators like the late Steve Jobs (who sent jobs over to China), or the owner and investor class (who like to act like their shit doesn't stink) that used to be called the leisure class back in the days when labor was spoken about (and each town had a pro-labor-newspaper to check the pro-business newspaper).

Beme is clearly a laborer—refusing to glorify consumerism, but working the crowd into a frenzy, even as he knows the corporate hip-hop establishment will call what he does "shit." He can turn the tables, though, as he raps to say he's too busy making shit to buy their shit:

Cause i shit talk give me ex-lax
deeps a fine chick he's got the best tracks\

---

196   The line break suggests the deeper truth that shitting is the opposite of buying and what is needed in a culture that has eaten more than it can digest (Ezra Pound; Percy Byssh Shelley)

Excuse me deep I'm bout to shit on these
These rappers bowin down cause they Can't shit on me

Shit is not necessary synonymous with "Stuff," material goods one can buy if one's rich enough (dolphins swimming in a pool, for instance), as it seems in the chorus. It is more profoundly an action, and Beme's defense of the right to shit, and to shit talk, is one with his war against mere salvation-through-consumerism in "Rich." Rapping, the free improvisatory flow of words that are also tethered to the formalism of rhyme becomes ex-lax; its formality betters the "talking cure.[197]" When one is free to make the most outlandish gestures of braggadocio, one may get sick swallowing their own shit and need ex-lax. But the DJ's non-verbal beats are the ex-lax that can feed him, and heal him much more than the food/shit of these other word slingers.

If these rappers can't shit on him, make him hang it up to become their consumer, to accept their moral and/or aesthetic authority over his own, then he must shit on them. This contrasts with Berman's "personal responsibility" philosophy—for Beme, we must shit on each other in order for any true communication and mutual collaboration to take place; Beme dishes it out precisely in order to be strong enough to take it. Beme is not saying he prefers or needs rappers to bow down before him, coz it's clear he wants a challenge, and laments that he's not getting it from these rappers. I saw this in action when I invited him to speak to my class at Laney. I was fully prepared to let Beme lecture on his concerns or his art in this class; instead, he immediately began engaging the students by asking questions, and encouraging students (to make an ass out of themselves) and "shit" on him.[198]

---

197 http://chrisstroffolino.blogspot.com/2014/08/what-can-be-learned-from-rwanda-about.html

198 http://www.youtube.com/watch?v=4YhUJLlHkek

One may ask is the merely individual triumph over obesity and Big Food in this song sustainable without community support? The tug of years of addiction is strong, and sucks so many back down. Temptations are omnipresent and the attempt to avoid them can negatively impact one's social life. And, socially, the music world is notorious for its associations with drugs, and excess. The corporate media, and baby boomer music-critic establishment, love to push the myth that drugs make you a better musician, as if there's something intrinsic in music—or what is recognized as great popular music in this society—that demands drugs.[199]

It's easy to forget in this context that music is primarily a *healing* activity if we let it be (and bad music is that which has the power to make you sick)—not that it can be sold this way in the secular mass-culture America of the last century….unless perhaps it branches off into the field of "music therapy" legitimized by training in clinical psychology that has done less to heal people than music (unofficially) can.

And I sincerely believe that there would be less tragic stories of successful famous musicians if they had been recognized as *healers* at least as much as entertainers (and, yes, some people have to heal others to heal themselves).

Gospel music recognizes the healing function ("if the music's great, God is great"), but so does hip-hop even if it has to do in different terms, and, fighting on the level of connotations, Beme's song speaks in the language of "The American Dream" pushed by the Center for Consumer Freedom, yet manages to subvert it. And such songs could be more effective tools in the propaganda battle against the pushers of obesity and diabe-

---

[199] For instance, when the movie *Ray* made much of Ray Charles' fears that getting clean off heroin would take music away from him. The media's association of music with drugs, and black people with drugs, can doubly damn a black musician in the white "cultural imaginary."

tes-inducing foods than any current non-profit campaign trying to scold people into taxing soda to battle Berman and Company. And that's one of the reasons you won't hear a song like this alongside of "I'm In Love With The Coco."

But if we can ever get the loan for the radio station, or the MFA-In-Non-Poetry going, I'd love to offer him a job in either, or both, capacities. Maybe we can make music again (and my band won't reduce him to pale white indie rock).

3.

19. If Facebook Won't Listen, Will City Hall?

A. Techquity & Restoring The Local

As we saw in Chapter one, *Culture Crash* makes a persuasive argument that the 21st century globalized economy has played, and is playing, a major role in today's cultural and economic crisis, or as Jacques Depelchin put it, "the creative side of technology is overemphasized while its destructive capacity has been growing beyond the imaginable."[200] For instance, though technology is often sold as more environmental friendly ("we can go paperless, and save trees"), it doesn't take a rocket scientist to see how the glut of computers is actually more destructive to the earth (including increasing an addiction to oil from which plastic is made).

In addition, though technology is sold as being able to "connect" people, for instance, it has contributed to the loss of primacy that local face-to-face culture once had over the national and global. One result of this is that, "today's constituencies for justice movements are almost always dispersed and diverse enough that they can hardly be gathered in one place," as William Minter puts it.[201] Furthermore, it's not an accident that this trend parallels the increasing wealth gap, the rich getting richer and poor getting poorer (as the O'Jays sang back in '75) that can be seen in municipalities across this country (to say nothing of the 'global village'). The technocracy was not the primary cause, but certainly accelerated the process.

The question arises: if tech is so interwoven into the essence of contemporary American and globalized life, and culture, can

---

[200] Jacques Depelchin, "Cabral and the Dispossession (dehumanization) of Humanity)," *No Easy Victories*, 191

[201] William Minter, "Telling No Lies is Not Easy," *No Easy Victories*, 250

we *use* tech in different ways, ways that would emphasize the local and help rebuild decimated communities? Certainly people asked the same questions of earlier technologies of 20th century modernity in what—in retrospect—is called their infancy. Commenting on the new, modern, technology of radio in the first decade of its mass cultural rise, Bertolt Brecht wrote that the problem with radio is that it is one-sided where it should be two sided, *that it doesn't organize its consumers into producers!*

Today, the same may be said about the internet. This may be hard to see—for superficially, the internet allows more two way forms of communication than the radio, yet a close examination of the kind of news and views which many individuals (non-corporate regular folks) distribute reveals that the content commonly comes from the multi-national media conglomerates (CNN, FOX, MSNBC, for instance).[202]

Yet, this can change—for not long after Bertolt Brecht wrote those comments, an interesting thing happened: radio, in America, actually did become much more of a two way medium, in terms of content control. The large networks lost—or miscalculated and ceded—control of content, as locally owned and operated media outlets become more prominent from the 1940s through the 1970s.[203] Can radio, today, contribute to a more democratic culture than what the internet has afforded us? Or are there ways to use the internet in ways that more resemble the more "two-way" form of communication that radio once

---

202 Whatever good is coming from Black Lives Matters is the exception rather than the rule, and, besides, they're working locally too.

203 See my Radio Survivor series on the history of radio for a more detailed account: http://www.radiosurvivor.com/2011/06/02/a-history-of-radio-and-content-part-ii-jukeboxes-to-top-40/ It also must be said that radio didn't go far enough to becoming truly two-way in creating an interactive people's culture, and that eventually the corporations could crush it. In fact, they did so with the help of the internet—but in retrospect, radio went much further than the internet has, and shows any sign of becoming at present.

provided? I think so, but in order to do this we must learn to rethink what it means to think, and act, locally. It certainly doesn't mean placeless.[204]

Generally, in the official reality of America's mass culture today, the local is not presented as glamorous or consequential as the national level is.[205] This can be clearly seen in dominant attitudes towards both electoral politics and the entertainment industry. It's a well-proven truism that voter turnout rates are higher during a presidential election year and lower in "off years" in which mayors and city council members are elected. It's also true that the news media devotes far more time to national (specifically presidential) politics so that most people—even among those who know something about the three branches of the federal government and the role of corporate lobbyists and the "4th estate"—don't know how their local governments work and the large impact they have on their lives. National politics may exist for the common man and woman, but the local is often consigned to the "downticket" connoisseur.

In a way, you could say that the national news media uses the national governmental issues as a smokescreen to cover, obscure, the machinations of local power, to keep our attention misdirected and diverted into an area over which we have less control, and which ultimately may have less control over us. This is an ingenuous tactic used to neutralize opposition to the soft underbelly of globalized capitalism, as seen (if seen) in its local administrators or colonizers.

Locally, Oakland hasn't seen an exciting grassroots mayoral campaign that could galvanize its population since Bobby Seale's campaign over 40 years ago. When today's seemingly lo-

---

204 Pandora may be local in my town, but it's ultimately placeless, and that's not just its problem.

205 And the national also masks the global....but we'll save that for another time.

cally-based resistance movements (such as when Occupy Wall Street became Occupy Oakland) appear to gain a kind of traction, and media attention, they usually are portrayed as not able to pierce through these layers of obfuscation, and are primarily framed as visible confrontations with armed police forces—and perhaps the mayor insofar as she's "commander and chief," but rarely are they seen engaging in tactics that challenge the city's infrastructure, the employment, housing, educational, cultural and economic policies that affect the day to day life of the citizens and contribute to a lack of social justice and equity.[206] As a result of this, no wonder many young adults (such as Laney students) don't believe that they truly have the power to "fight city hall," or even that anything could be gained from such a struggle.

On the mass cultural level, the local may have even less prestige than it does on the electoral/political level. But, as with the electoral, people grow up believing that Drake's or Taylor Swift's culture is *their* culture. They are not taught that back in the day when senior citizens were their age that they could make a decent living, and do more to contribute to the local economy as entertainers, writers or artists who operated primarily locally or regionally (the local radio DJ, for instance) without having to live in either NYC, LA (or Nashville), the centers of today's mass-culture.

Furthermore, civics classes that were once a staple of K-12 public education are rarely taught today. In today's corporate dominated climate, teachers are encouraged to teach toward the standardized test, and if they include a component of civic analysis and engagement, they are accused of not doing their job properly or, being "too radical." Yet schools themselves have—for many—lost their glamour and practicality and this is

---

[206] This doesn't mean these movements aren't doing precisely that, but BLM's call for more structural changes in the city government, for the most part, is simply unreported.

because mass-culture reaches kids before school does, and has created a sense of glamour and consequence by which schools inevitably fail.

In order to change this, we probably have to act both nationally and locally and make demands or negotiate with our local congressman as much as the mayor. Otherwise, "act locally" becomes an empty term. As teachers, we can at least act by thinking....as long as we're thinking out loud, in the classroom, with our students to combat the disenfranchising miseducation mass culture encourages. This becomes especially urgent given a city in the midst of a cold civil war.

B. Beyond Placelessness: Or, Searching For Common Ground Amid The Culture Wars

Today, we're told that Oakland is entering a new era, as we're witnessing a rapid—if not exactly revolutionary—transformation in Oakland's real estate economy (which some refer to as a "boom"). Of course, there's a debate: is it better? Is it worse? Or some of both? Is the recent development throwing out the baby with the bathwater or, even worse, throwing out the baby and *replacing it with more bathwater?*[207] Indeed, there's a range of

---

207 Gentrification: Jerry Brown called it "Elegant Density," said it would make Oakland more like New York (how much time have he and mentee Schaaf spent in NYC?) I must make sure that my fight against what I call gentrification is not tangled in what they call my "New York snobbery." Certainly gentrification isn't going to make Oakland more like what I love and miss about NYC (circa 2000, coz yes it's accelerated there since I left too, though it must be a little slower there because the old street culture is more firmly rooted, the infrastructure less decimated, and it's still got its walking city which died before it got to take hold here?). In fact, a strong argument could be made that *gentrification is making Oakland even less like what was good about NYC (night life, for instance), less "elegant"* (if that's a positive word, and I like the alliteration of "the glamour and the grunge),

opinions from those who argue in rational tones of fiscal policy in the form of pro-development and anti-union fiscal hawks to those who argue in more impassioned terms of civic responsibility and human rights. Yet, amid all the talk of economic boom, Oakland has been steadily losing its middle class, its diversity—especially its black community—and even its culture. Yet the city still has a chance to begin to remedy this situation.

On a cultural level, long-standing less professional Oakland traditions (from BBQ around Lake Merritt to Choir practices at the Pleasant Grove Baptist Church) are under siege by new city bans and many of the new residents lured to the city by its rising rents and displacement of residents, residents for whom culture is primarily pricey restaurants. The culture clashes and economic clashes reveal a city profoundly undergoing an identity crisis, or even a civil war.

Can the pro-development forces and the anti-gentrification movement find common ground to create a world in which gentrification doesn't have to equal displacement and an increase in the wealth gap. I think so, so let's put these differences aside for a second—bracket them, suspend them—and imagine that everybody who lives in Oakland has at least one thing in common: *we love Oakland, we at least value Oakland*. We all want to see Oakland's economy and culture grow. In this light, it's important to revisit more closely the debate over resurrecting the Kaiser Convention Center's Calvin Simmons theatre—once a hub of Oakland culture—as a viable performance space.

According to the city's RFP, any proposal for what to do with this space should include "as many community benefits as possible" including "local and small business participation, commitment to living and prevailing wages, commitment to labor peace and opportunities for job training and mentoring, a high

---

less "cosmopolitan" which means the same as words like "diverse" or "multi-cultural" more beloved among the Bay Ayrians....

number of jobs created for a range of training and educational levels, and a provision of high quality public facilities and amenities." (Oakland Post, July 1-7, 2015).

In short, these guidelines seem straightforward in recognizing the need for a true center to Oakland culture.[208] A problem, however, arises when high-paid lawyers have been at work on a twisted interpretation of these words that resemble Orwellian double-speak in their ingenuity. We're told that the Orton proposal for use of the space is in accord with what these city RFP zoning guidelines demand to create a "multi-floor rehab combining office, flex, public access and food uses." Notice how "high quality public facilities and amenities" is transformed into mere "public access and food uses." The *facilities* won't necessarily be public, just the access. This sounds more like a store, or a hallway lined with stores and offices (and, reportedly, a brewery). It's clear that this proposal would "transform the majority of the interior of this building into offices for private business." In short, this empty public space will become a privatized shell of its former public/civic cultural glory.

By contrast, an alternative proposal from Creative Development Partners shows more understanding of the original intent of the city's zoning guidelines in ways that would better contribute to *the entirety* of Oakland's culture and economy: "The CDP proposal is built around community benefits, including creating 1,700 jobs and a career training program in partnership with Laney and Merritt College for jobs in hospitality, culinary arts, creative arts and landscaping, as well as a partnership with OUSD's Linked Learning proposal." This proposal, which "envisions the building as a hub for local music, cultural and performing art companies to use as a rehearsal and performance

---

208 I do recognize in the phrase "living and prevailing wages" the same kind of loophole-creating dissembling one may see in more famous legal phrases like "with all deliberate speed," but otherwise its message is very clear

space," clearly betters the Orton plan in its adherence to the *spirit* as well as the *letter* of the city's RFP, as well as the slogan inscribed on the building.[209]

The CDP plan to draw talent and "content providers" from the students of the state- funded community college across the street from it is a win-win situation for not only the city (and the developer who has found a way to make it turn a profit), but also would help Laney College successfully fulfill the hope of its mission statement (or ILO)[210] of community service and vocational training. Despite being underfunded by the state (and in the midst of an accreditation battle), Laney College is one of the few cultural institutions in Oakland that understands the meaning of the word "community." Nationally known not only for its "world class theatre program at community college prices," as Michael Torres proudly claims, but also its culinary, cosmetology, and construction program, Laney provides a pool of talent that is woefully underutilized by the city of Oakland to the detriment of both. And it is to the credit of the creative ingenuity of Randolph Belle and the CDP team that they have recognized how this can help create a better Oakland in which gentrification doesn't have to equal displacement and an increase in the wealth-gap.

Once again, however, the city has seemed to miss its opportunity, as they've all but broken ground on the Orton proposal.[211] But if it's too late to save the Kaiser Convention Center from the plutocrat's privatizing plans, it must be understood that this empty arena serves as a symbol of a larger vacuum left by the de-funding of Oakland's old infrastructure, but also of

---

209   *"AUDITORIUM OF THE CITY OF OAKLAND DEDICATED BY THE CITIZENS TO THE INTELLECTUAL AND INDUSTRIAL PROGRESS OF THE PEOPLE"* (1914).

210   Institutional Learning Outcome

211   http://postnewsgroup.com/blog/2015/07/27/city-asks-orton-development-rehabilitate-kaiser-convention-center/

the hope that we may yet regain what was good about the old Oakland. Beyond merely being a gesture of civic pride, an initiative like the CDP plan can both serve the need of consumers as well as those who value *"labor peace"* by providing high-quality locally-based affordable culture (arts and entertainment in the broadest sense of the words) that could foster a much needed alternative to the mass-cultural mediocrity that has colonized Oakland (The McDonalds-like culture of Hollywood whose business-as-usual is to rob from Oakland's economy and communities on a daily basis).

Oakland's got talent, and many people (human resources) who are willing and eager to work here, who would *prefer* to stay here and give back to the community rather than resigning themselves to be part of the brain-drain exodus of innovative creative sensibilities to LA or NYC, for instance. These people, however, need incentives to stay here and currently this city is not providing them. It's not even on any legislative agenda, in any way beyond such lip-service as the mayor's toothless "Made In Oakland" campaign promise.

Given the economic crisis and heightened cultural conflict in Oakland, "Made In Oakland," sounds like a great idea, but her policies have clearly fallen short of this slogan.[212] When it comes to Oakland culture, she perpetuates the policies of outsourcing that drain Oakland's economy, and fail to utilize the talents, and serve the needs, of the vast majority of people who live here. For the Mayoral administration, and others in position of cultural authority, Oakland Culture—at least when it comes to the arts and entertainment (its professional sports teams are outside the scope of this essay), means venues such as the Fox Theatre, which mostly features national acts at the expense of Oakland residents.

---

[212] Just as they fail to measure up to another recent corporate-sponsored slogan associated with Oakland, "strength in numbers."

Even such "local" 21st century success stories as Pandora—as locally-based cultural content providers—merely march to the tune or beat set by Hollywood, et al, to become glorified "distributors" compared to, say, 50 years ago when, only a block away from where Pandora's corporate headquarters now stands, Oakland's KDIA radio station, while not strictly locally owned, at least broke local artists and employed local celebrity "content providers" like DJ Roscoe who helped make—and not merely reflect—national trends, in less of a "one way street" way.

C. Schaaf's "Black Arts District" & The Role Of Locally Owned Media

In February of 2015, the mayor symbolically declared a long stretch on 14th Street in downtown Oakland as a "Black Arts Movement and Business District."[213] This could be an amazingly positive wealth-generating win/win initiative that could benefit *all* of Oakland did this gesture have any practical teeth (dedicated funding, institutional oversight); it could help restore some of the local cultural self-determination that Oakland's black community lost after the systematic destruction of the 7th street entertainment and business district a half-century ago. After all, Oakland's culture, which has largely been a black culture, is a legacy every new resident who calls Oakland her home should be proud of, or at the very least curious about. But it's generally been swept under the rug, or never considered seriously as part of a comprehensive practical solution to Oakland's ills (which some—a very powerful minority—of course don't see as ills). What—beyond empty words—could a possible Black Arts District look like?

Marvin X. Jackmon, and company, have brilliant ideas, and

---

213 It was formally recognized by City Council a year later in January 2016

we need to encourage such homegrown innovative creativity that doesn't originate from big tech's think tanks and big real estate's boardrooms, but rather from "the academy of the corner" to create a *cultural export* that could help Oakland's economy. In considering such possibilities, the tech companies are of course welcome to contribute to the discussion as long as they don't dominate it, and deny the central importance of a grass-roots (worker owned or at least operated) entertainment venue and arts center that is clearly rooted in the local, from the ground up (we already have enough trickle-down cultural and economic initiative, and look where that's gotten us).

One example I should mention before closing is the role of radio—good old fashioned terrestrial broadcast radio—in helping to create this.[214]Although Pandora and other Oakland Corporate Tech Firms tell us the days of radio are largely a thing of the past, and not a worthwhile arena for the expenditure of venture capital (or even cultural capital), the fact that the most powerful international media conglomerates currently cling tightly to their ownership of the three (3) radio stations licensed by the FCC to be broadcast from Oakland shows that radio still has a power, and that that power—in its current form—serves a particular agenda, an agenda that, no matter how you slice it, is resolutely anti-Oakland culture.

Some argue that national and international culture clearly offers a much more exciting, wider array of options than limiting ourselves to emphasizing culture made here in Oakland, yet surveying the corporate culture currently being imported into,

---

214 Charles Hamilton, Stokely Carmichael's collaboration on the Black Power manifesto, wrote:
"For blacks to gain control of a significant portion of the electronic media would be the most important single breakthrough in the black struggle, and would justify every bit of time, talent and resources expended toward its achievement." (1971, "Blacks And Mass Media")

and colonizing, Oakland, I believe we should at least consider that this statement is not a self-evident truth. Again, Oakland's got a wealth of talent; it's the venues for it that are lacking.[215] And, in an era in which the city is in a mad rush to sell off its assets to private developers, we may have to struggle even harder for our cries for more of these civic venues to be heard.

The fact that corporate conglomerates have systematically hurt Oakland's culture and economy through their control of the programming of these radio stations is barely a blip on the radar on most people's thinking of how to improve Oakland; this is due to purposeful miseducation (For instance, how many Oaklanders today even know about former mayor Elihu Harris's valiant, if ultimately failed, attempt, to keep Oakland's radio programming local? How many even know Oakland *has* a radio station?). But, with concerted effort, we could remake these broadcast outlets into a positive good for anybody who truly values the "Made In Oakland" slogan.

It also goes largely unsaid that these corporate owners of Oakland's airwaves are actively violating FCC regulations that demand that programming must originate in the city to which they're licensed, and must serve the public interest of the community in which they are located. This illegal corporate maneuvering has become standard operating procedure across the country as these regulations are not enforced (thanks to the lobbyists' revolving door, for instance), a form of taxation without representation people feel helpless to fight against when there's so many seemingly more immediate problems (racial profiling, police brutality, to name but two). Yet, at root, the corporate control of radio, gentrification and the PIC are part of the same phenomenon.

I don't have to be so fatalistic to agree with those who say,

---

215 As I'm sure Malik and Khafre of Hip Hop For Change would agree with if they weren't too busy working their buts off to ameliorate the situation.

"you can't fight city hall" to agree with those who argue "it's much harder to fight Clearchannel and Disney who in many ways have more power than City Hall." I'd like to hold out some hope that City Hall, in fact, could be persuaded to become our ally in the fight against Clearchannel, et al.

Our demands our simple: the city should help provide economic incentives, and remove economic obstacles, for a team of locally-based culture workers and investors to buy (or at least manage) at least one of these radio stations from the corporate behemoths on the condition that this station will be part of a job training and job creation program for the citizens of Oakland. Ideally, this would be a commercially self-sustaining station that would mandate advertising rates that are affordable enough so that locally-based small businesses in Oakland could advertise (we don't need Geico and Chevron to survive, and I would not be adverse to forbidding such entities to advertise on this station).

Ideally, there would also be one non-commercial station (not merely an LPFM station like the Peralta School District's 96.7FM, that doesn't even reach all of Oakland, but more like San Francisco's listener-supported KPOO 89.5) that would serve underserved populations, emphasizing educational programming (again, in the broadest sense of the word), working closely with Oakland public schools, trade schools and colleges and the diversity of Oakland's musicians and artists: a true working class (and world class) radio station. Of course, these stations should have a "world wide" internet component, but they would be clearly connected to a place, a venue, a locally run art and entertainment center (even if this can't happen on the site of the former Kaiser Convention Center)—either in the "Arts District" or in the so-called "Black Arts District."

Whether you work for Pandora or are an (ex-)Black Panther, think about what would happen if we got even *one* radio station; *every faction (or demographic niche) could be heard*: There's room for everybody. But unlike the Web, with its alleged democracy, such eclecticism can bring more people together through the radio, first and foremost because of the of the local emphasis and secondly because the mere finite number of radio stations render each more meaningful. The essential connection with a place gives it an added purpose if we compare it to Pandora—a purpose based in a commonality of locale, to help create a better Oakland, to provide more opportunities for Oakland listeners, musicians, and other culture producers and content providers. It can allow the various communities (and "individuals") to air out the conflicts—even in a danceable way—and find some unity in diversity against a common enemy—to go beyond the war between those taking over and those they're driving out. What we create locally—if given a chance—can be at least as good as what is imported, or imposed, from without. Say it like a mantra—and radio is a perfect vehicle for that....

In Conclusion....

This admittedly broad outline could at least be a discussion starter. I believe that such a plan for an Oakland Auditorium/Radio Station, in working closely with OUSD, could, in the long term, decrease drop-out rates, by giving hope to the disenfranchised that education truly means something as well as serve the public need for a new cultural hub that could do much to revitalize Oakland culture so that it may rival the current culture we too often import from Hollywood or NYC at Oakland's expense. This could help reduce poverty, crime, joblessness, and the general disenfranchisement that is epidemic in this city (I'd even argue that—in the long term—it could even have more positive effects in reducing hypertension, depression, and obesity than in the quick fixes Kaiser Permanente and other HMOS push).

And, yes, I understand that Oakland's City Council and the Mayor's office could only do so much against the corporations—and that we need to work on many fronts—for any plan would be likely to take the form of a "public/private partnership" at first in order to have a chance of getting off the ground—on city, country, state and federal levels (it shouldn't be too difficult to get Oakland congresswoman Barbara Lee's ear with a well-developed proposal), but if the city can use what muscle it does have to advocate for this—rather than blocking or turning a blind eye to it—we can promise you this, we got your back! And if the city can't help this become a reality, we'll find others who can; in a city of over 60% renters, we do, after all, have the power to vote you out of office—at least until you drive even more of us out of here. So, this is a matter of some urgency; the time for action is now!

Works Cited:

https://oakulture.wordpress.com/2015/07/28/as-development-boom-bubbles-oaklands-arts-scene-increasingly-troubled/

http://www.insidebayarea.com/breaking-news/ci_28533280/artists-angered-developers-challenge-oaklands-public-art-requirement

http://www.bizjournals.com/sanfrancisco/blog/real-estate/2015/07/oakland-kaiser-convention-center-orton-crowdfund.html

20. The New 7th Street

It is the false question of integration that, not at all paradoxically, has set the white and black communities more than ever at division......and, with that one word, (whites) smashed every Black institution in this country, with the single exception of the Black Church......Integration was never considered a two-way street. Blacks went downtown, but whites did not come uptown. This helped Black restaurants, in Atlanta, for example, to go bankrupt."
James Baldwin, Evidence of Things Unseen (pg. 22-25), 1985

When I read the story of 7th Street,[216]
I remember what Cynthia Ohene—
The one black woman in my creative writing class—
Sad, back in 2004 (before a white
Student guy got all riled up, and shouted:
what does this have to do with poetry)
that blew my mind, and made me question
my inherited assumptions & habitual beliefs:
that segregation—
if compared to today's so-called integration—
may have actually helped black businesses grow....[217]

---

216 http://www.foundsf.org/index.php?title=The_Rise_and_Fall_of_Seventh_Street_in_Oaklandhttp://www.foundsf.org/index.php?title=The_Rise_and_Fall_of_Seventh_Street_in_Oakland

217 **Close Reading Civic Poetry III (an excerpt)** Oakland is in the midst of a Cold Civil War between the majority of the people who live here and the people the real-estate developers promise to lure here. City officials have thus far tried to smooth over the conflict between the two sides by seeming to side with both and downplaying any conflict of interest. On one hand, the city declared the "14th Street corridor" a Black Arts Movement and Business district. The mission and vision of this district is music to my ears. In fact, we could *line it as poetry*, and call it a "found text" (like the kind of "dry text" Kenny G., for instance, would love to "massage"):

The law forbidding black musicians
from playing at white clubs
made more whites go to the black owned ones
before the rot of TV set in
with Brown v. The Board of Education

& when I read the story
of the premature demise of 7th street,
I know for a fact that Oakland
would be a better place today,
and the future could be brighter
for all its citizens
than any techies and developers provide,[218]

The creation of this district
also sets the stage
for bringing resources
and government support
to preserve existing institutions
and support a new generation
of Black Artists and culture makers...
Official designation by Oakland....
creates a means for funneling arts
and culture grants to the Black community."
"We're also looking to adopt a public lands policy,"
said Council Woman Lynette McElhaney. (*Oakland Post*, Jan 13-19, 2016).

The "poet" side of me wants to say, "funnel, baby, funnel!"

218   On the other (and bigger) hand, the city is selling off this land in the heart of the Black Arts District to developers such as Bay Developers and Wood Partners. When asked about the absence of affordable housing and other community benefits in the apartment complex she proposes to construct smack dab in the heart of the Black Arts District, Maria Poncel of the Bay Development Group, replied:

"This actually fulfills the goal of safer streets and activates the ground

> if 7th street would have had a chance
> to grow, would not have been nipped

floor [with retail stores]." Similarly, Brian Pianca of Wood Partners argues. "We're providing housing, greater safety along the street. We don't have a community benefit as some may define it, but that activity is the benefit." *Both safer and more activated!* It almost sounds too good to be true. I also have to admire Pianca's rhetorical brilliance in redefining "community benefit."

Safety is a selling point. We all want safer streets, right? But do higher rents cause more safety? Who would these neighborhoods be safer for? Would it be safer for the vendors of the black arts district? Or is "safer" code for whiter, a rhetorical sleight of hand that had been perfected during the era of white flight (from the 50s through the 70s)?

Perhaps Ponce's most striking use of language is when she waxes poetic about *activating the ground floor* she calls the street (or sidewalk). Don't we all want our ground floor activated? I'm sure the young black folks peaceably congregating on the sidewalk outside the 15th Street galleries—with a bass guitar, drums, dancing and a microphone open to anyone who wants to try out a rap—are working to activate that ground floor, and make the neighborhood safer, and doing a good job at it until the curfew police clears them out to make more room for the kind of "activation" we see at other recent *non-affordable housing* developments. Or is it true that high—priced restaurants are the only way to truly *activate* the neighborhood (in the spirit of what Jerry Brown called "elegant density") because, of course, the people who can afford those rents would never want to be caught dead eating any great healthy meal if it's too cheap?

Here, we see, in stark contrast, the conflict of interest that our city officials are charged with adjudicating, yet the government once again shows that in any conflict of interest between these two sides, they will side with the minority (the developers) over the vast majority. Councilwoman McElhaney, for instance, is "worried" or "concerned" that imposing "impact fees" on these developers could "deter more developers" from coming to Oakland. I try to put myself in McElhaney's shoes, especially since she is a loud champion of the BAM district (and has argued that it means nothing without dedicated funding and a public lands policy), and thus has some populist cred.

in the bud by development...
and renewal...
Did they need the WW2 economy
Historians say
7th street was already in decline by 1960
(and such decline explains the need for the Panthers)
but its ghosts still haunt this city
what could have been? what could be today?

A black arts district[219]

---

219 Yet, McElhaney's statement reveals who's in control, and can translate to: *We can't fight the developers, but must do their whim!* Are the developers' feelings that fragile? Do they need to be "babied," or handled with "kid gloves?" Do they really need more wealth gap? One can understand why some have claimed the city suffers from a kind of "battered wife syndrome" (though that term trivializes battered wives) even as their actions scream "I am loyal....to the developers, and the failed (or very successful, wink, wink) policies of the scions of trickle down economics." (as an anarchist I know puts it, "she's afraid they'll kill, or otherwise, destroy her").

But what if elected officials stopped trying to sell the city cheap, and realized that it can take or leave any of these developers' proposals, that these developers may *act* coy, but really want something you got more than you need what they got. Call their bluff. I ask councilwoman McElhaney, what do you really have to lose by prioritizing non-profit developers, or acting as if public land is intended for the public good? What if the city actually realized this BAMBD could be a selling point that could help lure community-minded residents (some of whom may currently be homeless) who have a stake in sustaining and creating a vibrant Oakland culture and economy?

Can a common ground be found? Can the developers truly be good neighbors and co-exist with the Black Arts and Business District? In order for this to be a reality, we must first compel these developers to formally acknowledge its existence. To the end, this city must, at the very least:

Publicize the Black Arts District widely as a site of community   re-

Can we stop them from unmaking it
long enough so we can make it?

Give Qilombo funds, and I'd advertise it
and give my students at Laney extra credit
if they could advertise it, or propose their own.

We could go on a field trip and distribute fliers
in the tech districts (we don't have to go far
as they are surrounding us)
just like Hip hop for Change canvassers
to help this arts and business district thrive
and by extension Oakland itself[220]

---

juvenation, just as the developers brag and advertise about the Koreatown/Northgate (Kono) neighborhood (a designation that largely ignores the Muslim community in that corridor.

Let the developers, and the future tenants of these buildings know they are moving into a Black Arts District (if they want a white arts district they got more than enough other neighborhoods, most notably that Uptown neighborhood anchored by the Fox Theatre) so that they won't be shocked into calling the police when confronted by neighbors who are (sometimes) loud.

Show how this Black Arts District could help all of Oakland by creating a cultural export that would benefit all residents of Oakland.

Let a thriving, supported, Black Arts district, compete on equal footing with the boutique store with its $500 jeans that brag about being made by prison labor (Perhaps the art sold at the BAMBD would be made by prison labor too, but the middleman would be cut out; all proceeds of those sales will be put in an account that the incarcerated can use to dig his or her way out of the money she owes this privatized prison for her "hospitality").

220   It may not be too late to demand that the developers help *activate* these ground floors in conjunction with the more democratic steering committee of the Black Arts Movement district, that some-

by creating a cultural export
that would put Oakland on the map
to counter its negative publicity
as the city with the fastest rising rent prices since 2010
accompanied by an increase in crime & homelessness
to counter its negative reputation
as a city whose culture is dominated by Hollywood occupiers
and their Pandora proxy states.[221]

---

how these developers can see that their interests can be better served by working with BAM rather than trying to ignore it, pave it over, and cover up its murals, for the Black Arts district could help create entertainment that even the white residents of these luxury (I mean "market rate") towers will wish to see, hear and partake in, and not out of any sense of charity. Since Councilwoman McElhaney is largely responsible for heightening the conflict, by pitting these two opposed interests against each other in promising them the same land, she should be at the forefront of bringing these two factions to the negotiating table *on equal footing*.

I'll leave it to Donte James and the Department of Race and Equity to determine whether the city's decision to grant the developers *carte blanche* is yet another proof of ongoing systemic racial disparities, but it is a question every city official should be asked (and clearly it has class and cultural dimensions).

221   http://postnewsgroup.com/blog/2016/01/21/fight-gentrification-qilombos-upcoming-art-gallery/

21. Appeal to Musicians
(for shane frink)

I'm still enough of a "punk"
To be skeptical of the cloying Mr. Moral Highground
I fear my recent essays have become…

Very rarely is any appeal successful persuasion
Unless we appeal to others' self-interest.

In this case, I wanna appeal to the musicians and dancers
Who don't give a shit about politics
Who, even if they did, don't have any time
to do anything about it
(except maybe sing a song like
Reaganomics killing me, killing you, killing me, killing you)
Who just wanna rock—or make beats
Or make art music for galleries or schools
Or calming ballads and tear jerkers
Who are artists and entertainers, dammit!
Just trying to get gigs and not lose too much money
As a vocation demoted to a vacation in the hobby lobby….[222]

---

[222] Say, you're in a band, musical ensemble or other art-project in which the whole is greater than the sum of its parts, and you're going to have to break up due to what the press may call "musical differences," which, in your case, means: two core members are being priced out and have found a more clear path to "getting back on their feet" in cheaper cities that have more vital music scenes thousands of miles away. Your little group is a victim of gentrification and those who remain are going to have to make a living as a session musician or side-person in a touring band which may not be as creatively fulfilling or as easy to put your soul into as that local band where you could live close enough to each other to woodshed with a less-transient plan for a longer term project. So you take the show on the road, even though you never really believed in the myth of "adventure" so many 20-somethings may adhere to ("living the dream, dude").

> How much time do you waste
>> Trying to get gigs—looking for new places
>> After the old ones get shut down
>> Trying to make it on the Pandora stream
>> On a Sisyphusian uphill battle
>> Against the corporate musicians
>> Paying too much rent for rehearsal spaces you can't
> sleep in
>> Reinventing the wheel?[223]

For you, that "adventure" myth is an outgrowth or extension of the old-fashioned quintessentially "American" pioneering spirit you saw more from the perspective of the trail of tears and those whose heroes have always (killed) cowboys. But you got a few hungry mouths to feed so (despite your misgivings), off you go, to Winnepeg in a Winnebago, and in a Montana snowstorm on the way back, it flips over

---

223 So when you heal from the broken bones if not the trauma of your drummer's death, you may find yourself with this crazy notion of a package tour on a boat down the Mississippi River (from Minneapolis to New Orleans), or a cross-country train tour (co-sponsored by Amtrak) because you believe in "Strength in numbers." Musicians could bring their kids on this boat or train (and then, later, you could do Euro-Rail, or Africa-Rail, or a cruise that performs at every Mediterranean dock it stops at). Your musician friends like this idea, but you haven't been able to convince a venture capitalist. Soon the record stores that stocked your music are gone, and the college radio station that played your music illegally sold to a corporation (RIP KUSF)

In the meantime, you're searching for a way that you could sustain yourself (plural) as musicians right here in your hometown with its major league baseball, football and basketball teams. If the city can support these teams, certainly it could support a cultural entertainment/arts center, and locally-owned radio station. Or, failing this, you could do what so many other musicians in the 21st century are doing: learn Protools!! Learn how to program beats, the musical

You're basically already donating your time
Doing volunteer work, selling yourself short
On a dead end street, right?

Every musical group
Usually has at least one person
Who's responsible for getting gigs
(some of the best musicians suck at this
and I know some bands who purposely don't fire
their weak link because he earns his keep getting the gigs)

and they would increase their *visibility*
by working with, or you could say "adopting"
a local non-profit to be a house band for,
to write a theme song for
whether #BlackLivesMatter

---

equivalent of coding! Become a one-man band, or a quiet microband that doesn't have to worry about offending the new gentrified residents who like to make noise complaints but love the loud bomb sounds of gaming....

And you may find that just about every other musician—who never bought into the ageist youth culture mandate to hang it up by your 30s (unless you can afford "pay to play")—struggling with something similar—the money you make doesn't even pay for a regular access to a rehearsal space or studio time or even new gear. A corporate conscience gnaws in your ear, "that's coz you suck!" and you try to drown it out, and at one glorious "breakup show" blow your amps pumping up the volume to drown out the voice of these naysayers! "Take that!" it was an amazing warehouse party. Hell, even the cops who showed up couldn't resist dancing, though their bosses demanded they enforce the "you suck" ordinance, and another warehouse space bites the dust....and another amazing bassist is incarcerated while Justin Bieber gets off for posing a far greater danger to others in his expensive murder weapon called a car....

The #OaklandCreativeNeighborhoodsCoalition
Or other housing jobs and education activists.[224]
These other activists are all

---

[224] Meanwhile, a local reopened mid-sized Art-deco theatre touted by the Mayor, City Council and the Chamber of Commerce, as a glorious indication, a beacon or a shiny "point of light" of a newly *revitalized* city (as if that somehow justifies their pro-inflationary real-estate policies they call "growth" when the only thing growing you can see is the wealth gap) brings in mostly "famous" niche acts who are not from this town to drain cash from this city; this theatre is a kind of gated community that, except in rare cases, is *forboten* to local talent. And, you listen as the city culture's tzars say they choose to do so because of consumer demand: "more people *want* these outsider touring bands! There's simply not enough *demand* for local musicians."

And these culture tzars sound like a broken record, a record as broken as the long-disappeared locally managed (if not quite owned) commercial R&B radio station was, a record as broken as all those local "ma and pa" record labels, shops and stages up and down San Pablo in the 60s are, as broken as Tupac Shakur (who had to leave Oakland to make enough money to continue to be able to make music) if not Too $hort who also had to leave Oakland to make it...

And it may occur to you that there's a burning need for a "Buy Local" campaign that goes far beyond those "Support Your Local Musicians" bumper-stickers or fortune-cookies you often find near the Charity Hospital. Ah, charity, and often the phrase "Support Your Local Musicians" smells like Charity spirit, stinks up the joint, as if it's telling the listeners and consumers, *"go out of your way, lower your standards. It's for a good cause! (we all know The Coup can't really get you dancing and speak to your soul as much as, say, Drake).* But you want to defend the artists who don't want, or need, to become national *superstars*, but would honored to be "one hit wonders" or "cult artists" or funk brother session sisters, and who knows that music is generally more healthy in small venues....and, if you were mayor, or city council, you'd offer incentives to keep musicians here rather than becoming "too big for Oakland."

Fighting for things that impact you directly
(what good is being able to get gigs
or your quarterly checks from Warners for 52 cents
if you've been priced out of the city?)

The activists may need to be persuaded
That you, musicians, would be giving them
Even more than they'd be giving you.
But, yes, activists, if you need
To get 30,000 signatures
To place a rent-control initiative on the ballot,
Holding a dance party will be a more efficient way
To get these signatures
And maybe even galvanize a movement
In a spirit of unity and diversity—

22. Inside Oakland's Art (& Housing) Crisis: A Dialogue

"There is no institutional understanding that the arts are an economic engine for the city, they are not just a cynical lure to make a neighborhood pretty to attract outside investors," Pamela Mays McDonald, Oakland Creative Neighborhoods Coalition and External Affairs Chair for Oakland Art Murmur[225]

D: Did you know that Oakland recently received an NEA grant for the purpose of creating a cultural plan to preserve our art? I sure didn't....

B: It's probably a tiny bit of money, and won't do any of us any good.

D: You're such a cynic. But at least it shows they recognize that art has value...

B: But what do they mean by "art?" Do they mean only painters with an easel, or the arts in the broadest sense? Does it include musicians?

D: The article doesn't say. Nor does it say if it will include poets and writers. We don't even have a good locally based press...

B: They probably call that "culture" instead of art...

D: And they probably call musicians "entertainment" instead of art...

---

[225] http://theregistrybayarea.com/will-oakland-lose-its-artistic-soul/

B: They certainly don't consider outdoor BBQs in public parks "art"

D: But theoretically, in a democracy we can *be part of* the discussion. After all, they declared 14th St. The Black Arts and Business District, and the Black Arts Movement's all about art in the widest sense of the word (including music, poetry, and activism). Certainly, that's a good sign!"

B: But that's *all* it is....signage! Beneath those signs, Wood Partners and the Bay Development group (to name but two) are building condos that are diametrically opposed to the intent and work of this district.[226]

D: Well, at least the mayor shows up at parades with a big smile in her *Art Snail!*

B: She moves so slow, a snail is a greyhound by comparison. She won't even resurrect the Oakland Arts Commission until she appoints a Cultural Affairs Manager! She offers no timeline, but says "work is underway."

D: She's been listening to those outside consultants from Bloomberg who are forming a working group—get this—to study *Oakland's art ecosystem!*

B: They're studying us?? Smells like colonization to me. Why doesn't she just ask the artists, the musicians, the stand-up comics, those who need cheap and convenient culture, those with a sense of civic pride and a day to day stake in improving the city, but are thwarted?

---

[226] See Chapter 20

D: Judging by City Hall's actions, it seems they don't *want* to support arts.

B: Can it be possible that the majority of people who voted for her—her base in the Oakland hills may even be *afraid* of the arts?

D: you never *hear* anybody boldly claiming *Don't Fund The Arts*....but I know when I talk to other low-income folks who don't see themselves as artists that funding the arts is a much lower priority than creating and sustaining affordable housing....It's a little hard to rally the lumpen behind the cause of "art."

B: I understand their resentment, maybe it's not worth it to fight for "art"—for if we can take care of providing affordable housing, it will take care of art.

D: Or we can convince these "non-artists" that the two issues are the same, that supporting the arts will actually create more jobs for them and more affordable housing much more than wasting tax-dollars on a Bloomberg working group, task force think tank. Besides, a lot of these "non-artists" are really artists, and have more of a stake in local art than they might think... We have to take back the word "art" from the rich! (not that they can't have it too!)

B: So what should we do? Show up outside city hall with placards that blare: WHAT ARE YOU DOING WITH THAT NEA MONEY?

D: Why not? But if we're visual artists, we gotta make those placards pretty, at least as pretty as graffiti, or murals from the Community Rejuvenation Project?

B: It may be more important to blanket Facebook, Instagram and Twitter to catchy memes.

D: That's what they want us to think—that *that* has more power—to keep us more divided, but, sure, we could work that front too…

B: Maybe the poets will join us, and write a poem called "HOW ARE YOU SPENDING THE NEA MONEY?"

D: Maybe, but knowing the poetry world, it will take a few years to get published anywhere people see it, and it will be accused of being outdated by then….or the poem would get rejected for being too "strident."

B: That could be where we musicians come in, put that phrase to beats. After we record it, we can get in cars and bikes and blast it around town….hold a dance party in San Antonio Park….a contest for dance songs on this theme open to any resident of Oakland (and those recently priced-out). Dance songs bring people together! All songs are welcome. Imagine the industry that will result, the activated ground floors, and streets. Recording time will be donated. Visual artists and dancers will be enlisted. This could be funded by the NEA grant!

D: That's circular logic. You can't promise to pay people with the money you don't have yet.

B: The city, state, and federal government do that all the time! Okay, maybe it's better not to worry about money yet—that always stops any innovative thinking even before it gets a chance to start….We don't need money if we can work with students and those artists and activists who are already fighting for this cause, and who have already brought some people together. We just have to convince them that we can *give* them something with our art if they help create contexts for it....

D: Makes sense to me. Hiroko Kurihara, from Mayor Schaaf's Artist Affordable Housing and Workplace task force, might be someone to try to work with. I like the way she talks.

B: I didn't even know the mayor had an Artist Affordable Housing and Workplace task force! That sounds like a joke.... it gives me an idea for another song, *We are the Artist Affordable Housing And Task Force,*" (trying to sing it to the tune of "We are the Village Green Preservation Society"); we could create an ad hoc band named that!

D: But listen to what she says, she wants to create "a city-wide cultural district that would try to reap funding from the statewide California Arts Commission budget. That way, Oakland's art community won't be divided. There's a little pot of money, and then all these competing interests end up squabbling over scraps. We can't really do that if we're gonna really try to coalesce, and build a cultural arts-based community."

B: Well, it *sounds* better than anything coming out of the mayor's mouth. I like her broad vision. She seems to get the spirit of "unity in diversity" I'm talking about. I like what she says about stopping "squabbling over scraps," but it's easier said than done.

D: Not if there's strength in numbers, and by working together on a "city-wide level" we are able to bring more money in.... from both the state and the federal governments.

B: But the city has this terrible policy of sending back funds unused....

D: Or squandering them on consultants, working groups and task forces

B: Apparently, the city leaders don't even know that every empire has fallen when the bureaucratic class takes over and the creative class falls by the wayside... Anyway, Kurihara is just talking about government funding. We should be able to get money for the arts (including affordable housing for artists and non-artists who need art) from other sources......like, say, Big Tech

D: Big Tech, you've got to be kidding!

B: Well, Pandora's here, at the intersection of Big Tech and Music, right smack dab in the middle of Oakland, only a block away from where the great radio station KDIA used to be....

D: Pandora certainly shows no interest in cultivating and re-elevating a sustainable local music economy. Sad, because you think they'd be a natural ally, that they'd see how they'd benefit by forging strong connections with local Oakland music and art scenes to help brand a marketable, yet eclectic, Oakland cultural identity as a cultural export...

B: Maybe we should hold our demonstrations in front of their office. If you can't fight City Hall maybe you can convince big tech. And if Pandora doesn't come on board, maybe Uber could require its drivers play music from one of Uber's Local music channels (the passenger could choose from a wide variety of genres)...Certainly some of these techie hipsters must like to go to art galleries, read and dance...

D: They're probably into that Burning-Man "ecstatic dance" kind of stuff, and certainly wouldn't be down with helping to fund Hip Hop For Change….with no strings attached…"

B: Perhaps, but we can appeal to a sense of civic pride for *all* of Oakland, not just them. If we don't want to squabble over scraps, we can't let musical taste get in the way. This is what unity in diversity means. Yes, there's this nagging civil war over the soul of Oakland, and yes they may hate our culture…

D: And we may hate theirs

B: I don't hate it, I just don't *see* it. Their culture's like a giant *eraser*….made of *food* (and nothing but food)—-but even with this culture clash, or culture crash, we could still find common ground: *if nothing else, we all live here!* And if we can join forces, there will be more room for both *their* culture and *our culture*. All we have to do is convince them to value *what's here* more than the imported virtual culture from LA. This could be win/win, baby!

D: Of course, we'd have to convince some of *our* people of that too….

B: I don't think so, we can appeal to their needs, needs that are thwarted—so many young artists who give up on their art (as at least *one* of the many part-time jobs they must have to survive) because they see no hope, the young who don't yet realize that they're shooting their dreams in the foot when they're glued to the imported culture….

D: Those who complain about how the techies are taking over this city and driving them out, yet are dutifully enriching them by being glued to their smartphones and ipods….

B: Imported mass culture and Big Tech colonizers have such a way of seducing us from our intuitions and gifts at a young age.

D: As Stroffolino wrote, "One effect of today's globalized technological modes of communication is that one practically needs to make a message or proposal public to the surveillance medium of the interweb to even ask her next door neighbor for a cup of sugar, yet alone to hear their new song, etc. The spurious promise of democracy, freedom or autonomy comes with an increased alienation of neighbor and neighbor, which the ownership class prefers so that no unity of strength in numbers may challenge its cultural hegemony."

B: He bloviates! But I'm convinced we can help the kids have more *fun* creating their own art, and providing that "economic engine" that could fuel an Oakland cultural and economic renaissance, for all of Oakland.

D: Imagine, if you will, a locally-owned and operated radio station broadcasting from one of the city's many live/work warehouse space/art gallery that also holds dance parties and organizational meetings.....this station's programming would consist of at least 75% local programming (music, talk) with the purpose of helping to brand an Oakland cultural identity that would utilize the talent of Oakland's currently underused creative talent "content providers" and generate revenue for the city.....

B: Yes, but we have to find a new place first....

Bridges To Be

"so you're gonna be a bridge, bridge, bridge, bridge, bridge, but you're fallin' through the cracks."[227]

between past and present
between old and young
between talking and writing
between generalist and specialist
between students and teachers
between teachers and writers
between book review and academic essay
between one school of poetry and another
between poetry and music
between one type of music and another
between poetry and drama
between poetry and prose
between drama, dance, and diphthongs!
between art and criticism
between duty and pleasure
between art and activism
between introvert and extrovert
between settler and nomad
between art and entertainment
between education and entertainment
between "high" art and "mass" art
between elitist and populist, advanced and basic
between mfa programs and community colleges
between creative writing and critical thinking
between seminar & practicum
between poetry workshop & band rehearsal
between poetry workshop & multi-genre workshop

---

227   https://www.youtube.com/watch?v=AhRh-Sdkqb8

between art gallery and underground music venue
between arts activists and housing activists
between arts activists and radio activists
between musicians and art activists
between revolutionary manifesto and business plan
between page and stage
between "racial" and "non-racial" discourse
to burn the bridges
between The Center For Consumer Freedom
        and the childhood obesity epidemic &
between Euro-centric mis-education.....
                and so-called democracy
                    (to be continued)

CHRIS STROFFOLINO is the author of 7 books of poetry, including *Speculative Primitive* (2005), *Scratch Vocals* (2003), *Stealer's Wheel* (1999), and *Light As A Fetter* (1997). In 2016, Boog City published his play, *AnTi-GeNtRiFiCaTiOn WaR dRuM rAdIo*. He also co-authored a study (with David Rosenthal) of Shakespeare's 12th Night (IDG Books, 2001) as well as a collection of essays on (mostly) 20th Century Poetry, *Spin Cycle* (SD, 2000). Recipient of grants from NYFA and the Fund For Poetry, Stroffolino currently teaches at Laney College in Oakland where he sometimes steals time from grading to write essays and/or poems.

www.ingramcontent.com/pod-product-compliance
Lightning Source LLC
Chambersburg PA
CBHW020149090426
42734CB00008B/751